Men Learning Through Life

Men Learning Through Life

Edited by

Barry Golding, Rob Mark and Annette Foley

niace
promoting adult learning

Published by

© 2014 National Institute of Adult Continuing Education (England and Wales)
21 De Montfort Street, Leicester LE1 7GE

Company registration no. 2603322
Charity registration no. 1002775

The National Institute of Adult Continuing Education (NIACE) is an independent charity which promotes adult learning across England and Wales. Through its research, development, publications, events, outreach and advocacy activity, NIACE works to improve the quality and breadth of opportunities available for all adults so they can benefit from learning throughout their lives.

www.niace.org.uk

For details of all our publications, visit http://shop.niace.org.uk

Cataloguing in Publications Data

A CIP record for this title is available from the British Library

978-1-86201-828-0 (print)
978-1-86201-829-7 (PDF)
978-1-86201-830-3 (ePub)
978-1-86201-832-7 (Kindle)

All websites referenced in this book were correct and accessible at the time of going to press.

Printed in the UK by Marston Book Services, Abingdon.
Cover design by Book Production Services, London.
Designed and typeset by Avon DataSet Ltd, Bidford on Avon, Warwickshire, UK.

The views expressed in this publication are not necessarily endorsed by the publisher.

Contents

Foreword   **vii**
Acknowledgements   **xi**
Notes on contributors   **xiii**
Preface   **xvii**

Part One
Chapter One
Men learning through life   **3**
Barry Golding, Rob Mark and Annette Foley

Chapter Two
Men's learning in international settings   **20**
Barry Golding

Chapter Three
Men's health and wellbeing: Learning through the lifecourse   **34**
John Macdonald

Chapter Four
Empowering men to learn through literacy   **49**
Rob Mark

Chapter Five
The case for some men's spaces   **63**
Annette Foley

Chapter Six
Learning beyond the workplace   **77**
Barry Golding

Chapter Seven
Men and boys: Ages and stages   97
Annette Foley and Barry Golding

Chapter Eight
Men's sheds: A new movement for change   113
Barry Golding

Part Two
Chapter Nine
Men's learning in the UK   131
Rob Mark and Jim Soulsby

Chapter Ten
Men's learning in Ireland   148
Lucia Carragher, John Evoy and Rob Mark

Chapter Eleven
Men's learning in Portugal   164
António Fragoso, João Filipe Marques and Milene Lança

Chapter Twelve
Men's learning in Greece   179
Georgios K. Zarifis

Chapter Thirteen
Men's learning in China   196
Aijing Jin, Zhao Tingyan, Liang Hua and Barry Golding

Chapter Fourteen
Men's learning in Australia   205
Barry Golding and Annette Foley

Chapter Fifteen
Men's learning in Aotearoa/New Zealand   226
Brian Findsen

Chapter Sixteen
Men's turn to learn? Discussion and conclusion   244
Barry Golding, Rob Mark and Annette Foley

Index   260

Foreword

When I began my research into men and learning in the UK, I quickly found that this relatively unexplored terrain was a minefield. One female educationist asked me how I could 'live with' myself for tackling the subject! My response then was the same as it would be now: equality of learning access and opportunity should not apply only to one sex, even if that has been the case in the past. Acknowledgement that women have been discriminated against in education, as in so many other spheres of life, should not blind us to the possibility that *some* men may now be victims of that same injustice. I emphasise the word 'some', as I was at pains to do repeatedly in my published research. This attempt to avoid generalisation was clearly inadequate since it did not prevent a male educationist from rushing into print to fiercely contest my apparent claim that [all] men were 'not interested in learning', his experience having proved otherwise.

Yet it was abundantly clear from my examination of the evidence that some groups of men were indeed 'not interested' in any learning that was not related to the workplace. In fact, for a number of complex and interdependent reasons, many appeared to be highly resistant to anything that was described or perceived as 'education' or 'learning.' By the late 1990s, women composed the majority of students in most forms of post-compulsory learning in England, whether formal, non-formal or informal. While this could be perceived as a welcome development that was redressing some of the glaring gender inequalities of the past, it was raising concerns at a time of growing male unemployment and a gradually widening gap between male and female school and post-school performance.

My research was limited to the UK and, more specifically, England and it is of great interest to find evidence showing that similar concerns exist elsewhere. *Men Learning Through Life* is a much wider study, based on evidence produced in seven different nations in three continents. The diverse countries that are the focus of the study all have ageing populations. Some, in Europe in particular, also have high levels of unemployment among men of working age. The book's main concern is, therefore, how to make learning accessible to men who are not in work. As the editors state, there is a case 'for considering some men's disadvantage without applying the argument to all men'.

An interest in helping disadvantaged men should not be interpreted as a desire to push women out of the learning territory they have claimed. There are important social reasons to put the spotlight on men's learning. As the editors point out, lack of qualification, literacies and work poses significant risks not only to men's individual health and wellbeing, but also to those closest to them and, by extension, to wider society:

> *It is not in any country's interest to have a generation of bitter, angry and poorly educated, unemployed or under-employed men unable to comprehend what has changed, and turning irrationally, physically and aggressively on their fellow human beings (migrants, women, refugees, gay men, for example) as is occurring across most nations in Europe.*

Despite the fact that national education and training policies are increasingly directed towards education and training for work, the authors do not accept the simplistic premise that more education will automatically lead to employment. Instead they provide examples of successful community-based practice indicating that men of all ages can be attracted to non-work-related learning programmes, depending on the context and the way in which they are presented and run. The different chapters identify practical and creative ways of engaging men of all ages in 'places and spaces' that appeal to them. They outline a number of potentially transferable examples of good practice; communities of practice that are not perceived as patronising or coercive. In fact, some 'circle round education and health but lead to both learning and wellbeing without naming or foregrounding either'. The international men's shed movement, for example, is identified as an 'excellent example of a neat fit between men's learning and wellbeing'.

Barry Golding and his fellow editors Rob Mark and Annette Foley, as well as the large number of individual contributors to the book, are to be congratulated for producing such a wide range of perspectives on men and learning. This is a relatively new research field and the editors are right to stress that the evidence outlined is only a partial snapshot and that, dependent on information in English, they are only 'scratching the surface'. They acknowledge that very different gender participation patterns may be obtained in other countries. In some, as the Malala Yousafzai case so shockingly demonstrated, girls and women are prevented, often with violence, from engaging in any kind of structured learning. This could prompt the accusation that a spotlight on men's learning is not justified in a world where women still have to fight for full equality. On the contrary, however, such situations reinforce rather than negate the argument for a focus on men's learning, for those who seek to prevent girls and women from getting an education are in dire need of better and more enlightened education themselves. This timely book could provide a useful and informative starting point.

Veronica McGivney

Acknowledgements

The compilation of this book has involved many people who gave generously of their time, undertaking many different tasks so willingly. Without their help, this volume would certainly not have been possible.

We would like to particularly mention the very many people who contributed to interviews and discussions, whether as individuals or as representatives of community or voluntary groups and from places of work. The book is based on experiences in seven countries, with many of the chapter writers having the added challenge of putting thoughts and ideas together in another language. Their efforts have enabled us to compile a unique resource which we hope will be of value to a great many people involved with teaching, policy, planning, equity and access and research into men's learning and other related fields.

We would also like to thank the people who gave graciously of their time to review drafts and who gave us advice and support. While it is not possible to mention all these people, the editors would like to note the inspiration we have taken from the work of Veronica McGivney who had the courage and foresight to write about this important topic almost two decades ago.

Special thanks is due to the international men's shed movement, whose members have provided inspiration and demonstrated that what we are writing about really does make a difference to men's lives, families and communities.

We are aware of the many bodies and agencies that have encouraged the development of projects on men's learning in different countries and provided funding for a great many activities. We wish to acknowledge the advice and support of staff from the National Institute of Adult Continuing Education (NIACE) in the UK for their recognition of the importance of compiling a publication to meet the needs of an international audience in the broad field of lifelong learning.

Barry Golding, Rob Mark and Annette Foley, Editors and Authors

January 2014

Notes on contributors

Editors and chapter authors

Professor Barry Golding is a researcher in adult and community education in the Faculty of Education and Arts, Federation University Australia. His international research focuses on adult learning in community settings, with a specialisation in men's learning. Barry is President of Adult Learning Australia and a Patron of the Australian Men's Sheds Association.

Dr Rob Mark is Head of the Centre for Lifelong Learning at the University of Strathclyde, Scotland where he leads a centre that provides specialised teaching and research into older learning. Rob has worked as a teacher and researcher in the adult, further and community sectors. His research has focused on European lifelong learning, literacy and adult access to education. He is currently editor of *The Adult Learner Journal* in Ireland.

Dr Annette Foley is Deputy Dean in the Faculty of Education and Arts, Federation University Australia. Annette's research focuses on the value of adult and community education for health and wellbeing. Annette's other research interest involves vocational education and training and the value of adult pedagogies to engage disengaged youth.

Chapter authors (by country of residence)

Australia

Professor Barry Golding and Dr Annette Foley

Professor John Macdonald, at the University of Western Sydney, Australia, is Professor of Primary Health Care, Director of Men's Health and Chair of a drop-in centre for men at risk of suicide. John's work focuses on the social determinants of health. He is a Patron of the Australian Men's Sheds Association.

China

Dr Aijing Jin was an academic in China before her 2004 doctoral studies in Australia. A lecturer in the Faculty of Education and Arts, Federation University Australia since 2007, Aijing's main research and teaching expertise is in health and physical education curriculum, effective learning and cross-cultural teaching.

Professor Tingyan Zhao is Dean of the School of Social Development, Anshan Normal University, Liaoning Province, China. He has researched and published in China on social transformation and risk, social management and innovation and social work policy.

Liang Hua is a lecturer and doctoral student at Anshan Normal University, Liaoning Province, China. His main research areas are in public governance, social organisation and social work.

Greece

Dr George K. Zarifis is Assistant Professor of Continuing Education at the Faculty of Philosophy/Department of Pedagogy, Aristotle University, Thessaloniki, Greece. His research interests focus on adult educators' training and professionalisation, university continuing education and the comparative examination of adult learning policies and practices in south-eastern Europe.

New Zealand

Professor Brian Findsen works in the Department of Policy, Cultural and Social Studies in Education at the University of Waikato, Hamilton, Aotearoa/New Zealand. Brian has extensively researched adult and higher education in New Zealand and Scotland, specialising in critical perspectives on older adults' learning, social equity and international adult education.

Portugal

Dr António Fragoso is Pro-Rector at the University of Algarve, Portugal. António's research focuses on adult education, community development, non-traditional students in higher education and informal learning. António is co-editor of the *European Journal for Research on the Education and Learning of Adults.*

Dr João Filipe Marques is Assistant Professor at the Faculty of Economics of the University of Algarve, Portugal, and sociology researcher in the Centre for Spatial and Organizational Dynamics. João's research focuses on racism, ethnicity and identity in contemporary societies. He is a Board member of the Portuguese Sociological Association.

Milene Lança is a PhD student in tourism at the Faculty of Economics, University of Algarve, Portugal, and sociology researcher of the Centre for Spatial and Organizational Dynamics. Milene's main fields of research are tourism, sexuality and gender.

Republic of Ireland
Dr Lucia Carragher is a Senior Research Fellow in the School of Health and Science, Dundalk Institute of Technology, Republic of Ireland. Lucia's research interests lie broadly in the areas of healthy ageing and inequalities in health, gender and education. Lucia conducted the first national study of men's sheds in Ireland in 2013.

John Evoy is founder and Chief Executive Officer of the Irish Men's Sheds Association. Before this, John managed projects for County Wexford Vocational Educational Committee in the Republic of Ireland, including the award-winning Engage Programme, a community development training course for men. John is also the Australian Men's Sheds Association's European representative.

United Kingdom
Dr Rob Mark
Jim Soulsby is the originator of and facilitator for the European For-Age network and Research Associate with the Institute of Lifelong Learning at the University of Leicester. Jim is also Honorary Development Co-ordinator with the Association for Education and Ageing and an editor of its *International Journal of Education and Ageing.*

Preface

A book that focuses on the engagement of men in learning may appear puzzling to many people today. While the male sex may have in the past dominated the development of education, it is a strange irony that a growing number of men, particularly older men (though increasingly men of all ages), remains excluded from education and learning.

This is despite the fact that men have made a significant contribution to research and scholarly analysis in education and learning, as well as dominated the field of education, for many years. Recently, things have begun to change and the pendulum is now swinging against men's involvement. Indeed, men are now often minority participants in education across different sectors and areas of provision in many countries.

It is therefore the men experiencing exclusion that this book sets out to identify. We first seek to answer the question of why so many men are excluded and then reflect on what can be done to increase participation and to redress the imbalance that exists. We look at the particular characteristics of those experiencing exclusion and examine the ways in which providers of education can – and are – responding to this ever-increasing problem and what might be said to be examples of successful practice. In doing so, we consider how new types of provision are enriching the lives of individuals and their families for the benefit of society at large.

Below is an overview of what this book is about. This summary is intended to give the reader a snapshot of the problems and issues affecting learning across different continents, the success stories for individuals, communities and those whose job it is to provide for engagement in different countries, and the issues faced in bringing about transformation.

Synopsis of Parts One and Two

Part One, comprising most of the first half of the book (Chapters One to Eight) introduces and critically analyses some of the international research evidence surrounding men's learning. An introductory Chapter One provides a broad rationale and theoretical framework for analysing men's learning. The remaining chapters in Part One are organised around themes relating to men's learning. Specifically, they discuss men's learning: in international settings (Chapter Two), as it relates to learning and health and wellbeing (Chapter Three) and men's literacies (Chapter Four). Given the contested nature of 'men's turn to learn' arguments, Chapter Five makes a case for some places and spaces for men's learning for men, particularly for those men beyond paid work (Chapter Six), at different ages and stages (Chapter Seven) and through men's sheds in community settings (Chapter Eight).

Part Two has seven chapters, each focused on aspects of men's learning across seven nations located in three continents: in Europe (UK, Ireland, Portugal, Greece), Australasia (Australia and New Zealand) and Asia (China). Each chapter, contributed to or led by researchers based in those nations, is framed around recent research evidence that points towards practical initiatives and policies that increase men's level of engagement in learning in that national context. Given our book's theme, *Men Learning Through Life* Part Two seeks to identify new, practical and creative ways of working with and engaging men of all ages. Several of these chapters point to new ways of involving men in communities of practice as active participants in shaping their own learning.

Each of the seven national chapters in Part Two has been written around the following four broad research questions, but is customised by diverse researchers using different theoretical perspectives, as appropriate to diverse national contexts and available data.

- What prevailing socio-cultural factors affect men and their learning?
- What is the current learning and wellbeing situation for men?
- What practical initiatives encourage men's learning?

- In what ways are policy, practice and research shaped to accommodate men's learning?

The book's three editors contribute the final chapter. It includes a discussion and conclusions and seeks to identify and summarise what can be said about policy, practice and research into men's learning in the international context. It also identifies examples of good policies or practices in men's learning that can be shared in the international arena.

Synopsis of chapters in Part One

Chapter One, 'Men learning through life', provides the theoretical context for our book. It outlines a range of social and economic factors, including population ageing and the global financial crisis, that have led to an increase in the proportion of men not in paid work in many developed nations. This has often been accompanied by a decrease in many nations in the proportion of young men completing post-school qualifications. Evidence is advanced to show that men not in work, without formal qualifications or literacies face significant risks that can become intergenerational within families, with many men showing an aversion to formal education and training and reluctance to engage in lifelong learning beyond work. These risks include early and prolonged displacement from work and ongoing problems and issues across the lifespan that impact on learning, literacy, health and wellbeing. These crosscutting themes are central to the argument for reducing exclusion and recur throughout the book.

Chapter Two, 'Men's learning in international settings', critically examines new international research in the field on men's learning, originating recently from Australasia and Europe. It identifies particular groups of men who are adversely affected by educational exclusion in diverse contexts. These include men beyond work for a range of reasons (unemployment, early withdrawal from the workforce, early school leaving, disability and age retirement). It also includes men whose engagement with work, family and community is limited as a result of aversion to, avoidance of or exclusion from formal education.

Chapter Three, 'Men's health and wellbeing: Learning through the lifecourse', provides a background about why men's health and wellbeing is of concern. It particularly identifies the social determinants of health as a fresh way of thinking about men's (and boys') health. In addition, it draws some evidence-based connections between men's learning, wellbeing and health.

Chapter Four, 'Empowering men through literacy', focuses on ways in which literacies affect men's participation in learning. It is illustrated by recent research from Ireland that identifies low levels of literacy as a factor affecting men's participation in adult learning. The chapter looks specifically at findings from two recent studies of men's learning carried out in informal learning settings in Ireland.

Chapter Five, 'The case for some men's spaces', makes a case for creating some masculine-gendered spaces. It draws from feminist positions on equity and disadvantage to clear some theoretical ground for a case for male-gendered spaces for particular groups of men. The chapter examines the importance of health, wellbeing and community participation that some community spaces provide for men. It argues that being healthy and connecting with community brings about individual agency and is arguably a fundamental human right.

Chapter Six, 'Learning beyond the workplace', summarises what is known about men's learning beyond paid work. It deliberately emphasises learning through diverse contexts beyond paid work where informal, place-based, community pedagogies have been shown to suit such men and enhance their wellbeing. The chapter identifies the benefits of some men's 'communities of practice' that 'circle around' education and health, but lead to both learning and wellbeing without naming or foregrounding either. While such learning spaces tend to be common, they have previously been ignored or discounted for men in many contemporary education and training settings, policies and discourses.

Chapter Seven, 'Men and boys: Ages and stages', examines boys and men who have experienced disconnection from formal educational settings. It makes use of data taken from two Australian research projects looking at intergenerational learning. The chapter puts forward the case that for some boys (and men), there are health and wellbeing benefits associated with participation in structured mentoring relationships in community settings. The data shows that these relationships can provide positive emotional, social and cognitive benefits for men and boys.

Chapter Eight, 'Men's sheds: A new movement for change', provides a background and critical analysis of the learning attributes and implications of the international men's sheds movement. Men's sheds are identified as an excellent example of a neat fit between men's learning and wellbeing. Men's sheds, as a community-based, grassroots movement, illustrates many of the arguments that the rest of the book advances. Its thesis is that learning and wellbeing can be advanced by collective action by men themselves in community settings, if the circumstances are right. This, in essence, is when men are not treated as customers, patients, students or clients from negative, deficit or ageist models.

Synopsis of chapters in Part Two

The second section (Chapters 9 to 15) provides a window into the situation for men's learning in seven different national contexts.

Chapter Nine, 'Men's learning in the UK', examines issues and examples of men's learning, which have developed largely since McGivney's (1999, 2004) milestone research in this topic. While a gender gap in school education attracted attention as early as the mid 1990s, responses in UK policy and practice in adult education that are directed to men remain relatively few. The recent economic crisis in the UK has also led to renewed concerns about men of all ages who are not working or participating in education and training across the UK.

Chapter Ten, 'Men's learning in Ireland', is informed particularly by a recent, major, Irish men's shed research study. There has been a marked growth in interest in men's issues, including men's learning and health in community settings over recent decades that has led to the development of provision to meet the needs of men both in Northern Ireland and in the Republic of Ireland. The chapter is framed within the context of broader concerns around inequalities in gender relations, the political, religious and socio-cultural divisions that persist in Ireland, and the impact on men of all ages of the recent economic crisis in Ireland.

Chapter Eleven, 'Men's learning in Portugal', begins with the 'big picture' by examining some of the historical, political and social-economic factors impinging on adult learning in Portugal, focusing on and identifying why men's learning in community settings is something of a research lacuna. This is in spite of evidence of widespread disadvantage experienced in Portugal by men not in paid work, both as a consequence of the global financial crisis and widespread population ageing in rural areas. The chapter includes recognition of the importance of researching this field for future policy and practice.

Chapter Twelve, 'Men's learning in Greece', reveals that many Greek unemployment and social statistics are comparable with similar statistics in Ireland and Portugal. The Greek chapter focuses on research findings from two studies. The first involves data from a programme specifically oriented to the learning needs of socially disadvantaged older men (age 50+). The other research study involves interview data from a research project involving younger (18–30 years) unemployed men. Like other chapters in Part Two, this chapter identifies, describes and evaluates several examples of good practice involving men and learning in the Greek context.

Chapter Thirteen, 'Men's learning in China', provides an outline of some aspects of men's learning in China, including the poorly researched area of gender and older men's learning. The chapter also shows how a new emphasis on different forms of education is providing new ways to engage older people in learning. While the prospects for future research are good, the chapter is relatively brief because of the current paucity of accessible, critical or comparable Chinese research, whether written in English or Chinese.

Chapter Fourteen is a comprehensive review of 'Men's learning in Australia'. Until a decade ago, men's learning and wellbeing remained relatively poorly researched in Australia. This chapter summarises much that has happened since. Aside from men's sheds (addressed separately in Chapter 8), a range of other contexts beyond paid work are identified in which men are learning informally through community contexts.

Chapter Fifteen, 'Men's learning in Aotearoa/New Zealand', begins by emphasising how historically New Zealand has been perceived as a male-dominated society or 'blokes' world', a perception now seriously blown apart under globalisation. The chapter critically examines policies that have influenced the pattern of boys' and men's participation in schooling as well as adult and community education in New Zealand. Men's disengagement with varied forms of learning, including formal, non-formal and self-directed learning is considered, taking account also of ethnicity, age and social class.

In our final **Chapter Sixteen**, 'Men's turn to learn', we provide a critical synthesis, discussion and some conclusions. We draw some national and international conclusions based on the data and the literature examined in Part One, and the national policies and practices identified in Part Two. We reflect on and collectively discuss the increasing importance of learning beyond education and training in a narrow, vocational sense. Finally, we look closely at how men's learning in a lifelong and lifewide sense has tended to be devalued by recent neoliberal policies in many nations that rely on entry and re-entry into the education and training 'market'.

Finally, we tease out what it is about education that can (and does) turn many boys and men off learning and adversely limits men's and family wellbeing across the lifespan. Some issues which affect men's development are identified which require new thinking if men are to be encouraged back into 'learning for life'. These include focusing on getting men into paid work, not assuming that more education is all men need to return to work and tackling the issue that learning beyond work is tending to become a luxury for a few.

Part One

CHAPTER ONE

Men learning through life

Barry Golding, Rob Mark and Annette Foley

Introduction

This introductory chapter seeks, through a broad-brush analysis of a wide range of international research and data, to provide context for our book. It consists of four sections. The first sets the broad intentions and the main source of information for the two parts of our book that follow, including some limitations. The second section seeks to make explicit our interest in focusing mainly on men, particularly those men beyond paid work. The third section teases out some of our theoretical presuppositions about the process, purposes and value of learning that men experience. The fourth explains our reasons for overtly including and emphasising the seldom-theorised link between men's learning and wellbeing.

In its totality, this introductory chapter provides an outline of our equity and evidence-based case for acknowledging worldwide changes and trends that have made this book timely, particularly for men not in paid work, including a 'big picture' view of men learning through life in international settings. It begins to delineate a range of social and economic factors, including the global financial crisis and population ageing, that have led to an increase in the proportion of men not in paid work in most developed nations. This increase has been accompanied by a decrease in many nations in the proportion of young men completing post-school qualifications.

Evidence is advanced in later chapters to show that men not in work, without formal qualifications or literacies, face significant risks to their wellbeing. These risks can become intergenerational within families, with many boys and men of all ages, often with low formal literacies, showing an aversion to formal education and training and a reluctance to engage in course-based learning beyond paid work. These difficulties have been exacerbated by the global financial crisis. They include early and prolonged displacement from work, an ageing population and problems with learning, literacy, health and wellbeing at different stages across the lifespan.

Our starting presuppositions

As researchers in adult education we are keen to provide evidence for our case, which is essentially that gender is relevant to how some (but not all) men engage with learning and what kind of learning they best and most effectively engage with at different stages of their lives. Our research interest, as in our book title, is in *Men Learning Though Life*. Our particular interest is in how men who are not in paid work learn and get access to lifelong and lifewide learning. By lifelong, we mean learning from cradle to grave. By lifewide, we mean learning across all domains of life at any age. We are also interested in how the link to learning can help men, their families and communities in what can be a very difficult time of their lives, particularly with their health and wellbeing.

While we are not arguing that there are significant or fundamental biological differences that have an impact on men and women's learning abilities, we are exploring some real, learning-related gender differences that affect men, both positively and negatively, in intersections with other variables such as culture, place, class and income. As Connell (2013) recently noted, 'the actual psychological differences between women and men are few and far between, and very small when they do appear'. Severiens and Geert (1994, p. 498) reviewed theoretical and empirical findings in research on gender-related learning styles and concluded that there were small but consistent gender differences: in essence, 'men were more often interested in the course for the qualifications they offer. Women, on the other hand, are more interested in learning for learning's sake.'

We also acknowledge that sexism, socialisation and discrimination tend to, in a global sense, put most women at a significant disadvantage in relation to most men in most areas of life, including education, family and work. Leach (1998, p. 11) observed that 'in most countries men occupy overwhelmingly the well-paid and secure jobs available', leaving 'women in casual poorly paid and insecure jobs, usually in the informal sector, where they have to work long hours, often in hazardous conditions, just to secure economic survival'. Globally, 'Lack of education makes access to information and services difficult for women, and limits their mobility, share in decision making and life opportunities' (p. 11). Further, a 'lack of education disadvantages women in their participation in both productive and community spheres: the two spheres of activity which conventionally confer status on individuals' (p. 12). This theme of status and identity in productive and community spheres is one we return to often in this book, specifically in relation to men not in work.

However, up until 1994, in most Western countries women:

> had not been at a disadvantage with respect to men in the sense of leaving with less education since about 1980 … However they still leave school with fewer opportunities for continuing their education and poorer prospects in the labour market. (Severiens and Geert, 1994, p. 487)

Our book provides new evidence that some but not all access and opportunities have changed for some men (and women) in the two decades since 1994, and in the decade since McGivney first opened up the 'Pandora's box' of men's learning in the UK (McGivney, 1999a, 2004).

Sources, limitations and qualifications

Our research about men's learning that informs this book comes from five main literature sources. Aside from the small amount of literature specifically about men's learning and wellbeing, some of the literature we draw on comes from the research (including our own in Australia, Ireland and the UK) into the nature and benefits of informal, social and situated adult and community learning that has particular resonance with men's lifelong and lifewide learning. Other insights are drawn from larger surveys or research in which men are not the main subjects of study, but which consider men as a discrete sub-group as part of a wider study. The fourth set of literature consulted involves studies of learning later in life. The final set is about learning in community contexts (such as through sport, emergency services and community men's sheds), which has only recently been studied through the lens of learning and/or wellbeing, and rarely as a valuable learning context for some men.

5

While this book contains chapters and important new insights from several non-English-speaking countries (Portugal, China, Greece) we are otherwise limited to literature and data available in English. Most of the adult male-specific studies in the fields of adult learning and wellbeing we have accessed in English tend to come from the United Kingdom, Australia and Ireland. While the US and Canada are large and important sites for practising and theorising education, it is important to note that we were unable to find researchers or sufficient research to generate national chapters on men's learning in Canada or the US. Meantime there would appear to be a need for new approaches. Approximately 20 US war veterans have been committing suicide *each day* since at least 1999 (Kemp and Bossarte, 2013), and soup kitchens, mainly for men not in paid work, are common in cities in both countries in 2014. Despite men comprising half of the world population, Australia and Ireland have the only national men's health strategies in the world and, together with New Zealand and the United Kingdom, are the main sites for the recent and rapid proliferation of community men's sheds along with some associated, very recent research.

Our broad intentions

Concerns about men's attitudes to and involvement in lifelong and lifewide learning and wellbeing have recently emerged in many countries. There is a growing interest in many nations in finding ways to increase boys' engagement in school and post-school learning as well as men's engagement in life beyond paid work, including programmes and practices that will contribute to men's learning and wellbeing in contexts and life stages outside of and beyond paid work. We regard *Men Learning Through Life* as particularly important and timely, in the context of a combination of elevated men's unemployment as an outcome of the recent global financial crisis, population ageing, early withdrawal of predominantly less formally educated working-class★ men from paid work and concerns about men's functional literacies, health and wellbeing. In addition, there is the persistent and highly publicised anxieties about boys' perceived underachievement and growing concerns among education providers about the difficulties they face in recruiting men to their courses and programmes (McGivney, 2004, p. 1). While our book

★ Working class is a term widely used in UK literature but less well used in some other national contexts.

is not about boys, given that all men were boys and many men become fathers we make a case in Chapter Seven for considering boys in the book's 'bigger picture'.

While there is an almost complete lack of accessible books available on this specific subject in English, there are insights on the topic we are interested in exploring embedded within literature in and beyond the UK, Ireland and Australia. Veronica McGivney's ground-breaking work, also published by NIACE, *Excluded Men: Men who are Missing from Education and Training* (McGivney, 1999a) and its five year follow-up study, *Men Earn Women Learn: Bridging the Gender Divide in Education and Training* (McGivney, 2004) are notable exceptions. There is also a growing realisation of the typical, narrow, pigeonholing of men as amenable mainly to individual vocational benefit through training, and of the need within men's health policies, (Ireland, 2008; Australian Government, 2010) to link men's learning policies and practices with broader wellbeing strategies for men of all ages.

While there is growing evidence from research in several different, mainly Anglophone, countries about what works in improving learning and wellbeing for different cohorts of men, this is a very new and inter-disciplinary field. Our inclusion, in Part Two of this book, of insights from diverse European, Asian and Australasian nations is by no means global, but is seen as sufficient to begin to assemble, examine and analyse evidence from theory, research, policy and practice in this newly emerging field. It is deliberately inclusive of case study examples from seven world nations to provide not only some theoretical lenses but also practical and arguably transferable examples of good practice in men's learning and wellbeing across diverse national and cultural contexts. Our aim has been to produce a book that is useful, authoritative, original and well informed, but written in a way that minimises professional and theoretical jargon, making it accessible to diverse readers of English in equally diverse national and cultural contexts.

Gender and masculinities

While we discuss learning and masculinities in more depth in Chapter 5, from the outset we stress that we are not making a case for a certain, essential 'gender order' on the basis of false dichotomies and archaic beliefs about the nature of each sex or aside from history. However, we are exploring the question of value (or otherwise) of social and cultural differentiation between men and women, specifically as it relates to learning and wellbeing, a question that also lies at the heart of feminist theory. Scott (1996) in *Feminism and History* argues that sexual difference, indeed that all forms of social differentiation, cannot be understood apart from history. As the European Society for Research into the Education of Adults (ESREA) Network on Gender and Adult Learning noted in the invitation to their 2013 European Conference:

> *The normative power of the messages associated with the gender carries penalties for people of both sexes, which may constitute real obstacles to individual freedom to learn and to make decisions, to choose areas of study to professional domains, to participate in civic and political organisations in the community, or even to be responsible for the management of family life … Such inequalities continue to contaminate undoubtedly the way men and women exercise their citizenship and how they evaluate themselves as members of a fully democratic society.* (NGAL, 2013, p. 1)

Furthermore, we are not seeking to directly compare women with men to invoke some sort of generalisable, empirical difference in terms of learning and wellbeing. What we are doing, however, by focusing specifically on men's experiences of learning and wellbeing in this book, is drawing out some aspects of men's experiences of learning and the impact on their wellbeing, that we argue are important to try and better understand.

One thing we do not do in this book is blame all men or suggest that all women or all gendered aspects of learning are the cause of 'the problem' (whatever the problem might be), or to argue for quick and easy answers. We acknowledge that while there are multiple ways of being a man (Connell, 1995), many men (and boys) subscribe to a very narrow view of masculinity that has a tendency to limit their engagement as lifelong learners beyond work. We also acknowledge that some men, for a range of reasons, have a problem with some forms of adult education practice. In part, this is because they perceive it as a women's domain, and in part because they have been socialised and enculturated to embrace masculinities that do not include positive attitudes towards learning, which they perceive as female gendered practice. Given that the consequences of these negative perceptions can limit men's wider potential and wellbeing throughout life, it is something we should at least talk about.

Following on from the early work of McGivney (1999a) and O'Rourke (1999), we go beyond asking and exploring whether or not men's absence is the result of exclusion or election, to identify places and pedagogies where men *can* learn through sharing, connection with and practising some aspects of masculinities in contexts that are beyond paid work, and which are neither negative nor hegemonic. Paraphrasing some of Tett's (1996) words, made in the context of theorising about single-sex work in adult education, our specific interest is in for which men, in which contexts and for which purposes does learning not work, and particularly where can it and does it work for these same men. This line of inquiry has been enhanced by recent European research in the gender and adult learning literature (Ostrouch-Kaminska, Fontanini and Gaynard, 2012) referred to later in Chapter Five. What will become evident, despite our focus on men, is that many of the gendered pedagogies that work for many men beyond paid work may also work for many women whose confidence and self-esteem has been similarly damaged by difficult life, family and work circumstances.

What we do acknowledge is that the process of gender socialisation through school, further education and family, combined with strong cultural norms and expectations in most nations, has produced strong and persistent gendering by field of study and types of work for both men and women. This trend towards men's and women's occupations, referred to in the literature as 'occupational segregation', can result from a range of differences aside from discrimination, including gendered preferences and gendered differences in skills and education (Singapore, 2000). In most nations, cultures and families, men have tended to do more of the paid work outside of the home for longer than most women, and most men die several years earlier – up to 12 years earlier in some Eastern European nations. Conversely, most women have tended to do much of the unpaid caring work involving children and family and, partly as a consequence, the paid work women do is typically more broken, less secure and relatively poorly paid.

Our argument is not about moral panic about men or boys learning. Rather, we regard it as timely to reflect on the evidence in the context of widespread population ageing, combined with men's withdrawal in many (but not all) nations from involvement in adult and community education, other than that which is overtly vocational and youth-oriented. Our book complements the findings from the recent and extensive UK *Inquiry into the Future for Lifelong Learning* (Schuller and Watson, 2009) that mapped out a future for lifelong and lifewide learning but barely touched on issues to do with gender, and men in particular.

While we identify men in many nations as relatively advantaged in the workplace, we focus on common characteristics of groups of men and boys seen to be at risk through not being in paid work. We also examine common difficulties in many nations that affect men displaced from work, including those whose age (and age discrimination in employment) precludes them from paid work. These issues have come to a head with the severe downstream effects of the global financial crisis in the four European nations for which chapters are included in this book.

Our approach in the book is distinctive and deliberate in that we see learning as being much more than acquiring individual, new knowledge. We are perhaps more interested in those men of all ages who are shut out from learning as adults in diverse contexts for whatever reason, than we are about men who are already lifelong learners by virtue of their formal education. Like Coombs and Ahmed (1974, p. 8), we are particularly focused on the power and potential of informal education as part of a lifelong process, 'by which every individual acquires and accumulates knowledge, skills, attitudes and insights from daily exposure to the environment – at home, at work, at play'.

As McGivney noted in her book, *Informal Learning in the Community*, people (men and women):

> *often choose familiar, non-threatening or stereotypical learning activities as a starting point [which] gives them the confidence to progress to something different. Providing 'safe' first learning options has therefore been found a useful strategy for widening participation and helping people to develop other learning interests.* (1999b, p. 46)

The difficult irony, as we demonstrate in the chapter about community men's sheds (and which is similarly demonstrable in research into community centres and neighbourhood houses), is that safe and effective spaces in which some men and some women can develop other interests are sometimes gendered.

We identify some of the learning issues that affect men's wellbeing and also link some of the wellbeing issues back to learning. This includes consideration of the learning experiences and outcomes that are valued by men, particularly those capabilities that allow men to exercise control over their lives and wellbeing, in roles that are not framed around deficit or ageist models, as patients, students, clients and customers.

It is important in our book about men's learning to tease out some of the similarities and differences which women experience in terms of learning and wellbeing. We stress that internationally, on average, women remain relatively disadvantaged compared with men on a wide range of learning, income and wellbeing criteria. We also identify women's and girls' recent increased access to education as one way towards redressing some of these historic disadvantages. Throughout the book we explore whether, for what reasons and with what consequences particular groups of men are missing (and or/excluded) from education and training in international contexts, as Veronica McGivney suggested in 2004 in the UK.

There is a considerable participation gap which exists for certain groups of men and women, though this is not universal or in the same direction, for reasons explored in the chapters that follow. We acknowledge the problems experienced by women, who also face unemployment and redundancy. For this reason, in Chapter Five we include consideration of feminist theoretical frameworks to examine in/equity and in/equality associated with particular groups of both men and women and their experiences of disadvantage, income and wellbeing. The struggle for women's rights is discussed along with the ongoing need to widen access to education and employment for women. We seek to demonstrate that access to certain occupations is often limited and roles are still comprehensively gendered in many nations. For many women, there is still the additional burden of work and home responsibilities, which are often not shared equally by men, even in some very developed nations. The implication of this for men's learning programmes is examined, as is the opportunity to learn from the experiences of the women's movement.

Recent research into men's learning has identified the importance of place-based pedagogies for men in several nations. In Part Two, our book examines some innovative learning environments and programmes that tend to engage men of all ages in diverse national and policy contexts. Given the relative dearth of men as learners in formal educational settings in later life, we seek to emphasise the learning function that life beyond work plays for men and some ways in which lifelong and lifewide learning policies can be reframed to actively engage men of all ages. We also establish and emphasise the strong relationships between men's work identities, group affiliation and learning.

We provide new evidence in Part Two that community contexts are becoming critically important for the increasing proportion of men who are not in paid work for much of their later lives. We include consideration of the learning that occurs through men's participation in a range of community organisation types and contexts, many of which have not previously been critically examined as learning organisations. In doing this, we identify new and innovative research approaches for working with men.

While our book is about men, we are acutely aware that boys' school performances and completion rates have declined in many countries in recent years. This book therefore includes an examination of the evidence and builds a case as to why initial education for boys should receive particular attention. We put forward a case for new ways to understand and value education in order to break intergenerational cycles of aversion to learning for some men and some communities. Recent studies in the UK, as part of the *Inquiry into the Future of Lifelong Learning* (Schuller and Watson, 2009), have identified the importance of looking at and balancing learning across the lifecourse. This book uses the data from some of these UK-based studies as a springboard to explore how men's different ages and stages affect their need to learn in other national contexts. We also consider why and how men need to learn to adapt to changes across the lifecourse, particularly to unanticipated identities and circumstances beyond paid work and in later life.

Presuppositions on the process, purposes and value of learning

We begin our discussion about the purposes of learning with some basic assumptions about lifelong learning, neatly summarised by Rubensen (2000) in a discussion questioning lifelong learning policies and adult readiness to learn in international settings. These assumptions apply to men and women. Rubensen notes that '[i]n order for lifelong learning to become a reality, people should live in a context that encourages them to want to learn' (p. 2). Rubensen identifies an early 'first generation' of ideas about lifelong learning with its roots in humanistic traditions and utopian visions, followed by a 'second generation' of ideas from the late 1980s of lifelong learning 'almost exclusively structured around an "economistic" world view' (p. 2).

The International Adult Literacy Survey (IALS) data, first available in 1997 (OECD, 1997), and the recently completed Program for the International Assessment of Adult Competencies (PIACC: OECD, 2013), have created something of a 'third generation' of concern by pointing to the huge impact a family's literacy culture has on functional literacy. It also identified the large and widening gulf in adult learning participation, in countries including Australia and the USA, between those with university degrees and those who had only limited primary education. In essence, those with the most education are the most self-directed to seek and get access to the most lifelong learning. Further, the IALS data pointed to the 'long arm of the job' (in addition to the above 'long arm of the family'), where those in work also get the most lifelong learning. Rubensen summarises this by stressing that 'every country in the IALS faces major challenges in extending lifelong learning to the least qualified' (2006, p. 7), and concludes that:

> lifelong learning for all can only be achieved in a society that actively engages and makes demands of the literacy skills of all its citizens. It is conditional on a working life that promotes the use of literacy, and a society where people are encouraged to think, act and be engaged. (ibid.)

We identify a very recent 'fourth generation' of concern based around the emerging evidence of relationships between learning and wellbeing, with people not in paid work (for any reason). We identify older people as being most vulnerable to both diminished health and wellbeing, and with the most limited access to the learning and life skills necessary to stay well. These learning and wellbeing issues have previously been identified in Europe, with a combination of exhortations about changing men's behaviour and altering the power balance between men and women. Indeed, the report on the EU's Fifth Framework Programme on European Research Network on Men in Europe (European Union, 2003) was pointedly titled *The Social Problem of Men* (Hearn et al., 2004). The programme identified 'a correlation across many countries between poor health, including the health of men, and various forms of social disadvantage associated with factors such as class and ethnicity' (p. 2).

While it recommended that education programmes should be set up, their purpose was to encourage 'men [to] devote more time and priority to caring, housework, childcare and the reconciliation of home and paid work.' While we have serious concerns about positing all men as being '*the* social problem' we agree with the authors' qualifications that 'top down social policy initiatives may be insufficient to change men's behaviour'.

Merriam and Caffarella (1991, p. 138) identify four broad approaches to conceptualising learning, most simply described as behaviourist, cognitivist, humanist, and social or situational. Each approach is seen as having its distinct, respective purpose to produce behavioural change, develop capacity and skills, become self-actualised or autonomous and to fully participate in the community. While we acknowledge value in all approaches, our main interest in this book is about the latter two approaches, particularly the value of learning for and by men in informal communities of practice *through* life, including across the lifespan and across all aspects of life, in effect, through lifelong and lifewide learning, the twin policy platforms of Adult Learning Australia. Our inclination towards studying the value of humanist and social or situational learning is associated with our focus on men not in formal education or training, where research (already alluded to) suggests that men with the lowest formal literacies have the most to gain from learning, particularly if its formality can be minimised and if men's agency can be maximised.

While each of these academic learning theories of Merriam and Caffarella (1991) construct the locus of learning, its purposes and the role of the educator in a somewhat different way, in reality most learning involves aspects of all four approaches, with more emphasis on the learner and less on the educator when moving from the first to the fourth approaches. It is also useful to consider how adult learners think about learning. Säljö (1979) asked adult learners what they understood by learning, eliciting five broad categories of responses, three of which were cognitive and acquisitive (increasing knowledge, memorising and acquiring facts), in effect about knowing *that*.

We suggest, like Smith (1999), that the other two categories are qualitatively different and potentially more radical and transformative for men beyond the workplace, by way of making sense of subject matter and the real world, but particularly about interpreting and re-interpreting understanding and reality in different ways. In this way, learning becomes less about a single truth and more about multiple ways of knowing about life and the world, a perspective we would argue is increasingly important in an interconnected and globalised world in which all people have 'the right to learn throughout life as a human right' (Smith, 1999, p. 8), particularly to make sense of and contribute to life beyond work. It is also consistent with widespread moves in all education sectors to make learning more learner-centred, supported by relatively recent, widespread application of theories about constructivist learning and post-structuralism.

Finally, and importantly, our interest in humanist and social or situational learning is tied up with evidence and understandings that the value of learning goes well beyond the individual. Learning also builds networks, trust, reciprocity (give and take) and social connections that, as Field (2005, p. 1) notes, helps people build social capital and advance their interests by co-operating with others. The conundrum here for men's learning, for men not in work and not otherwise engaged in a learning activity, is that for adults generally,

> the highest level of positive attitudes towards an active approach to learning [is] among those who [are] actively engaged, whatever the activity; these are followed by those who are actively hostile; while those who are indifferent show the lowest levels of positive support to an active approach to learning. (Field, 2005, p. 6)

Why focus on men beyond the workplace and across the lifecourse?

We argue that empowering men with the desire and opportunities to learn and contribute to families, partners and communities across the lifecourse, including beyond paid work, is clearly beneficial to individual men's quality of life, with obvious and direct benefits to women and children as well as to other men, along with society at large.

Gender studies has developed in universities during the past three decades in most Western nations, but focuses mainly on women and studying and teaching about men mainly from a feminist perspective. While feminist theory has positively influenced contemporary academic thinking, there has been a tendency for it to sometimes be underpinned by negative and hegemonic views of masculinity, in some instances coming from a position of *misandry* (hatred or dislike of men and boys (Wilson *et al.*, 2010)). It is pertinent to ask why there are so few studies

15

of gender, aside from men's studies by women from feminist perspectives, and whether it is time to create a male studies discipline.

Misan (2012) suggests that such a discipline might take stances, some of which we have we have tried to adopt in this book. It would be multidisciplinary. It would avoid the existing tendency towards ideological advocacy and defensiveness and accommodate the diverse contemporary contexts and experiences of males, including those that adversely affect their partners, families and wellbeing. It would consider men's and women's experiences and contribution to the family and community beyond work, and develop theoretical, arguable and practical alternatives based on evidence.

Why emphasise the link between men's learning and wellbeing?

Despite trends within educational settings to acknowledge learning more from constructivist, contextual and communitarian viewpoints, rather than acquisitive and individual ones, evidence that learning has value for wellbeing across life has been difficult to analyse and assemble in one place. However, some serious studies of the link between learning and wellbeing are emerging. Cooper *et al.* (2010, p. xvii) is the best example we can find, albeit limited to the UK, of an attempt at a 'true integration of neurosciences and social sciences to provide interventions for the enhancement of mental capital and wellbeing for the individual and society'. Read in tandem with Schuller and Watson (2009), it provides a strong case, which we argue in this book specifically in relation to some men, for acknowledging the debilitating, often lifelong effects on wellbeing of childhood learning difficulties, of the downsides for families and communities of placing an undue emphasis on paid work identities, and of the particular and related health and wellbeing difficulties for people of any age who are not in paid work and who are socially disconnected. Rather than negatively concentrating on these difficulties, our book is premised on positive findings of research that show that the subjective wellbeing of adults depends not so much on their health as on a range of contextual and social factors, among which social engagement plays an important role (NSA, 2013). Our fundamental argument is that learning and social engagement can be mutually reinforcing at any age, and that wellbeing can be a positive outcome of both.

These understandings about wellbeing are supported by the well-known World Health Organization social determinants of health (WHO, 2003). Regardless of national and cultural context, men and women on average have significantly diminished wellbeing through adversity associated with unemployment, inadequate income, housing or health services, unforeseen climatic and life events, relocation (particularly as immigrants or refugees) and environmental exposure, both general and work related.

Lifelong learning is implicated in these understandings and addressed in our book for several important reasons. Men with less limited access to learning (including learning available to men in the workforce) that suits their needs, preferred pedagogies, locations and socio-cultural contexts are much more likely to be subject to one (and often many) of these adversities in the first place. They are also more prone not to recover from adversity because of their more limited access to the resources, networks and capital (social, mental, physical, educational, family, community, skills and qualifications) required to recover. Finally and importantly, men's wellbeing (mental and physical) is more likely to already be diminished by one or more of the following: substance abuse, lack of exercise, depression, obesity and early death, all with obvious adverse effects on partners, families and children. For all of these reasons, exploring the associations between men's learning and wellbeing globally at a time when longevity is increasing and unemployment and levels of young men's unemployment are historically high, is regarded as both important and very timely.

Conclusion

We have set the scene for our book by presenting this introductory chapter in four main sections. In the first we framed the intentions of the book and the main sources of information for the book. The second section discussed the intention and key focus of the book, that is, our interest in focusing mainly on men, particularly those men beyond paid work. The third section discussed some theoretical presuppositions about the process, purposes and value of learning that men experience. Finally, the chapter clarified our reasons for explicitly including and emphasising the seldom-theorised link between men's learning and wellbeing.

References

Australian Government (2010) *National Male Health Policy (Australia)*. Retrieved 28 May 2013 from www.health.gov.au/malehealthpolicy

Connell, R. (1995) *Masculinities*. Cambridge: Polity Press.

Connell, R. (2013) 'The male vs female brain: Is it all in the mind?' *The Age* (Melbourne), 2 February, p. 15.

Coombs, P. and Ahmed, M. (1974) 'Attacking rural poverty: How nonformal education can help', in B. Israel (Ed.), *Research Report for the World Bank*. Baltimore: John Hopkins University Press.

Cooper, C., Field, J., Goswami, U., Jenkins, R. and Sahakian, B. (2010) *Mental Capital and Wellbeing*. Chichester: Wiley-Blackwell.

European Union (2003) 'Men and social problems: A new approach'. Retrieved 8 January 2008 from www.europa.eu/research/social-sciences/knowledge/projects/article_3551_en.htm

Field, J. (2005) 'Social capital and lifelong learning', *The Encyclopedia of Informal Education*. Retrieved 3 June 2005 from http://infed.org/mobi/social-capital-and-lifelong-learning/

Hearn, J., Muller, U., Oleksy, E., Pringle, K., Chernova, J. *et al.* (2004) *The Social Problem of Men: Final Report (2000–2003)*, EU FPV Thematic Network: The Social Problem and Societal Problematisation of Men and Masculinities. Luxembourg: Office for Official Publications of the European Communities.

Ireland (2008) *National Men's Health Policy 2008–2103 (Ireland)*, Retrieved 28 May 2013 from www.dohc.ie/publications/national_mens_health_policy.html

Kemp, J. and Bossarte, R. (2013) *Department of Veterans Affairs, Suicide Data report 2012*, DVA Mental Health Services, Suicide Prevention Program (no place indicated, USA). Retrieved 19 November 2013 from www.va.gov/opa/docs/Suicide-Data-Report-2012-final.pdf

Leach, F. (1998) 'Gender, education and training: An international perspective', in C. Sweetman, (Ed.), *Gender, Education and Training*, Oxfam Focus on Gender. UK: Oxfam Professional, pp. 9–18.

McGivney, V. (1999a) *Missing Men: Men who are Missing from Education and Training*. Leicester: NIACE.

McGivney, V. (1999b) *Informal Learning in the Community: A Trigger for Change and Development*. Leicester: NIACE.

McGivney, V. (2004) *Men Earn, Women Learn: Bridging the Gender Divide in Education and Training*. Leicester: NIACE.

Merriam, S. and Caffarella, R. (1991) *Learning in Adulthood: A Comprehensive Guide*. San Francisco: Jossey-Bass.

Misan, G. (2012) 'Why Australia needs a male studies course'. Presentation to Victorian Male Health Gathering, Moorabbin, 16 November.

NGAL: Network on Gender and Adult Learning (2013) 'Invitation to conference on Private(s) worlds(s): Gender and informal learning of adults', ESREA, University of Coimbra, Portugal, 10–12 October.

NSA: National Seniors Australia (2013) *Staying Connected: Social Engagement and Wellbeing among Mature Age Australians*. Canberra: National Seniors Australia Productive Ageing Centre.

OECD: Organisation for Economic Cooperation and Development (1997) *Literacy Skill for the Knowledge Society*. Paris: OECD.

OECD: Organisation for Economic Cooperation and Development (2007) *Lifelong Learning for All*. Paris: OECD.

OECD: Organisation for Economic Cooperation and Development (2013) *OECD Skills Survey*. Retrieved 18 November 2013 from www.oecd.org/site/piaac

O'Rourke, R. (1999) 'Men on the margins: Towards an account of men's experience of adult education', Paper to SCUTREA Conference, 5–7 July, University of Warwick.

Ostrouch-Kaminska, J., Fontanini, C. and Gaynard, S. (Eds.) (2012) *Considering Gender in Adult Learning and Academia: (In) visible Act*. Warsaw: Wydawnictwo Naukowe.

Rubensen, K. (2000) 'Adult's readiness to learn: Questioning lifelong learning for all', Paper to Australian Association for Research in Education, Sydney, 4–7 December.

Säljö, R. (1979) 'Learning from a learner's perspective, I. Some common-sense conceptions', *Reports from the Institute of Education, University of Gothenberg*, 76.

Schuller, T. and Watson, D. (2009) *Learning Through Life: Inquiry into the Future of Lifelong Learning*. Leicester: NIACE.

Scott, J. (1996) *Feminism and History*. Oxford: Oxford University Press.

Severiens, S. and Geert, T. (1994) 'Gender differences in learning styles: A narrative review and quantitative meta-analysis', *Higher Education*, 27, pp. 487–501.

Singapore (2000) *Occupation Segregation: A Gender Perspective*, Manpower and Paper No 1/00. Singapore: Ministry of Manpower.

Smith, M. (1999) 'Learning theory', *The Encyclopedia of Informal Education*, Accessed 3 January 2008 from www.infed.org/biblio/b-learn.htm

Tett, L. (1996) 'Theorising practice in single-sex work', *Studies in the Education of Adults*, 28 (1), pp. 48–63. Leicester: NIACE.

WHO: World Health Organization (2003) *The Social Determinants of Health: The Solid Facts*, Second Edition, R. Wilkinson, and M. Marmot (Eds.). Copenhagen: WHO.

Wilson, N., Parmenter, T., Stancliffe, R., Shuttleworth, R. and Parker, D. (2010) 'A masculine perspective of gendered topics in the research literature on males and females with intellectual disability', *Journal of Intellectual and Developmental Disability*, 35 (1), pp. 1–8.

CHAPTER TWO

Men's learning in international settings

Barry Golding

Introduction

This chapter critically examines new and emerging international research in the field of men's learning, which tends to come mainly from Australia and Europe. It deliberately builds on the first major work on men's learning by Veronica McGivney (published by NIACE, McGivney, 1999; 2004). It also identifies particular groups of boys and men who are adversely affected by educational preclusion in diverse international contexts. These particularly include men of all ages who are beyond paid work for a range of reasons (early school leavers, unemployed, withdrawn from the workforce, with a disability or in age retirement). It also includes men whose engagement with work, family and community is limited by exclusion from, active avoidance of, or aversion to formal education. The chapter provides a rationale and theoretical framework for focusing throughout this book on the needs of men whose limited knowledge of formal learning cultures, new information technologies and functional literacies preclude them from accessing, participating in and benefiting from lifelong and new learning.

What is meant by learning?

This chapter adopts a strong presupposition that valuable adult and community learning, at its best, for many men, is more bottom-up than top-down, and more relational and contextual rather than individual, cognitive and behavioural. It contends that the learning process is most powerful in community contexts in which men simultaneously engage with each other around issues of culture, identity and difference and learn *through* life (Comerford, 2005), rather than through formally prescribed content, process or teaching in formal educational settings, thus the title of our book.

Given our interest in the power of bottom–up, relational and contextual learning, it is unsurprising that our particular interest is in the less formal learning often taking place beyond dedicated learning contexts. Herein lies a dilemma in the literature about what to call it (Smith, 2003; Colley, Hodgkinson and Malcolm, 2002; Golding, Brown and Foley, 2009). If we call it 'non-formal 'or 'informal' learning, we are, in essence, privileging and setting it in false opposition to learning that is fixed, formal, taught and accredited. Even going down the path of seeing informal learning as being found only in *situated* communities of practice, in the Lave and Wenger (1991) sense, in contrast to formal learning, is also a dead end, since all knowledge is situated in some context. For each of these reasons, we concur with Colley, Hodgkinson and Malcolm that there are:

> *few, if any, learning situations where either informal or formal elements are completely absent. Boundaries or relationships between informal, non-formal and formal learning can only be understood in particular contexts.* (2002, p. 1)

That said, including everything as 'learning' and not distinguishing between the formal and accredited and 'the rest' makes the measurement tasks of researchers and policy makers much more difficult, particularly if lifelong and lifewide learning is considered to occur in all contexts down to individual reading, including use of the internet, for example. Livingstone (2000), working in Canada, used the iceberg analogy to suggest that the bulk of learning remains hidden below the more obvious, smaller but more visible, formal and accredited learning. In Australia, the National Centre for Vocational Education Research (NCVER, 2009) have picked up the analogy in their discussion of informal learning, to claim that 'We should only recognise learning if it is of a high quality' (where 'people are gaining the right knowledge and are applying it in a safe and effective way'). This is a contention with which we disagree. It opens up a raft of other questions about learner agency and intention through life, quite apart from the questions about the value of learning through doing, the importance of serendipity, the value of learning through making mistakes, and particularly about who decides what is the 'right knowledge' in a society with a now unlimited potential to post and access knowledge on the internet. Finally, it is important to acknowledge, as Hager (1998, p. 533) notes, that 'learners themselves, influenced by prevailing assumptions about education and knowledge, are often unaware of the significance, range and depth of their informal knowledge'.

Theories about why men engage in learning (or not)

Our interest in men's engagement (or not) in learning raises the important question of why, and whether, men deliberately engage in (and in many instances avoid) learning. Our answers, given the diverse contexts and life circumstances in which individuals and groups of men find themselves, will also be diverse, and dependent on which theories of learning are used as lenses for the analysis. McGivney (1990) summarised six better-known theories of engagement in learning by adults related to their participation, later discussed by Smith (1998). These have to do with:

- Maslow's (1954) *theory of hierarchy of needs*;
- *congruence theory*, linking adult self-concept to the nature of education (Boshier, 1973);
- *force field theory* (Cross, 1981), where motivation emerges from the interaction of expectancy (of personal success and positive consequences) and 'valence' (the positive and negative values assigned to learning);
- *life transitions theory* (Sheehy, 1976), where people are more likely to participate in education through changes in life circumstance (job, break up of relationships, having children, bereavement, retirement);
- *reference group theory*, where people identify with the social and cultural group to which they aspire or belong (McGivney, 1993);
- *social participation theory* (Courtney, 1991), where reasons for learning are connected to the associated social roles and rewards.

In the 15 years since 1998, several other influential theories have grown in importance in the English-speaking literature and become movements, the most influential of which comes from French sociology, particularly from Bourdieu (1986), Foucault (1988) and the broader field of post-structuralism. These theories have been particularly useful in theorising adult education because they address the interrelated issues of power and knowledge and the role of different forms of capital. While Foucault (1988) sees power as 'ubiquitous' and beyond agency or structure, Bourdieu (1986) sees power as culturally and symbolically created, and constantly re-legitimised through the interplay of agency and structure through 'habitus': socialised norms or tendencies that guide human behaviour and thinking. Habitus is of particular theoretical relevance in the context of this book, given that it is created through a social, rather than individual, process leading to patterns that are enduring and transferrable from one context to another, but that can also shift in relation to specific contexts and over time. Nevertheless, habitus 'is not fixed or permanent, and can be changed under unexpected situations or over a long historical period' (Navarro, 2006, p. 16).

Delineating the research field

Much available literature, research and policy on education for adults is written in English and from Western liberal democracies. It is focused on the initial acquisition of formal educational skills and qualifications primarily for economic and employment purposes. This is particularly relevant today in the neoliberal political setting. Our specific interest in this book is in the broader value of men's informal and lifelong learning, including for other purposes and across the lifecourse. Using Pollard's (2010, p. 362) typology, our interest goes mainly to the second and third strands of philosophical and political thinking on educational purposes to be found in contemporary Western democracies, which are essentially concerned with social cohesion and inclusion, and wellbeing respectively. Our particular concern is that the first strand tends to see teaching and learning linked mainly or solely to economic productivity. While seductive in policy terms, this is only a very partial view of the wider benefits of learning.

While we acknowledge, with Pollard, that the three strands are 'deeply interconnected' (2010, p. 362), and accept that there is a persistent correlation between school and post-school educational success and employment, like Gorard (2010) we are more concerned about the persistent flipside for some men. That is that lack of success in learning is typically correlated with increasing difficulties through life, in and beyond paid work, and that many of these difficulties are closely related to family

23

background and where and when people are born. Further, our concern is that many of these difficulties go well beyond the individual and can become intergenerational and familial.

Our strongest caution and concern in this book is to avoid repeating what schools and post-school educational institutions and governments do, by simplistically linking and promoting educational qualifications and employment for all men because of persistent statistical correlations, without acknowledging the underlying inequity of using and promoting prior education as the main or only variable for selection to employment. As Gorard puts it, when we take a lifecourse view, qualifications, rather than being a causative agent, can alternatively be seen as 'a substitute variable summing up the prior individual, economic social and economic determinants of "success" at school and beyond' (2010, p. 359). As Gorard concludes:

> *Educators do not select their potential students, nor employers their employees, on the basis of their socio-economic status, ethnicity or age, as this is both unfair and illegal. However, they do select them on the basis of a substitute variable – prior education – that sums up, and is very heavily correlated with, such background factors. What is the sense in that?* (Gorard, 2010, p. 358)

Much educational discourse is premised on the idea that access can be universalised and participation maximised if young people and adults can somehow be encouraged to overcome impediments or 'barriers' by accessing the desirable education on 'the other side'. Gorard's scathing critique of 'barriers to learning' is a good starting point in a critical examination of men's learning. Gorard uses UK data to show that once family background, sex and age are accounted for, 'none of the measurable variables in adult life makes any difference to the quality of the predictions' (2010, p. 357) about adult participation in learning. Gorard concludes that 'We need to revise our complacency that the existing set-up for learning is appropriate for all, and that the reluctant learner need only be lured back 'on track' (p. 357). Indeed, most adult non-participants in formal learning are not put off by barriers, 'but by their lack of interest in something that seems alien and imposed by others' (p. 357).

A useful way of perceiving barriers, in the context of our book about men learning through life, is to acknowledge that there are factors beyond the contextual, institutional, informational, situational and personal/dispositional barriers identified by Cross (1981), elaborated by Bailey and Coleman (1998) and WRC (2003) and summarised by TSA (2009, p. 20) in the NALA Irish men's learning study. It is the closely related three personal and dispositional barriers identified by Corridan (2002) which emerge in most recent research to do with men's learning related to socially excluded men. The first is the accumulation of often-negative early school experiences that other forms of learning come to be negatively associated with throughout life. The second is the embarrassment and shame that some men experience associated with literacy and learning difficulties in more formal educational contexts. The third is the male culture of ridicule about pursuing something like learning, which some male peers regard as inappropriate and not masculine. At worst, what some men can and do experience in some educational contexts is neatly summarised from Owens' (2000) research as:

> *a deeply internalised sense of powerlessness ... which is rooted*
> *in early school experiences and in the wider cultural milieu*
> *wherein the dominant ideologies of the social order and masculinity*
> *dictate one's way of perceiving and being in the world.* (TSA,
> 2009, p. 21)

What has boys' underachievement got to do with all of this?

Factoring boys' education into our discussion is essential for three main reasons. The first is that boys become men, and the influences they gain about education are carried with them to manhood. The second is that many men go on to become role models as fathers and later grandfathers, including to boys. The third reason has to do with a trend towards boys' underachievement, particularly in areas of the world that have experienced higher growth in educational attainment rates (Jha and Kelleher, 2006, p. 5). Internationally, the data on gender and education, while intriguing, are far from consistent. While girls (and women) remain significantly educationally disadvantaged in relation to boys (and men) in many world nations, particularly in sub-Saharan Africa, the Arab States, Latin America and the Caribbean, school life expectancy data (SLE: the average number of years of schooling individuals can anticipate) confirms that girls exceed boys in educational access and educational success in many Western nations (Jha and Kelleher, 2006, Table 1, p. 5).

Debates around boy's underachievement are plagued with 'three persistent myths', identified and debunked by Jha and Kelleher (2006, pp. xiii–iv) that we are keen not to reinforce, by extrapolation, into our own work with men. The first is that this is about 'boys versus girls'. In fact it is never one or the other. Indeed the United Nations Development Programme's (UNDP, 2002) Millennium Development Goals commit signatory states to eliminating gender disparities in education in any direction. The second myth is that boys' underachievement is a spinoff from a 'war of the sexes', and necessarily related to the gender of teachers. The third is that boys' achievement at school should be measured against that of girls.

These myths aside, Jha and Kelleher trawled the literature then available and concluded that some of the causes of boys' underachievement, particularly in languages and the humanities, were fairly universal, while some others were context-specific (2006, p. 39). They stressed in advancing these causes that most societies are primarily patriarchal, and that gender relations remain in favour of men in more than one way. The first of these causes is perhaps less important in many developed, urban economies, and relates to social, economic and occupational practices that keep boys away from school. Similarly, the second cause relating to a paucity of places for boys tends not to apply in school sectors, where primary participation is becoming universal. It is the third cause: conformity to masculine gender identity and the feminisation of schools, that was identified in the work of Jha and Kelleher as most important and common. While this cause is debatable and not fully discussed in our book, it has some likely implications for research to do with men's learning in community settings, and is consistent with very recent research on male health-seeking behaviour undertaken by beyondblue in Australia (Mousaferiadis, 2012).

In essence, what Jha and Kelleher (2006) report is that some boys' and men's close conformity to traditional masculine gender identities clash with the demands of feminised education. While academics theorise about other, less traditional ways to be masculine or feminine, most boys and men, particularly those with limited and negative experiences of education, are socialised into often fairly rigid aspects that define masculinity as being about 'physical and mental toughness, the capacity to control emotion, capability for sexual conquest and fatherhood, and not with being feminine' (Jha and Kelleher, 2006, p. 43). For Mousaferiadis (2012), key universal themes for men (in a study designed to reduce the impact of depression and anxiety for men in the Australian community) were very similar: it was about men maintaining control, a preference for action and physically engaging rather than talking, and in relation to their wellbeing, a hesitancy and difficulty talking about it in either theory or reality. Our study of men's sheds in Chapter Eight returns to these themes, including Mousaferiadis' (2012) finding that most Australian men were more comfortable and more likely to 'look out for a mate' (a close male friend) than themselves.

What do recent tertiary education participation data show?

The pattern of men's participation in learning is neither simple nor easily generalisable. It varies by nation, sector, level and field of study, and has also varied over time. Chapters from seven different nations later in this book are illustrative of this diversity. Nevertheless, there have been attempts to globally link participation by gender in upper secondary school to participation by gender in vocational education and training (VET). UNEVOC (2006), for example, undertook a complex statistical study using existing global data to analyse to what degree gender inequities at upper secondary school impact on gender disparity (in either direction) on technical vocational education and training (TVET). It looked first to see whether more boys or girls in upper secondary school could be correlated with more men or women in TVET. It concluded that there was a 'complex pattern' but no such general relationship (UNEVOC, 2006, p. 62). However, it did conclude that the more equitable a nation was in terms of gender parity, the higher the percentage of TVET participation. Golding (2010) used some of the same data as part of a follow up study with an Australian focus.

Nevertheless, there are some recent trends if the focus is on men's participation in education in particular sub-regions of the world. I illustrate these trends in this section using recent OECD data from the tertiary (mainly higher education) sector, acknowledging that extrapolating to other, unlike nations will not necessarily reveal the same patterns. I acknowledge here that gendered relativities in tertiary education participation (differently defined and measured across nations) are not necessarily indicative of gender relativities in other adult education sectors, including VET and adult and community education (ACE). We also note that the global financial crisis since 2008 has greatly elevated unemployment in most nations, dating these statistics.

The first trend is that in most relatively developed nations, such as those in the OECD, women are increasingly more likely to commence higher education, in many nations significantly more likely than men. OECD (2008, p. 70) data show for the 26 OECD nations with data, females comprised more than 50 per cent of new entrants to tertiary education in 22 nations, with an average of 54 per cent across all 26 nations and 55 per cent for the 19 EU nations. OECD nations with higher proportions of women commencers included Iceland (60 per cent), Norway and the UK (59 per cent), Portugal and New Zealand (58 per cent).

By contrast, most males in developed nations are more likely to be in employment. While, in all OECD countries, males of working age (25–64 years) are significantly more likely than females to be in paid employment regardless of level of education attained (OECD, 2008, pp. 151–2), the difference between the percentage of males and females in employment reduces with higher education levels. Across all OECD countries, 82 per cent of males of working age were employed, compared with 64 per cent of females. Conversely females are more likely to be unemployed than males in most OECD nations, regardless of education levels (OECD, 2008, pp. 153–4). Across all OECD countries, five per cent of males of working age were unemployed, compared with six per cent of females. Females on average in the OECD earned less in paid work than males. Males of working age earned significantly more than women from paid employment, regardless of education level (OECD, 2008, p. 175).

Trends in women's participation in adult learning observed by McGivney (1999, 2003) in many developed nations and the UK will since have altered. McNair (2007, pp. 18–19) more recently identified broad changes in gender roles in the UK in the four decades since 1970. While the proportion of women in the workforce increased significantly, pay remained heavily biased in favour of men. Over the lifecourse, men and women tend to spend equal amounts of time working, but in different ways and stages. Career patterns and many fields of work and study remain heavily gendered. Patterns of retirement for men still tend to be very different than those for women. As McNair puts it, men tend to climb higher, and fall faster. Women tend to have fewer chances but smaller disappointments. With increased longevity, women are also more likely to care for elderly dependents, their own children and grandchildren.

Looking at men's learning in adult and community education settings

When we look at learning outside higher education in particular nations, some of the generalisations identified above start to fall away. In Canada, for example, Myers and Myles observed that:

> *Among the least educated, women are slightly less likely than men to participate in adult learning although the difference is not significant. In contrast, among university graduates women are much more likely (1.6 times) than men to participate in adult learning.* (2005, p. 19)

While the benefits to learning are greatest for the least educated (Myers and Myles, 2005, pp. 21–2), in most developed nations there are significantly more women involved in adult and community education than men, particularly amongst older men. As Scott and Wenger (1995, p. 162) noted, older men tend not to want to become involved with older people's organisations that they perceive to be dominated by women. More broadly, as Formosa (2012, p. 13) observes, men tend to relate to a culture that encourages them to cling to traditional roles and patterns of behaviour, where it is believed that engaging in learning is for women rather than for men.

In dedicated community-based learning organisations for older adults such as the University of the Third Age (U3A) (Formosa, 2012, p. 13), all surveys uncover a positive women to men ratio, ranging between 2.5:1 in Spain, 3:1 in Malta and the UK, and 4:1 in Australia, for example. As Formosa (2012, p. 13) summarises, 'the low percentage of men signals strongly that for a number of reasons the organization is not attractive to them'. In Ireland, the gender breakdown of all participants in community and adult education is approximately 70 per cent female, 30 per cent male (O'Connor, 2007) and the proportion of men participating in adult literacy declined from 71 per cent in 1980, to 37 per cent in 2000 (De Brún and Du Vivier, 2008). One-quarter of boys in Ireland exit formal education before the Leaving Certificate, compared with only six per cent of girls (Cleary *et al.*, 2004).

Summary

In summary, the situation for men and women in adult education is neither simple nor the same for all men and all women. Nor is it the same everywhere, at all education levels or for adults of all ages. For example, while most women globally 'remain disadvantaged in the spheres of education work and social life' (Bowl and Tobias, 2012, p. 4), on average 'European women are better educated than their male counterparts' and 'the rate of women's access to education and training throughout life is now higher than men in all courses or company training' in most European nations (Ostrouch-Kaminska, Fontanini and Gaynard, 2012, p. 10). While we are careful elsewhere in this book not to blame 'feminism, women teachers and women themselves' (Bowl and Tobias, 2012, p. 4) for these positive trends in educational participation for women, our interest is in addressing the absences and silences on gender issues in adult education (Ostrouch-Kaminska, Fontanini and Gaynard, 2012, p. 10), particularly as they apply to men learning informally through life, beyond the workplace.

Our general interest in this book is in how learning can and does make a big difference to men's lives (and by extension to partners, children, families and communities) in contexts beyond paid work. Our specific interest is in the benefits of learning in less formal contexts by the least formally educated men of any age. Our underlying interest is why such men sometimes hold very different expectations and attitudes towards learning from women and most other men, and how we can prevent these attitudes from becoming intergenerational.

Conclusion

This chapter has examined research in the field of men's learning with a particular emphasis on groups of men and boys who have been adversely affected by educational preclusion in diverse international contexts. The chapter challenges the neoliberal view of learning as pertaining only to the acquisition of formal educational skills and qualifications primarily for economic and employment purposes and looks at the broader value of men's informal and lifelong learning, including for other purposes and across the lifecourse. The chapter examines the trend towards boys' underachievement, particularly in areas of the world that have experienced higher growth in educational attainment rates (Jha and Kelleher,

2006, p. 5). The chapter concludes with a discussion on the value of community education for health and wellbeing but highlights the concern that men are less likely to engage in learning than women.

References

Bailey, I. and Coleman, U. (1998) *Access and Participation in Adult Literacy Schemes in Ireland*. Dublin: NALA.

Boshier, R. (1973) 'Educational participation and dropout: A theoretical model', *Adult Education*, 23 (4), pp. 255–82.

Bourdieu, P. (1986) 'The forms of capital', in J. Richardson (Ed.), *Handbook of Theory and Research for the Sociology of Capital*. New York: Greenwood Press, pp. 241–58.

Bowl, M. and Tobias, R. (2012) 'Gender, masculinities and lifelong learning: entering the debate', in M. Bowl, R. Tobias, J. Leahy, G. Ferguson and J. Leahy (Eds.), *Gender, Masculinities and Lifelong Learning*. Abingdon: Routledge, pp. 3–13.

Cleary, A., Corbett, M., Galvin, M. and Wall, J. (2004) *Young Men on the Margins*, Dublin: The Katharine Howard Foundation.

Colley, H., Hodgkinson, P. and Malcolm, J. (2002) *Non Formal Learning: Mapping the Conceptual Terrain. A Consultation Report*. Retrieved 3 January 2008 from www.infed.org/archives/e-texts/colley_informal_learning.htm

Comerford, S. (2005) 'Engaging through learning, learning through engaging: An alternative approach to professional learning about human diversity', *Social Work Education*, 24 (1), pp. 113–35.

Corridan, M. (2002) *Moving from the Margins: A Study of Male Participation in Adult Literacy Education*. Dublin: Dublin Adult Learning Centre.

Courtney, S. (1991) *Why Adults Learn: Towards a Theory of Participation in Adult Learning*. San Francisco: Jossey-Bass.

Cross, K. (1981) *Adults as Learners: Increasing Participation and Facilitating Learning*. San Francisco: Jossey-Bass.

De Brún, T. and Du Vivier, E. (2008) *Men Alone in no Man's Land: A Study of the Needs of Socially Excluded Males in Dublin's Inner City*. Dublin: Dublin Inner City Partnership.

Formosa, M. (2012) 'Four decades of universities of the third age: past, present, future', *Ageing and Society*, available on CJO2012. doi:10.1017/S0144686X12000797.

Foucault, M. (1988) *Power/Knowledge: Selected Interviews and other Writings, 1972–1977*. USA: Random House.

Golding, B. (2010) 'The big picture on men's (and boy's) learning', *Australian Journal of Adult Learning*, 50 (1), pp. 54–74.

Golding, B., Brown, M. and Foley, A. (2009) 'Informal learning: A discussion around defining and researching its depth and breadth', *Australian Journal of Adult Learning*, 49 (1), pp. 34–56.

Gorard, S. (2010) 'Participation in learning: Barriers to learning', in C. Cooper, J. Field, U. Goswami, R. Jenkins and B. Sahakian (Eds.), *Mental Capital and Wellbeing*. Chichester: Wiley-Blackwell, pp. 351–60.

Hager, P. (1998) 'Recognition of informal learning: Challenges and issues', *Journal of Vocational Education and Training* 50 (4), pp. 521–35.

Jha, J. and Kelleher, F. (2006) *Boys' Underachievement in Education: An Exploration in Selected Commonwealth Countries*. London: Commonwealth Secretariat and Commonwealth of Learning.

Lave, J. and Wenger, E. (1991) *Situated Learning: Legitimate Peripheral Participation*. Cambridge: Cambridge University Press.

Livingstone, D. (2000) *Exploring the Icebergs of Adult Learning: Findings of the First Survey of Informal Learning Practices*. (Canada) Retrieved 2 April 2009 from www.oise.utoronto.ca/depts/sese/csew/nall/res/10exploring.htm

Maslow, A. (1954) *Motivation and Personality*. New York: Harper and Rowe.

McGivney, V. (1990) *Education's for Other People: Access to Education for Non-participant Adults*. Leicester: NIACE.

McGivney, V. (1993) *Women, Education and Training: Barriers to Access: Informal Starting Points and Progression Routes*. Leicester: NIACE.

McGivney, V. (1999) *Excluded Men: Men who are Missing from Education and Training*. Leicester: NIACE.

McGivney, V. (2003) 'Participation and non-participation: A review of the literature', in R. Edwards, S. Siemenski and D. Zeldin (Eds.), *Adult Learners, Education and Training*. London: Routledge, pp. 11–30.

McGivney, V. (2004) *Men Earn, Women Learn: Bridging the Gender Divide in Education and Training*. Leicester: NIACE.

McNair, S. (2007) *Demography and Adult Learning: Thematic Paper 1, Inquiry into the Future of Lifelong Learning*. Leicester: NIACE.

Mousaferiadis, T. (2012) 'Putting the spotlight on male help seeking behaviour', Presentation to Victorian Male Health Gathering, Moorabbin, 16 November.

Myers, K. and Myles, M. (2005) *Self-assessed Returns to Adult Education: Life-long Learning and the Educationally Disadvantaged*, Research Report W35. Ottawa: Canadian Policy Research Network.

Navarro, Z. (2006) 'In search of cultural interpretation of power', *IDS Bulletin*, 37 (6), pp. 1–22.

NCVER (2009) *Informal Learning: At a Glance*. Adelaide: NCVER.

O'Connor, M. (2007) *Sé Sí: Gender in Irish Education*. Dublin: Department of Education and Science.

OECD (2008) *Education at a Glance 2008*. Paris: OECD.

Ostrouch-Kaminska, J., Fontanini, C. and Gaynard, S. (Eds.) (2012) *Considering*

Gender in Adult Learning and Academia: (In) visible Act. Warsaw: Wydawnictwo Naukowe.

Owens. T. (2000) *Men on the Move.* Dublin: AONTAS National Association of Adult Education.

Pollard, A. (2010) 'Evidence-informed principles from the teaching and learning research programme', in C. Cooper, J. Field, U. Goswami, R. Jenkins and B. Sahakian (Eds.), *Mental Capital and Wellbeing.* Chichester: Wiley-Blackwell, pp. 361–7.

Scott, A. and Wenger, G. (1995) 'Gender and social support networks in later life', in S. Arber and J. Ginn (Eds.), *Connecting Gender and Ageing: A Sociological Approach.* Buckingham: Open University Press, pp. 158–72.

Sheehy, G. (1976) *Passages: Predictable Crises of Adult Life.* New York: Dutton.

Smith, M. (1998) 'Participation in learning projects and programmes'. Retrieved 3 January 2008 from www.infed.org./mobi/participation-in-learning-projects-and-programmes/

Smith, M. (2003) 'Learning theory', *The Encyclopedia of Informal Education.* Retrieved 11 January 2014 from www.infed.org/mobi/learning-theory-models-product-and-process/

TSA (2009) TSA Consultancy, *Men and Literacy: A Study of Attitude and Experiences of Learning.* Dublin: NALA.

UNDP (2002) *Human Development Report 2003: Millennium Goals: A Compact among Nations to End Human Poverty.* New York: Oxford University Press.

UNEVOC (2006) *Participation in Formal Technical and Vocational Education and Training Programmes Worldwide.* Paris: UNEVOC International Centre for TVET.

WRC (2003) WRC Social and Economic Consultants, *Accommodating Diversity in Labour Market Programmes.* Dublin: Equality Authority.

CHAPTER THREE

Men's health and wellbeing: Learning through the lifecourse

John Macdonald

Introduction

This chapter draws on new data and insights from international research to provide a background to the question of why men's health and wellbeing is a matter that deserves looking at in more depth. It also aims to offer some insights into men and learning in the context of their health and the ways in which a social determinants approach to health can enrich an understanding of men's health and learning.

For some time, thinking about men's health, both in academic writing and in policy and programmes, has been carried out within two main frameworks: a bio-medical one and what might be called a social-psychological one, based on notions of 'masculinity'. While both of these approaches may have useful insights, they are increasingly being shown to be an inadequate basis for a comprehensive approach to men's health, including the structuring of men's health policies and of programmes aimed at 'educating' men about their health.

The emergence on the world public health scene of the enormous amount of evidence concerning the *social determinants of health* (SDOH) presents a fresh way of thinking about men's health. The World Health Organization (WHO) has led the field (WHO 2003, 2008) and many scholars throughout the world are adding to the available evidence of the impact of social and political environments on people's health (Marmot, 2005; Macdonald, 2010). The systematic study of social determinants, social epidemiology (Berkman and Kawachi, 2000), is described as looking for the 'causes of causes', not just of disease but also of health. This approach calls for consideration of diverse local contexts, societies and populations. There is a considerable body of research on the social determinants of women's health (Wuest *et al.*, 2002; Anderson, 2006) as well as the inspirational Australian Longitudinal Study on Women's Health (ALSWH, 2013), which has spent two decades looking at women's physical and psychosocial health over the lifespan.

Yet, interestingly, the SDOH approach has rarely been adopted when looking at men's health, though there are a few exceptions (Macdonald, 2006; Department of Health and Ageing, 2010). This lack is regrettable, since the SDOH approach offers an obvious way of constructing a rational and balanced framework for looking at and building policies for male health. This chapter sets out to redress this situation by applying the social determinants approach to male (boys' and men's) health. Such a perspective is usually described as a 'lifecourse' view of health: looking at the different stages of a person's life and the health needs and challenges of each stage. This prompts a brief comment on the different 'health' learning that takes place or should take place over a man's lifecourse.

How we see the issue determines how we see 'solutions'

Two illustrations from real-life incidents are offered here which usefully illustrate the point I wish to make: that views and policies of male health and wellbeing and the 'health education' which flows from these are generally shaped by the two bodies of thinking already mentioned – the medical view and the sociological academic view, the latter strongly influenced by theories of 'masculinity'. I am director of a drop in centre (The Shed) for men (mainly Aboriginal men) at risk of suicide (Macdonald and Welsh, 2012). The two illustrative incidents took place at that location.

In the first incident, a young female student social worker visiting The Shed was explaining that the problem with men's health is that 'They (men) don't speak', and 'They don't get in touch with their feelings'. She affirmed this confidently since she had studied the 'theory' of men's psychology just two weeks ago in class. I asked her to turn around. Puzzled, she did so. A man was in deep conversation with an actively listening mental health worker who is available to men who come to

The Shed. The student seemed not to be aware of the contradictions in what she was saying and what she was seeing. She was not convinced by anything I said or by what she could see: she continued to insist that 'men don't talk'. She had studied the matter and the visual evidence wasn't enough to challenge the view of men that she had learned about. I attribute this blindness to the dominance in sociology of theories of 'masculinity', particularly of 'hegemonic masculinity' (Connell, 1987; Connell and Messerschmidt, 2005). These theories have been nuanced in recent years, but they have helped build a professional discourse which holds that men are 'hard wired' to dominate and compete, tend towards violence and suppress their feelings.

In the second incident, a van visited the same shed. The van offers check-ups on blood pressure, body mass index and the like and suggests referrals to local doctors; it is excellent at what it does. The interest is particularly in diabetes, potential heart attacks and strokes, all-important conditions in the health landscape of these men. Aboriginal men experience the lowest life expectancy in Australia and, as a group, have the worst health outcomes of any population in Australia. The Australian Indigenous Health*InfoNet* points out the underlying causes:

> *Indigenous male health is also affected by contemporary structural and social factors, including economic opportunity, physical infrastructure and social conditions. These factors, known collectively as the 'social determinants of health', are manifest in measures such as housing, education, employment, access to services, social networks, connection with land, racism, and rates of imprisonment. Indigenous males suffer substantial disadvantage for all of these measures during their childhood, as adolescents, and throughout their adult years. It is important to consider these social determinants in addressing the health of Indigenous males as it is here that resilience can best be supported and reinforced.* (Thomson *et al.*, 2010; Australian Indigenous HealthInfoNet, p. 1)

The Aboriginal men in western Sydney (the largest single Aboriginal community in Australia) make up one of the most disadvantaged populations in the country. An average of five men a day kill themselves in Australia, as does one woman. But suicide is tragically even more common among Aboriginal men, who:

*are more likely to die from almost any cause and at any age than
are non-indigenous males, have the lowest life expectancy, and
high rates of substance misuse, suicide, and incarceration*
(Brown *et al.*, 2012)

Housing and job insecurity, and frequent incarceration (the Indigenous population of New South Wales is around 2.5 per cent, but it makes up almost one-quarter of the prison community), often on account of court orders to do with domestic violence, are part of the regular context of the lives of many of these men. Stress is endemic. One day I asked the two health workers in the van about their work, and slipped in a question about stress: 'Did you ask the men what was going on in their lives?' The response was swift. 'We deal with health issues here, mental health is another department'. I respectfully withdrew. We cannot risk alienating those who provide a service to men who have much less access to health check-ups than the rest of the Australian community.

My point here is that medicine has a clinical focus, of course. Beyond this particular men's shed, and as illustrated by International Men's Health Congresses, the global focus on men's health is clearly on the clinical, generally the prostate and erectile dysfunction (Macdonald, 2012). Pharmaceutical companies have a particular interest in fostering this view of 'men's health'. When attention is moved away from the narrow, clinical view of men's health, it focuses either on male health magazines about abdominal 'six packs' or better sex (no bad things, but a limited perspective), or on telling men to behave better, to stop 'men behaving badly'. In the academic world, this negative view of men is promoted in the writing on 'masculinity' already referred to; if men are ill then the problem must be men themselves.

These two pathologising streams of thinking (with consequences for policies and practice concerning men's health and health education) can come together, with the authority of both medicine and academia; the result can be quite negative approaches. One classic example is the Men's Health Policy of the Australian Doctors' Reform Society (DRS):

*The DRS recognises that there are particular issues for men
which affect their health. These issues can arise from the process of
socialisation to compete and dominate in social and political spheres
which can foster violence. As a result of this, many men experience a*

*number of psychological difficulties, a reluctance to acknowledge and
address their own health issues and diffidence in approaching health
services.* (Doctors' Reform Society, undated).

This is the policy of a group of progressive doctors, seemingly unin-
terested in men commuting long hours to work for their families, men
killing themselves, men doing hard physical jobs which threaten their
health: everything is caused by their compulsion to 'compete and dominate'. Thus, education for health would consist of telling them to change.

A fresh approach: The social determinants of male health

There has been such a wealth of research on the social determinants
of health in recent years that it is easy to make a case for adopting this
perspective to frame professional responses to the health needs of any
population. There is by now a vast amount of evidence that physical and
mental health, in addition to being influenced by genetic and behavioural factors, are deeply influenced by the social, economic and cultural
contexts of people's lives over their lifespan. An easily accessible text
demonstrating the evidence for the importance of social determinants
(the material, emotional and other social contexts of our lives) on people's health in general can be found in the World Health Organization's
2003 document, *The Solid Facts*: 'People's lifestyles and the conditions in
which they live and work strongly influence their health and longevity'
(WHO, 2003, p. 8). The document argues that although medical care
can prolong survival after some serious diseases, the social and economic
conditions that affect whether people become ill are more important for
health gains in the population as a whole.

Macdonald argues that health and illness can no longer be reduced to
biological functioning or malfunctioning, or, indeed, to personal behaviour. He goes on to argue that:

> *typical examples are the links between diabetes or cardiovascular
> disease and social context. Such perspectives on population health
> have led to the growth of social epidemiology, the study, not only
> of the spread of disease in communities, but of the contextual
> circumstances of both disease and health: the social, cultural and
> political environments which either foster or threaten the health of*

populations and subpopulations in our societies. (Macdonald, 2006, p. 456)

There is much talk of the need for evidence-based health policies (Brownson *et al.*, 2009). The SDOH perspective put health policies and practice, and also the approach to education for health, on a more solid, evidence-based foundation. Recent valuable work has been done to improve service provision to women, and attempts have been made to incorporate a fuller understanding both of women's life contexts and perspectives on their own health into professional practice. This must be applauded and seen as an exemplar that could be applied to male health policies. The *Australian Longitudinal Study on Women's Health*, started in 1995 with long-term funding to follow a cohort of 40,000 women, goes some way to supply evidence to ensure good-quality outcomes for women (ALSWH, 2013).

The Australian Male Health Policy announced the funding of a similar national male health study, the first of its kind. The study, consistent with the social determinants approach, is following boys and men over the lifespan. Many of the contextual influences on people's health start in early childhood and develop and are enhanced or diminished by their ongoing life experience, a point returned to later in the context of health and learning. The building of evidence over time, such as through the longitudinal study, will supply a broader base for programmes of male health.

Health and learning over the lifecourse

The social determinants approach helps to conceptualise health as something dynamic, the result of interactions with multiple environments over time. The world literature on the subject, as well as our own study on male suicide (MHIRC website), helps to show that health consists of positive interactions with our total environment: familial, school, community, political and physical. Managing these interactions well makes for strong health, whereas lack of good interactions with these factors in our environment, especially if these difficulties accumulate, has a deleterious effect on our health (Macdonald, 2005). The field of scientific study which studies these effects, psychoneuroimmunology, reports, for example, that:

> *adverse events, stress etc. can increase susceptibility to upper respiratory*
> *tract infections, hostility can increase the likelihood of heart disease,*
> *while conversely, strong social support and an optimistic attitude*
> *by the patient can prolong the life expectancy of a cancer patient.*
> (Leonard and Myint, 2009, p. 166)

These are measurable effects. Positive interactions release a flood of health enhancing hormones: excessive negative stress has the opposite effect.

> *Studies of the behavioural changes elicited by the cytokines*
> *interleukin (IL)-1, IL-6 and tumour necrosis factor have*
> *demonstrated that cytokines activate specific cytokine receptors on*
> *neurons and glial cells and thereby directly influence brain function.*
> (Leonard and Myint, 2009, p. 165)

Studies of the interaction between adverse events and behavioural and immunological responses in this new field of psychoneoroimmunology (e.g. Leonard and Myint, 2009) help to identify the health/illness effects of positive/negative interactions with the environments as physiological and not just 'all in the mind'. In essence, positive or negative interactions with the total environment shape wellbeing or illness, not in a linear but in a holistic sense.

Our own study of male suicide (MHIRC, 2013) is relevant in this context because this research has reinforced the idea that the interactions which go a long way to building health (including physical health, as in strengthening the immune system) are interactions which either reinforce our sense of being valued, or diminish it. If a child is loved, she/he has a good chance to flourish physically and mentally; if abused, the opposite can happen, with disastrous long-term effects in terms of coping with life. If older people feel valued, their immune system is strengthened and, of course, their psychological health is as well. The study led us to think of the social determinants of health as 'lifelines': the important threads that hold us in life (or not).

Male health learning across the lifecourse

What has all of the above got to do with men's learning? The connection between the social determinants of health and learning is not a difficult one to make. For a long time educators have been rediscovering that 'learning' is not just about the acquisition of 'facts' and certainly is not only something that happens in formal settings like classrooms (Candy, 1991). Learning is also not being subjected to facts that help to change behaviour, as in the version of 'health promotion', which consists of telling people what to do, or not to do: not to smoke, not to drink too much and to practise safe sex.

Public health has, for understandable reasons, often been dominated by clinical or behavioural dimensions of health and disease. An example would be smoking and its negative health effects and prevention initiatives. There is plenty of clinical information available on the negative impact on health of smoking; there are also many programmes aimed at stopping people from smoking (behavioural change). Graham, researching smoking by women, concluded that:

> *Despite the emphasis on maternal smoking in epidemiological studies,*
> *little attention has been paid in psychological and social research to*
> *the experience of smoking in the context of poverty and motherhood.*
> (Graham, 1987, p. 47)

Graham emphasised the importance of taking context into account: considering the social determinants of people's lives before rushing into interventions such as health promotion about the dangers of specific harmful practices. Without naming it, Graham also showed gender to be an important social determinant of health: in this case the isolation and disadvantage of the women targeted.

At least one lesson should be learned from Graham's work: before giving people recommendations on how they should change their behaviour or about their 'lifestyle', it is important to take into account the circumstances of their lives, with the preoccupation of valuing them where they are, and supporting them towards healthier lives. Our own research points to the importance of 'life context' health promotion rather than 'lifestyle' health promotion (Macdonald, 2005, p. 145). This may be of particular importance for men since, as has been said, the professional culture seems focused on preventing men from 'behaving badly'.

Moreover, we should remember that 'learning' throughout life is, importantly, about being enhanced in our sense of self and our ability to deal with the things life throws at us. What Deci and colleagues (and many educators like them) were saying decades ago about learning in the school context applies to learning at all stages of life, in whatever context:

> *The acquisition and retention of facts are important but are by no means enough for excellent education. Correspondingly, the central features of optimal adjustment are feeling good about oneself and acting volitionally to satisfy one's own needs while being attuned to and concerned about the social surround.* (Deci *et al.*, 1991, p. 326)

In the context of male health, this insight into the essential links between learning and sense of self worth, reported here in the context of formal education, casts light on all stages of life. All significant interactions, especially long term interactions, involve some form of learning and have an impact on health, either strengthening or weakening it.

The perspective of SDOH in the context of male health encourages the provision of environments that allow the boy and the man at the various stages of their lives to flourish to the fullness of their capacity. For example, in the case of the health of boys, since much of a child's life is spent in school, we should be asking: 'Does the school environment provide a growing boy with occasion not just to develop his brain, but his whole self?' The seemingly uncontested assumption that boys are unruly in school and that the frequent diagnosis of Attention Deficiency Hyperactive Disorder is beyond question should raise questions for all those genuinely concerned with boys' learning and education.

Conclusion

In conclusion, some of the implications of taking a social determinants approach to male health and learning are identified at four stages across the lifespan: in early life, in schooling, in work and in life beyond work.

Early life

Early life is a critically important social determinant of health (WHO, 2003) and lays the foundations for our later physical and mental health. Young boys in the family context in the first years of their life are given lots of knowledge but also acquire their fundamental sense of self. This should include the sense that it is okay to be a boy and take pride in themselves as well as respect of others, including girl children. There seems to be a 'culture' in the West that presumes that women (and girls) are always more deserving of supportive health interventions since they are assumed to have poorer health outcomes than males. This may not be the case: a Finnish study draws attention to the poorer health of boys in many instances:

> *The data confirmed earlier findings that boys have more biological health problems than girls. The gender differences were most striking for perinatal health indicators, mortality, asthma and intellectual disabilities. This is in concordance with the results of previous Finnish studies, which have reported boys' excess risk for death … respiratory problems including asthma … and intellectual disability… . Gender differences in perinatal health did not much explain the gender differences in later childhood health.* (Gissler et al., 1999, p. 313)

In the face of such evidence, it is hard to argue that from the very start of life women are always more worthy of health support than men. And in the context of the social determinants of health, it reinforces the need for positive messages to boy children about themselves (Gissler et al., 1999).

Schooling

Schooling, as mentioned earlier by Deci et al. (1991), also involves learning, for both girls and boys, of course. In addition to instructing children in the '3 R's', schooling optimally builds on the self-confidence acquired in the home; boys at school learn more about themselves and society's expectations of them and how to interact with the wider world. Researchers such as Epstein et al. identified the decline in achievement of boys in schools in much of Western society (Epstein et al., 1998). Given the strong emphases in other chapters about the value of informal learning by men, it is sufficient to note that 'learning', both at home and in school, is much more than information gathering.

For example, bullying is a learned behaviour and school is often the place where it occurs:

> *Poor family functioning and especially domestic violence might promote bullying in several ways. Parents might show very little care for their children and not consider their feelings. As a consequence, a child develops a low empathy towards others. Badly functioning families might be characterised by a clear imbalance of power and aggression between members; children start to learn to dominate others and might even be encouraged in doing so. Domestic violence in this regard is relevant in explaining aggressive behaviour among children as a learned behaviour.* (Baldry, 2003, p. 175)

Although Baldry is mentioning boys in this context, she is careful to point out that girls also bully and that all efforts to reduce bullying/violence in school will have a positive 'learning' impact on young boys. The importance of positive male role models is clear, both in the home and at school. The paucity of male teachers in primary schools has often been lamented for depriving boys of positive role models during a very formative stage of their lives (Watson *et al.*, 2010).

One conclusion to this might be: if society wants healthy men it must have healthy boys (and vice versa). If healthy boys are desirable it is critically important to actively involve boys in schools to ensure that what goes on in schools helps young males to grow up, not only to be non-violent but also to have pride in themselves as males. Willis' famous, early book (1977) about the impact of 'secondary modern' education on young English working-class boys' sense of self and aspirations (low) remains a classic piece of work on the unofficial 'learning' that goes on at schools. Such education (secondary modern), said Willis, makes boys 'ready to labour'. Hopefully societies have moved on since then, but there is a need to be vigilant to encourage true education in the way mentioned for all boys.

Learning at work and after work

A considerable amount of many men's lives is spent in the work environment. Much learning takes place in this environment, as identified in Chapter 6. While working, men acquire skills that help them support themselves and their families. Young men who join apprenticeship schemes can work and learn at the same time. The Australian National Male Health Policy highlights that the workplace can be good contact point with men for health services:

> *Health checks in the workplace are an important means of raising awareness about health issues and reducing barriers to access by bringing health checks to males. Workplace health checks, such as the Workplace Men's Health Program offered by Foundation 49, the Tradies Tune Up … or the Transport Workers Union's Healthbreak screening program, can identify health risks, provide educational materials, pick up on occupational health risks like sleep apnoea, and refer participants to health care services.* (Department of Health and Ageing, 2010, p. 21)

But, of course, learning is not only about acquiring skills. In the workplace, as at school, a man's sense of value, of self worth, is either strengthened or diminished. He learns his worth, to some extent, in the long hours spent at work. The famous Whitehall study launched by Michael Marmot shows conclusively that having a measure of control over your work adds years to your life: the social gradient (where you are in the ladder of authority, in this case at work) is directly correlated to your health and longevity (Marmot *et al.*, 1991).

Learning beyond work

In summary, enough has been said here to indicate the importance of seeing 'outside the box' and considering the vital links between health and the learning about oneself that goes on at all stages of life for boys and men. Just as in the area of health, it is critically important to stop thinking that health is restricted to what goes on in hospitals and through health service provision (which are really necessary, but mainly there to fix what has gone wrong). So, too, we must stop thinking of 'learning' or even 'education' as something that takes place for men and boys exclusively in schools or other institutions. The lifecourse perspective on health, which is part of a social determinants approach, encourages seeing 'learning for health' for men as having to do with creating positive environments which allow men not only to learn facts about health, but also to acquire skills and confidence to navigate through life's changing circumstances. This wider sense of 'education for health' is what has been referred to in the last few years as 'health literacy' (Nutbeam, 2009). It is not just about understanding words, but being empowered to engage successfully with those things which either build health or threaten it.

References

ALSWH: *Australian Longitudinal Study on Women's Health* (2013) Retrieved 7 May 2013 from www.alswh.org.au

Anderson, J. (2006) 'Reflections on the social determinants of women's health exploring intersections: Does racialization matter?' *Canadian Journal of Nursing Research*, 38 (1), March.

Australian Indigenous HealthInfoNet, *Review of Indigenous Male Health*. Retrieved 16 October 2012 from www.healthinfonet.ecu.edu.au/population-groups/men/reviews/our-review updated 2010.

Baldry, A. (2003) 'Bullying in schools and exposure to domestic violence', *Child Abuse and Neglect*, 27 (7), July, pp. 713–32. Retrieved 7 May 2013 from doi:10.1016/S0145-2134(03)00114-5

Berkman, L. and Kawachi, I. (Eds.) (2000) *Social Epidemiology*. New York: Oxford University Press.

Brown, A., Scales, U., Beever, W., Rickards, B., Rowley, K. *et al.* (2012) 'Exploring the expression of depression and distress in aboriginal men in central Australia: A qualitative study', *BMC Psychiatry* 2012, 12:97. Retrieved 7 May 2013 from www.biomedcentral.com/1471-244X/12/97

Brownson, R., Fielding, J. and Maylahn, C. (2009) 'Evidence-based public health: A fundamental concept for public health practice', *Annual Review of Public Health*, (30), pp. 175–201.

Candy, P. (1991) *Self-direction for Lifelong Learning: A Comprehensive Guide to Theory and Practice*. Jossey-Bass: San Francisco.

Connell, R. (1987) *Gender and Power: Society, the Person and Sexual Politics*. Sydney: Allen and Unwin.

Connell, R. and Messerschmidt, J. (2005) 'Hegemonic masculinity: Rethinking the concept', *Gender and Society*, 19 (6), pp. 829–59.

Deci, E., Vallerand, R., Pelletier, L. and Ryan, R. (1991) 'Motivation and education: The self-determination perspective', *Educational Psychologist* 26 (3 and 4), pp. 325–46.

Department of Health and Ageing (Australian Government) (2010) National Male Health Policy, Canberra. Retrieved 7 May 2013 from www.health.gov.au/internet/main/publishing

Doctors' Reform Society (undated). Retrieved 20 July 2010 from www.drs.org.aupolicy/8-gender-health.aspx

Epstein, D., Elwood, J., Hey, V. and Maw, J. (Eds.) (1998) *Failing Boys? Issues in Gender and Achievement*. New York: Taylor and Francis.

Gissler, M., Järvelin, M., Louhiala, P. and Hemminki, E. (1999) 'Boys have more health problems in childhood than girls: Follow-up of the 1987 Finnish birth cohort', *Acta Pediatr*, 88: pp. 310–14. Retrieved 7 May 2013 from www.ncbi.nlm.nih.gov/pubmed/10229043

Graham, H. (1987) 'Women's smoking and family health', *Social Science and Medicine*, 25 (1), pp. 47–56.

Leonard, B. and Myint, A. (2009) 'The psychoneuroimmunology of depression', *Human Psychopharmacology Clinical and Experimental*, 24, pp. 165–75.

Macdonald, J. (1994) *Primary Health Care: Medicine in its Place*. London: Earthscan.

Macdonald, J. (2005) *Environments for Health*. Trowbridge: Earthscan.

Macdonald, J. (2006) 'Shifting paradigms: Social-determinants approach to solving problems in men's health policy and practice', *Medical Journal of Australia*, 186: pp. 456–8.

Macdonald, J. (2010) 'Health equity and the social determinants of health in Australia', *Social Alternatives*, 29 (2), pp. 34–40.

Macdonald, J. (2012) 'The need to change our way of looking at men's health: Australian perspectives', Future perspectives for intervention, policy and research on men and masculinities: An international forum. Retrieved 7 May 2013 from www.mensstudies.com

Macdonald, J. and Welsh, R. (2012) 'The Shed at Mt Druitt and the social determinants of Aboriginal male health'. MHIRC UWS. Retrieved 7 May 2013 from www.menshealthweek.org.au/TheShedPaper.pdf

Marmot, M. (2005) Social determinants of health inequalities, *The Lancet*, 365(9464), pp. 1099–104.

Marmot, M., Stansfield, S., Patel, C., North, F., White, I. *et al.* (1991) 'Health inequalities among British civil servants: The Whitehall II study', *The Lancet*, 337(8754), pp. 1387–93.

MHIRC: Men's Health Information Resource Centre (2013). Retrieved 23 June 2013 from www.uws.edu.au/mhirc

Nutbeam, D. (2009) 'Defining and measuring health literacy: What can we learn from literacy studies?' *International Journal of Public Health*, 54 (5), pp. 303–5.

Thomson, N., Midford, R., Debuyst, O. and MacRae, A. (2010) 'Review of Indigenous male health'. Retrieved 7 May 2013 from www.healthinfonet. ecu.edu.au/male_review

Watson, A., Kehler, M. and Martino, W. (2010) 'The problem of boys' literacy underachievement: Raising some questions', *Journal of Adolescent and Adult Literacy*, 53 (5), pp. 356–61.

Willis, P. (1977) *Learning to Labour: How Working Class Kids Get Working Class Jobs*. Westmead: Saxon House.

WHO: World Health Organization (2003) *Social Determinants of Health: The Solid Facts*, R. Wilkinson and M. Marmot (Eds.). Retrieved 7 May 2013 from www.euro.who.int/__data/assets/pdf_file/0005/98438/e81384.pdf

WHO: World Health Organization (2008) *Social Determinants of Health: World Commission on Social Determinants of Health: Final Report*. Retrieved 7 May

2013 from www.who.int/social_determinants/thecommission/finalreport/en/index.html

Wuest, J., Merritt-Gray, M., Berman, H. and Ford-Gilboe, M. (2002) 'Illuminating social determinants of women's health using grounded theory', *Health Care for Women International*, 23 (8), pp. 794–808.

CHAPTER FOUR

Empowering men to learn through literacy

Rob Mark

Introduction

In this chapter, I examine how a lack of literacy skills can affect men's participation in learning and the potential impact which participation can have on men's lives and wellbeing. The chapter draws on findings from two research studies of men's involvement in literacy in informal learning settings in Ireland. The studies were funded by the National Adult Literacy Agency (Lalor *et al.*, 2009) and the Changing Ageing Partnership (Mark, Montgomery and Graham, 2009). The research provides evidence about issues affecting men's participation in adult learning and literacy provision as well as how older men learn in non-formal and informal learning contexts.

Background

Throughout the industrialised world, the problem of illiteracy has advanced to the top of the policy agenda, largely as a result of the International Adult Literacy Survey (IALS, 1994). There has been a radical rethink of the need to confront the problem of illiteracy and its impact in modern industrial democratic societies. While there is acceptance that literacy has a profound impact on life chances, there is less agreement on what to do about this.

An understanding of the meaning of literacy ranges from the ability to read and write, to a more complex set of abilities, which include understanding other forms of communication such as body language, pictures, maps and video, to the lifelong, intellectual process of gaining meaning from a critical interpretation of the written or printed texts. The United Nations Educational, Scientific and Cultural Organization defined literacy as the:

> *ability to identify, understand, interpret, create, communicate and compute, using printed and written materials associated with varying contexts. Literacy can therefore be said to cover a continuum of learning that allows individuals to achieve their goals, to develop their knowledge and potential, and to participate fully in their community and wider society.* (UNESCO, 2004, p. 1)

A literate community is a dynamic community where individuals exchange ideas and take part in debate. The complexity of meaning has led to a focus on the uses of literacy that are constantly evolving along with advances in technology. New types of communication are emerging, and the ever-wider availability of communication, such as the internet and mobile technologies, now encourages greater social and political participation. Equally, illiteracy can be seen as an obstacle to a better quality of life and can even breed exclusion and violence.

Literacy is essential for social and human development and has the ability to transform the lives of individuals and their families. It could be said to be an instrument of empowerment to improve the health, income and lives of both men and women. The International Adult Literacy Survey (IALS, 1997) revealed lower literacy levels among older age groups than other sections of the population. Difficulties with literacy can make some older people feel self-conscious about taking part in any form of learning, including creative and recreational activities (AONTAS, 2008, p. 6), especially if there are negative attitudes towards ageing in society. Marginalised and socially disadvantaged older people lack the confidence and self-esteem to seek help in such an environment.

Survey findings referred to by McGivney (1999, p. 23) show that men with low literacy levels or few qualifications and a history of unemployment are under-represented in all types of education and training, and account for only four per cent of literacy learners over the age of 60. In the longer term, the most vulnerable male group, and those who are particularly disadvantaged in the job market, are those with poor literacy and numeracy skills, including older workers and the homeless (McGivney, 1999, p. 32).

Lalor *et al.* (2009, p. 19) note that the proportion of men participating in adult literacy education in Ireland has declined since 1980, when 71 per cent of participants were male (De Brún and Du Vivier, 2008). They report that participation rates by males in adult literacy education in 2000 was 37 per cent, but note that even though the relative participation of males has reduced, the actual number of males engaging has increased. They suggest that throughout this time, adult education providers increasingly oriented activities towards women, and raise the question as to whether this orientation could account for the increasing take up of adult literacy education by women.

This participation rate is not confined to adult literacy services. Lalor *et al.* (2009, p. 19) noted O'Connor's research into gender, which found that men have a lower participation rate than women in all areas of community and adult education, the breakdown being approximately 70 per cent female, 30 per cent male (O'Connor, 2007).

The National Adult Literacy Agency study

Lalor *et al.* (2009) conducted research for the National Adult Literacy Agency (NALA) into men's attitudes towards and involvement in literacy learning in Ireland. They sought to identify literacy issues among men, specifically those learning in informal settings, and also looked at the impact that a lack of literacy skills has on men's participation in learning.

The men were questioned in focus groups conducted over a six-month period in 2009. The men were drawn from five different community groups, from return to learning and a Traveller's learning group that included a homeless group. There was a total of 32 men, at least 15 of who were Travellers (47 per cent) aged between 40 and 70 years. Forty per cent lived with family members and 12 per cent lived alone. Fifteen per cent had left school before completing primary education (i.e. staying in education to 12 years of age) and only 8 per cent of the men had completed second level education (staying in education to 15 years of age). The men were following programmes in basic and advanced computers, communication skills and mathematics.

The men consulted in this research recounted largely negative memories of school as a result of regular and often brutal corporal pun-ishment and informal segregation based on social class, which meant many of the children were ignored, left to their own devices or allowed to fall behind with schoolwork, including reading, writing and numer-acy. As a result, many of the men participating in the discussions had left school early with enduring negative memories and attitudes toward education and learning.

The men elicited feelings of embarrassment and humiliation, particu-larly in situations where they had to rely on the kindness and under-standing of others in order to complete certain tasks. Many of these men had particular difficulty with staff members in financial institutions and social services. However, others reported feeling no embarrassment at disclosing their difficulties. The men's difficulties with reading, writing and numeracy had an impact on the level of participation in community and social activities. The majority of men believed that their literacy dif-ficulties held them back and prevented them from becoming involved in these activities as much as they would like.

The focus group discussions revealed a variety of reasons that moti-vated these men to tackle their literacy difficulties. These motives related to the individual, the community and the family. Some of the men chose to return to education because they believed the opportunity to learn had been missed or lost the first time around. Others believed that returning to learning would enable them to make a contribution to the community. A number of the men acknowledged that their literacy dif-ficulties were the main cause, if not the sole reason, for their withdrawal from, or lack of engagement in, community activities. A number of the men wanted to improve their mathematical and computer skills, as well as their literacy skills in order to keep up with the demands of their children for help with homework. Others recognised that their own experiences of education shaped their desire to strive for a better quality education for their children.

A major theme identified by the men was the benefits which lit-eracy engagement can provide for individuals and their families and the knock-on effects that these benefits can have on the communities in which they live. These benefits include improved literacy, self-respect, self-confidence, pride and being able to interact socially with other men. In some cases, the satisfaction they felt from overcoming dif-ficulties spurred the men to think about engaging further in learning opportunities. Other benefits included improved abilities to communicate with one another, and to listen to and respect each other's opinions.

The research also found that many men in semi-skilled and low paid manual employment were now experiencing various difficulties at work due to an ever increasing emphasis on literacy, including computer literacy, in the workplace.

Men were also found to develop coping strategies to assist them in dealing with literacy problems. The most common coping strategy adopted by the men was reliance on their spouse or partner, particularly in relation to tasks such as form filling. However, the men also identified strategies such as developing excuses and thinking on their feet in order to get themselves out of situations that required literacy skills. Some of the participants, particularly those tackling their literacy problems as part of a workplace learning initiative, spoke of their reliance on colleagues when it came to reading, writing and numeracy and were conscious of how this reliance on colleagues could sometimes lead to a strain on workplace relations.

The Changing Ageing Partnership study (2009)

A further study carried out in Belfast, Northern Ireland, and funded by the Changing Ageing Partnership (Mark, Montgomery and Graham, 2009) examined the attitudes and experiences of older men with literacy needs who were learning through participation in informal community learning activities and in literacy classes set up with men's literacy needs specifically in mind. The study examined the older men's attitudes and experiences of learning, and sought to find out what kind of provision would encourage older men to engage in learning through active community involvement.

The study also examined older men's attitudes towards learning in non-formal and informal learning contexts. In particular, it identified what was seen as attractive, common and different about group settings where older men could learn together, as well as new and better ways of engaging with older men through active community involvement beyond the workplace, especially for those men not in paid work. In addition, the study looked at the nature and benefits of this engagement for the wellbeing of older men, their families and their communities from the perspective of literacy learners who had been attending a class in three different places over a period ranging from two weeks to three years.

A total of 57 men participated in the study, which gave unique insights into older men's learning experiences from the perspective of those who lived in polarised districts of the City of Belfast during a time of civil unrest and uncertainty. At an individual and community level, many of the men had been involved in paramilitary activity. In addition they were affected by issues such as alcoholism, poor physical and mental health, depression and the effects of living in a society with deep political and cultural divisions, in environments where education was not seen as important or of value.

Findings revealed that many of the men experienced an awakening to the benefits of learning, especially regarding history and heritage that 'armed' them with information and knowledge. The study identified evidence of the capacity of community-based organisations to provide contexts that could address disadvantage, particularly social exclusion, unemployment, stress, substance abuse and underdeveloped literacy skills. Through informal learning environments, all aspects of lifelong and lifewide learning were being practised and enhanced, with the added benefit of a positive impact on men's health and wellbeing.

The men attended classes in two community centres and in a hostel for homeless adult males who had alcohol dependency or mental health issues. The men were attending a two-hour-a-week literacy class using computers as a method of learning. The centres were located within areas of social deprivation that had experienced social and political unrest. The learning centres were funded by the European Social Fund to support the delivery of literacy, numeracy and ICT (information and communications technology) training through a peace and reconciliation initiative drawing in people from both sides of the conflict. All of the participants, except one, were learning in a classroom environment at the time of the interviews. The learners were interviewed both individually and in focus groups.

The reasons men joined classes ranged from rehabilitation owing to drug and alcohol addiction or homelessness, to building skills for work. The organisations were accessible in that they were open all year round and on most days of the week.

Motivation to attend the men's literacy class included the desire to learn to use computers and improve literacy skills. A safe, flexible, supportive environment that was alcohol free also appealed greatly to the men attending from the hostel. The benefit of one-to-one counselling, especially in dealing with personal issues, and growing self-esteem to cope with education were also highlighted. Learning provided relief from boredom, especially for hostel residents on a restrictive rehabilitation programme, and a way of 'filling in the day'. This view was expressed – with an added appreciation of incidental learning or learning by stealth – in the following comment, 'It's a good pastime and you're learning at the same time'.

The feature of attending classes that related directly to life being enjoyable as well as educational was highlighted as important by most interviewees. Finding a setting that is informal and relaxed where 'there's no blackboard and no dress code', in which they could bring in a cup of tea 'as if you were at home', eased the way and facilitated learning.

The 'second chance' opportunity of adult learning to further knowledge, try something new and different and to confer with others while listening and learning collaboratively provided learners with the 'adventure school should have been', as it was described by one learner who was deeply affected by civil unrest. For him, 'the majority of it [school] turned into a nightmare'. Negative experiences of school included being punished or being put to the back of the class for 'those that were slow in their English … [while] those that were good were always given more attention'. There was awareness that school triggered memories of failure and lack of ability, together with an element of rejection and isolation. At the same time, some men regretted not paying greater attention at school and felt the problem rested with them.

Some men indicated that coming to the literacy programme had increased their confidence in communicating. For example, 'It makes me feel good within myself. Definitely makes me feel good in myself'. Another reason for underachievement, highlighted by a different participant in a separate literacy group, was the violence in Northern Ireland during childhood. One participant noted:

> There's a lot of people from my own place in life – for want of a
> better word – that's very clever people, very underestimated people,
> but they didn't get the education. … I'm talking from an age group of
> 50, your education system was blew out of the water by the violence.

He went on to describe how difficult it was for children like him, especially boys, from working-class backgrounds in areas of unrest in Belfast to apply themselves at school, as there were too many distractions, including 'hate and misinformation'. He explained that a very specific reason for attending adult literacy classes was to mix with people, to be exposed to different views and to get away from ingrained ideas.

This 'chance for change' was described by another learner, who regarded a self-development course, 'Key to Change', as pivotal in his progress and necessary as preparation for the literacy class and beyond. Without the residential, on-site nature of the hostel rehabilitation pro-gramme, these men said that they would not have been involved in training. In addition, the activities of the hostel and interaction with others in class and outside of it provided the opportunity to learn how to talk about problems and be accountable to staff and peers. Refer-ring to how much others were learning and enjoying the class showed the extent of their influence as role models. For this reason, there was a sense of purpose with 'directed activity'. Even though the learning environment was relaxed and informal, it brought routine – and there-fore structure – to life. This appealed to those learners who, in their 50s, had not undertaken any learning prior to entering 'the house'. It also appealed to a divorced man living on his own. He described 'drip-feeding' his problems in class as therapy.

Interviewees described the relevant, everyday nature of the content of adult literacy classes, which helped them to improve spelling and vocab-ulary and catch up on what they missed by finding out where they went wrong. Four of the six learner participants felt they were readdressing skills 'left at school' or which they 'didn't progress on'. Another referred back to literacy skills from schooldays, saying, 'You did learn it all, long time ago'; the skills had been forgotten, especially when grammar was not needed in previous work situations and there had been a lengthy time lapse with age. A relevant point in these comments is the view that literacy skills have already been covered or learnt, but then forgotten, left behind (unused) or have gone wrong somewhere. This may be a reason for the stigma that literacy creates as the men feel they should know or remember these previously covered skills, unlike other courses where the content is mostly new to participants, hence there is no embarrass-ment in not knowing.

The interviews revealed that the men had attended a range of literacy activities, which included the use of computers and technology, literacy, numeracy, counselling, history and personal development. The out-comes and learning from these courses and specifically the literacy and computer classes were many and varied. The older participants referred to a 'slow build-up'. Yet, with growth in confidence and knowledge came greater skills and insight into the potential uses for them. A positive attitude was also evident in statements such as, 'I'm getting there', 'I know I'll catch up' and 'I don't care if others are ahead of me'. With application of learning came a more self-assured and calm approach to study, which all the interviewees regarded as conducive to further learning. A new recruit to the class described being 'intense into it' and learning to cope with this. He was discovering how to feel more at ease with himself in order to risk trying new things. Interacting with other group members and overcoming fear and nerves helped this. All participants mentioned an experience of initial anxiety. Although confidence, self-esteem and assertiveness play an important part in alleviating this fear, being able to use and transfer skills outside the classroom situation was crucial.

The literacy learners who were interviewed cited many benefits on an individual level. Having fears allayed and experiencing a positive and educational 'school' environment that was missing in earlier years for these men brought many benefits: enjoyment, encouragement, confidence, stress relief, social skills, feel-good factor, feeling rejuvenated, banter or fun, relaxation, more learning, computer skills, self-respect and empowerment. The opportunity to get back on track involved learning what is manageable by taking on a short course, which then led one man on to further courses through other organisations, colleges and university. For him, a sense of control, discipline and accountability (in terms of his key worker) meant he could plan for the future, which previously appeared impossible because of alcohol abuse.

Interviewees repeated the benefits of increased confidence and feeling good about oneself, including being able to speak in front of a group. As well as having the words, means and freedom to express themselves in class, they benefited from an assurance of not being made a fool of. One man moved from being anxious about feeling behind others to realising that others had been there too and that he would catch up in time. This learner was referring to his computer skills, but the new skills also had an impact on his family, in that it opened up conversations, meant that he could keep up and not get left behind and could also communicate more. Other family members could also see his attempts to develop and the benefit of those things that were developing him. One insightful comment showed how learning affects participants and those close to them (who are happy to see their self-improvement), and how this reflects back on the participant, with the result that there is an all-round benefit. The learner said:

> *I'm not drinking on a daily basis the way I was before, and I'm doing other things that are bringing me along. So they're [family] much happier, you know, and of course that reflects back on me.*

For the community as a whole, the men reported benefits in sharing knowledge with others, getting involved with a group of people, getting to know people, developing friendships, speaking and sharing feelings, supporting an ethnic person in the group, and transferring skills to the 'outside' world (especially for hostel residents preparing for their return to life after the rehabilitation programme); most importantly, cited by three different respondents, was the benefit of being and feeling less isolated. As skills developed, the men's positivity and hopeful demeanour were evident to other, newer members of the group, and this had an impact on everyone's attitude to learning. The 'involvement' style of teaching and learning was described as 'most beneficial to bring people out and develop their skills'.

An important question was posed in trying to ascertain why older men do not enrol on – and why they drop out of – adult learning programmes. Retention of learners in adult literacy classes can be difficult for all age groups, although it is often helped by the personal support and mentoring offered through community-based education. The study participants were asked why older men, and literacy learners in particular, might drop out of courses or activities. Before commencing a course there is the issue of finding the right class to attend and getting used to the class. This included the teaching style as well as the content of the course. One learner said that 'a major factor' in shying away from doing courses was feeling stupid and not wanting everybody to see that you 'can't spell or can't add'. This interviewee also explained, 'Some people are not adequately prepared to write or do programmes', which affected their participation in courses. Two other interviewees reported that one of their peers had such serious difficulty with spelling that he left the class. Their view was that, despite every effort by the class tutors to help him address the problem, it was not possible to move beyond this major obstacle and he could not handle not being able to do it.

Other reasons for the lack of male participation were given as the men being shy and uncertain, being scared and panicked by taking so much in, having emotional problems and being on medication. The whole aspect of stigma was relevant as several learners referred to embarrassment, with one learner saying, 'It's hard to admit how much you lack and how much you've forgot'.

As well as citing frustration, another learner mentioned the danger of boredom setting in, which he had experienced as a peer tutor in having to integrate learners who joined the course late. His opinion was that having to go back to the beginning of the (computer) course slowed others down and created boredom for them, as well as stunting growth and damaging the sense of completion.

The men were more concerned with age than gender. They felt that younger learners want to do different things and have different attitudes to older men and that has a negative effect on the group dynamics. The learner who had later become a teacher made this comment. He understood learning from 'both sides' and was adamant that mixed age groups were not successful or satisfactory from either perspective.

Finally, some participants were concerned about bringing young men 'on board'. The view was expressed that older influential community leaders can mentor and encourage young men to 'get into education' as the means to a better future, and recommended financial incentives for unemployed men to get involved. In addition, having an input to the content of the course was seen as important.

Conclusion

Findings from both studies reveal a unique and complex picture, which provided much-needed evidence about older men's non-formal and informal learning needs. The Changing Ageing Partnership study showed that informal learning could be used as a strategy to avoid social problems, such as excessive drinking and gambling. Community-based organisations provide unique and powerful contexts in which older men can express all aspects of communication not available elsewhere in their everyday lives to develop their masculine identity, improve skills, socialise, support and mentor one another, interact in groups and seek further help when it is needed. The Changing Ageing Partnership study also showed enjoyment, belonging, friendship and mental stimulation as highly valued aspects of informal learning for older men that came about through following a hobby or interest rather than formal training. Within these community-based organisations, the men found a place where they could have an input into the design and content of learning, achieve a 'qualification' in receiving a certificate and aspire to leadership amongst their peers, all of which provide a sense of empowerment and achievement. These men are taking pride in realising the valuable influence they can have on others in their community by taking up positions as peer tutors.

Through informal learning environments, all aspects of lifelong and lifewide learning were being practised and enhanced, with the added benefit of having a positive impact on older men's health and wellbeing. Many research participants referred affectionately to the close connection and friendship amongst male group members, uniquely found in informal learning settings.

The key findings of the Changing Ageing Partnership project were that:

- Informal learning environments provide involvement in a closely-knit group with an interactive style of teaching. This is attractive because the men have a say in the course content and activities that were locally situated.
- A holistic approach allowing for peer support to deal with personal issues was found to be helpful to the men, especially those dealing with literacy difficulties.
- The reasons the men took part were said to be for enjoyment, to have a hobby, to provide a social outlet and for a sense of belonging, rather than for education and training.
- In an informal learning group, the men gained a sense of control, personal discipline, accountability, achievement, purpose, hope, increased confidence and feeling good about themselves.
- In a period of transition, men realised the positive influence of male peers on their identity.

A major theme identified by the men in both studies was the benefits that literacy engagement is providing for them and their families with a 'knock-on' effect on their communities. The need to develop programmes that help men of all ages to enhance their literacy skills and competencies, as well as promote self-esteem and positive self-worth, is also recognised.

The research shows that many men with literacy difficulties require a particular approach if they are to participate, in addition to supportive practitioners who are understanding, patient and offer a service which is radically different to the one remembered in school. In this respect, partnering with local agencies and organisations already engaging with disadvantaged men and who have a good understanding of their needs is more likely to be successful. Training for men who have successfully completed literacy programmes as peer learners to share their experiences with other potential learners may also have benefits.

Findings from both studies provide further evidence of a need for those with responsibility for providing adult learning and literacy to consider how best to promote men's wellbeing. The findings have implications for policymakers, service providers and those involved in organising and delivering programmes. Policymakers and those involved with the development of informal, community-based activities need to know more about the particular learning needs of men, particularly older men, if they are to tailor education services to meet their literacy needs.

References

AONTAS (2008) *Don't Stop Me Now! A Report on the Lifelong Learning Needs of Older People in Ireland.* Dublin: National Learning Organization of Ireland. Retrieved 21 May 2013 from www.aontas.com/pubsandlinks/publications/dont-stop-me-nowolder-people-research-2008/

IALS: International Adult Literacy Survey (1994 and 1997) *International Adult Literacy Survey.* Paris: UNESCO.

Lalor, T., McKenna, A., Doyle, G. and Fitzsimons, A. (2009) *Men and Literacy: A Study of Attitude and Experiences of Learning.* Dublin: National Adult Literacy Agency.

Mark, R., Montgomery, V. and Graham, H. (2009) *Beyond the Workplace: An Investigation into Older Men's Learning and Well-being in Northern Ireland,* Changing Ageing Partnership. Belfast: Institute of Governance, Queen's University Belfast.

McGivney, V. (1999) *Excluded Men: Men who are Missing from Education and Training.* Leicester: NIACE.

Murray, S., Kirsch, I. and Jenkins, L. (1994) *Adult Literacy in OECD Countries: Technical Report of the First International Adult Literacy Survey.* National Centre for Education Statistics. Retrieved 21 May 2013 from www.literacyworks.org/policy/pdf/literacyinoedcountry.pdf

O'Connor, M. (2007) *Sé Sí: Gender in Irish Education*. Dublin: Department of Education and Science.

UNESCO (2004) *The Plurality of Literacy and its Implications for Policies and Programmes*, Education Sector Position Paper 13. Retrieved 21 May 2013 from http://unesdoc.unesco.org/images/0013/001362/136246e.pdf

CHAPTER FIVE

The case for some men's spaces

Annette Foley

Introduction

My intention in this chapter is to address what could be seen as some tensions associated with the importance and value of gendered spaces in particular contexts. The gendered spaces that I refer to are those such as men's sheds, where older men can come together and develop friendships, form community bonds, share life experiences and skills and, as a consequence, attain health benefits that have direct and positive impacts on their families and their communities (Golding *et al.*, 2007). This chapter will put forward the case that in certain circumstances there is room for the existence and support of community gendered spaces for men that have the capacity to develop capabilities for individual agency (Sen, 1992).

I write this chapter with some reservations about what Rowan *et al.* (2002, p. 5) describe as the 'dangerous or hostile terrain' of gendered masculine spaces, with the associated concerns from some commentators that research which identifies men's disadvantage might take the focus off funding or support for programmes which address women's disadvantage, in terms of women's participation in – and outcomes from – education and training more broadly (Golding, Foley and Brown, 2008). For this purpose, I want to clear some ground by clarifying the intentions of the chapter and, by doing so, dispel some of the tensions around this argument.

It is important to stress at the outset that this chapter makes use of some feminist positions on inequity and disadvantage. That is to say that some feminist theorists and commentators broadly agree that some masculine structures and hegemonies not only have an impact on the capacity of women to achieve equal rights and citizenship, but also render some groups of men equally disadvantaged (Courtenay, 2000). Indeed, contemporary feminist theorists are as concerned with differences among men (and women) as they are about the differences between women and men. Certainly some of the differences involving men are dependent on their position in social structures, in other words the amount of power they have, and therefore on their capacity to access power and resources (Courtenay, 2000).

I support and acknowledge the position that has been developed comprehensively by feminists to analyse and interpret the notion of what it means to be a full citizen in a liberal democracy (Nussbaum, 2003), and the implications of unequal distribution of materials and resources that can restrict many women (and some men) from achieving full and equal citizenship (Fraser, 2002). My argument for the benefits of masculine gendered spaces that provide a site to develop health and wellbeing outcomes does not in any way diminish acknowledgement of and concern for the continued exclusion of women from full citizenship, and therefore full equality (Phillips, 1992).

Over the past two or more decades there has been extensive debate about the 'multiplicity of masculinities' that are inhabited and enacted in society (Paechter, 2003, in Emslie *et al.*, 2006, p. 2247). Most contemporary societies are characterised by men's institutional privilege (Messner, 1997, in Flood, 2003, p. 458) such that men in general receive a 'patriarchal dividend' from gendered structures of inequality' (Connell, 1995, in Flood, 2003, p. 458). According to Connell (1995), hegemonic masculinity is the idealised form of masculinity at a particular given time. It is the socially constructed, dominant gender that subordinates femininities as well as other forms of masculinity. It is the shaper of relationships between men and women and between other subordinated men; it represents power and authority.

For Connell (1995), the notion of masculinity or male dominance is played out or enacted in various ways, from hegemonic dominance to subordinate or less powerful configurations of male-gendered practices such as those of subordinate masculinities. These subordinate masculinities involve groups such as homosexual, black and working class men. No doubt many older and less formally educated men also inhabit this subordinate frame. The notion of hegemony involves control and power 'and having the ability to dictate the terms in which events are understood so that they appear "natural" and "normal"' (Donaldson, 1993, p. 644). 'White middle class men set the standard for other men' in relation to how men act (Kimmel, 1994, in Emslie *et al.*, 2006, p. 2247). Hegemony, particularly the form of hegemony that equates with power and dominance, requires men to show little emotion appear to be strong, tough and self-reliant. For many men, particularly those who are disadvantaged, unemployed or who are older, this hegemonic measure can leave them marginalised and under resourced and can have a negative impact on their mental and physical health.

Recent research in Australia indicates that men who are economically inactive make up a large and growing proportion of men in Australia. This lack of economic activity not only reduces economic growth in the country, but arguably and equally importantly has a significant impact on men's health and wellbeing and men's capacity to contribute or participate in community more broadly (Lattimore, 2007). Coupled with this, there is growing evidence that the very men who are most in need of adult education or vocational education and training are the least likely to access education due to their reluctance to commit to education programmes. This is in part because of preconceived ideas about adult education being for women, and in part because of negative experiences of schooling. Either way, commentators have argued that men's health behaviours and life choices are intrinsically connected to gender construction.

There is evidence that many men who do not fall within the privileged or dominant hegemonic frame experience health and wellbeing disadvantages. These disadvantages come in the form of men's health-related behaviours and beliefs — those beliefs that define men's identity as that of a man. Not living up to the hegemonic narrative of the ideal man has a significant impact on men's general health and longevity. Hegemonic masculinity, power and social inequity are important to understand when considering men's adoption of unhealthy behaviours, along with the social structures that foster unhealthy behaviour among men and undermine men's attempts to make healthy choices (Courtenay, 2000). Essentially, men are constructed and encouraged to use gendered, dominant health behaviours in line with socially constructed hegemonic pressures. Part of these behaviours involves rejecting health care as being 'girly' or weak. For Courtenay, to express oneself as a 'real' man by enduring physical discomfort, being involved in risk-taking behaviours and not attending to health care needs demonstrates the difference between men and women's health choices. For Courtenay, this type of behaviour fits into the socially constructed dominant male behaviour.

> *These behaviours serve as both proof of men's superiority over women and as proof of their ranking among 'real' men. A man's success in adopting (socially feminised) health promoting behaviour, like his failure to engage in (socially masculinise) physically risky behaviour, can undermine his ranking among men and relegate him to a subordinate status.* (Courtenay, 2000, p. 1390)

The pressure to live up to the idealised and dominant male measure, leaves many men at risk of experiencing mental and physical health problems through their desire to measure up to the 'power' male stereotype.

Men's and women's learning

Adult community education (ACE) in both the UK and Australia has been recognised broadly as providing health and wellbeing benefits for those who participate in the myriad of programmes it offers (Foley, 2007; Golding, Kimberley *et al.*, 2008; Lewis, 2012). It is also recognised as involving an outreach or social purpose for those who participate in its learning activities (NIACE, 2010). There is recognition that for older people, learning in ACE organisations involves interacting with others (Courtenay and Truluck, 1997) and drawing meaning from the learning setting that is relevant for them, whilst also providing enjoyment. Despite these benefits, there is considerable research to suggest that ACE, including neighbourhood houses in the Australian context, cater more readily for women. Indeed, Beckett and Helme (2001, p. 54) observe that 'older women are more than three times more likely to participate in adult education than men'.

In Australia, the history of neighbourhood houses, and ACE more broadly, involved women coming together under the then Australian Assistance Plan (APP) in the 1970s to re-skill. The main themes coming from community houses and learning centres was empowerment of the individual and providing a safe and nurturing environment for women to re-skill in order to get back into the workforce after staying at home to care for their children. A significant factor enabling women to link into neighbourhood houses at that time was a funding model that catered for childcare where women could leave their children to be cared for in the centres and houses whilst they learned (Foley, 2005).

At that time, neighbourhood houses and learning centres in Australia tended to be part of a grassroots movement that grew according to the needs of local people. Many of the programmes included computer skills, general education classes such as literacy and numeracy and pathway courses such as the Certificate of Liberal Arts. The success of neighbourhood houses then, as now, is associated with the informal, drop in nature of the houses and centres, where people can make friends in an informal setting, learn together and feel 'comfortable and un-intimidated' (Foley, 2005).

Previous work has been done to identify the factors that pose barriers for men to connect with adult learning (Golding and Rogers, 2002; McGivney, 2006; Foley, Golding and Brown, 2008). The results of this research indicate that negative experiences at school, fear of failure, negative attitudes about post-compulsory schooling, and attitudes that neighbourhood houses or learning centres are for women only, as well as men's perception that work is more important to male identity than that of learning, all create a resistance to men connecting to learning opportunities offered by these forms of community education organisations. McGivney (2006, p. 94) addressed these issues in her research in the UK where she emphasised the need for funding to follow the first stage development work of community education, 'engaging with people in the community, winning their trust, listening to them in order to increase the quality of engagement'. According to McGivney, for some groups of reluctant learners, the notion of learning or connecting with learning is completely outside their cultural frame. McGivney suggests that in the case of older men reluctant to engage with learning, there is no easy or short-term solution. She notes that issues of engagement involve:

> [p]sychological risks (of possible failure or ridicule); the social risks
> (of acting contrary to family or cultural norms) and financial risks
> (endangering welfare benefits and getting into debt) where there
> are no guaranteed employment or fiscal returns from learning.
> (McGivney, 2006, pp. 94–5)

The Australian men's shed movement has significant parallels with the grassroots development of the neighbourhood house movement in Australia in the 1970s. Today, not only do sheds exist and thrive across all parts of Australia but the men's sheds movement has also grown to include many sheds in the UK, Ireland and New Zealand. Unlike the so-called feminised learning spaces offered in adult community education organisations, men's sheds cater for and fulfil men's require-ment for engaging with lifelong learning. Sheds can vary according to the different organisations that run and fund them and the activities that individual sheds focus on. Hayes and Williamson (2006) have cre-ated a typology in which sheds have five functional categories. These categories include occupational, clinical, recreational, educational and social outlets for men to engage with and benefit from. Despite these differences there are common factors facing men who participate in shed programmes. These factors involve men looking for friendship, health benefits and a place to be away from the home. Arguably these categories and common factors provide for the men who attend their respective sheds a masculine, 'friendly' learning space that lends itself to, or caters for, specific male requirements, and does not leave the men feeling compromised in terms of their identity and sense of masculinity.

There are mixed views from commentators about the values and effectiveness of gendered, masculine spaces for men to come together, make friends, share ideas and learn. While some research even sug-gests that men prefer to engage in learning opportunities if other men are involved, such as male teachers, other workers and all male stu-dents (Pugh, 2002), opinions differ on whether and what engages or attracts men to learning (McGivney, 1999). Other commentators reject the notion that some men are marginalised or disenfranchised from learning on the grounds of their gender. Tobias and Bowl (2012), for example, looking at data drawn from two international surveys, exam-ined the relationships between educational attainment and age (25–65 years), level of schooling, geography, occupation and participation among different groups of men and women. In their analysis, Tobias and Bowl (2012) concluded that the differences between male and female patterns of participation in education were small when com-pared with other factors such as age, geographic location and occupa-tion. Tobias and Bowl suggested that these other factors appeared to have a far greater influence than that of gender in influencing men's participation in adult education. The study, however, did not include people over 65 years, nor did it involve consideration of incidental or informal learning.

Certainly the evidence of men coming together in men's sheds, learning informally from each other and gaining value from their connection to programmes in the shed, is clear through the significant international expansion of shed-based programmes. There is a strong argument to suggest that men's sheds or men's learning spaces and programmes provide men with choice to participate in an environment that allows them to feel comfortable and which makes significant contributions to their overall wellbeing, their connection to community and their ability to develop capabilities to better their life opportunities.

Health, wellbeing and community participation are clearly important and desirable qualities for citizens, both male and female, young or old. Being healthy and connecting with your community brings about individual agency and is arguably a fundamental human right (Sen, 1997).

Capabilities for wellbeing

The notion of wellbeing has received significant attention from governments and researchers over the past few years – in particular, the notion that learning has positive benefits on an individual's wellbeing. Wellbeing is understood as providing satisfaction with life, feelings of happiness, being fulfilled and contributing to the community (Field, 2009). According to Field, wellbeing is:

> associated with such social qualities as confidence, optimism about the future, a sense of influence over one's destiny, and social competences that promote satisfying and supportive relationships with other people – and not simply with an absence of diagnosed illness, disability or dissatisfaction … It also, critically, involves the resilience needed to deal with hard times as and when they occur. (2009, p. 4)

Certainly adult educators have consistently emphasised the re-creative function of informal learning and the importance of personal wellbeing through the gathering of resources for capabilities (Field, 2009), such as resilience, social and community connectedness and civic engagement for the health of individuals. In fact, many would argue that informal learning, such as participating in men's sheds or citizens involvement in community or leisure activities, is connected with what Sen (1997) describes as involving human capabilities.

Governments and international agencies regularly debated the idea of rights. Moral questions about human entitlements are fundamental questions and often relate to what is meant by 'rights', what basic human rights are and how these rights and entitlements should be understood and distributed.

> *When we speak of human rights, do we mean, primarily, a right*
> *to be treated in a certain way? A right to a certain level of achieved*
> *well-being? A right to certain resources with which we may peruse*
> *one's life's plan? A right to certain opportunities and capacities with*
> *which one may, in turn, make choices regarding one's life plan?*
> (Nussbaum, 1997, p. 274)

Nussbaum, who has written extensively on human rights and human capabilities, claims that political philosophers and thinkers, when considering the idea of equality and human rights, have tackled the question by asking whether the idea of equality involves equality of resources, the equality of wellbeing and opportunity or the equality of capabilities (Nussbaum, 1997). Nussbaum draws from the extensive work of Sen (1997), who made several key contributions to economics and development studies, when he developed ideas involving personal wellbeing, agency and freedom through his pioneering work on the capabilities approach and its importance in debates concerning quality of life.

Sen (1997) puts forward the argument that an individual's worth is not evaluated merely as economic activity, but rather by recognising the diversity of humanity and drawing attention to the disparity that exists for individuals, such as by gender, race, class, caste or age. Sen focuses on embracing human agency and participation. He accomplishes this by emphasising the role of making choices and acknowledging that different people, different cultures and different societies may have different aspirations and values that make significant contributions to an individual's wellbeing; that is, a person's wellbeing is related to their capabilities. Human capabilities, he argued, reflect a person's real opportunities and positive freedoms through a choice of lifestyles. Sen argues that to achieve human capabilities, subjects must be able to act freely and have the capacity to choose. For Sen, these are the features of a 'good life' (Clark, 2007).

At its core, the capabilities approach is centred on the development of an individual's agency; that is, what an individual 'can or cannot actually do' (Sen, 2010, p. 261). People's agency and capacity to be able to do things can be hindered by factors or barriers such as social and environmental conditions, access to resources, sense of identity, age, gender and so on. Sen also acknowledges the external barriers that impede an individual from converting resources or commodities into capabilities. These resources and commodities can come in the form of education for disadvantaged groups, such as for men not in paid employment who may have mental and or physical health barriers, or pre-constructed, negative ideas or barriers to education. Barriers may also include 'income deprivations' and 'adaptive attitudes', since people's expressed preferences may be conditioned by acceptance of restricted agency due to discrimination or disadvantage (Lewis, 2012, p. 526).

Sen's capabilities approach has been criticised by some for failing to supplement his framework with a coherent set of capabilities (Williams, 1987; Nussbaum, 1988). Nussbaum's version of, or extensions to, Sen's capabilities approach involves a list of capabilities that, she argues, 'isolates those human capabilities that can be convincingly argued to be of central importance in any human life, whatever else the person pursues and chooses' (Nussbaum, 2000, p. 74). These capabilities involve ten principles enumerated under the following headings: (1) life; (2) bodily health; (3) bodily integrity; (4) senses, imagination and thought; (5) emotions; (6) practical reason; (7) affiliation; (8) other species; (9) play; and (10) political material control over one's environment (Nussbaum, 2000). Arguably, many of Nussbaum's principles are catered for in men's shed organisations and help to develop the capabilities of the men who attend.

The capabilities approach has developed momentum in recent years and has been used to investigate poverty, inequity, wellbeing, social justice, gender, social exclusion, health, disability, ageing, child poverty and identity, human needs, rights and security (Clark, 2007). The approach can be used as a framework to theorise the wellbeing of men in gendered spaces, such as men's sheds, where research tells us that men are being provided with choices to participate in communities that facilitate benefits to men's health, such as friendship, connectedness and so on, through choices that develop men's capabilities just as neighbourhood houses have done for many women (and some men) in the Australian setting over many years.

There is a clear argument drawn from research on men's learning and wellbeing (Golding *et al.*, 2007) that lifelong and lifewide learning, including incidental and informal learning delivered from learning spaces and learning opportunities that cater for the different needs of particular groups of men, develop capabilities through men's connections with learning, through the development of friendships, social participation and learning new skills that, in turn, develop men's agency. What these learning spaces and places produce is considerable practical and of economic value to the community, with 'benefits that are significant for partners, families and carers as well as to the health and well-being of men who participate' (Golding *et al.*, 2007, p. 27). This benefit to men and their communities picks up on Sen's ideas about the social good and wellbeing of society as a whole. Capabilities used to theorise wellbeing through particular learning spaces for particular men offer a 'rich set of goals for our full human dignity' (Walker, 2004, p. 2). For Sen, capability-based assessments of justice are not to be judged in terms of resources or primary goods (or skills), 'but by the freedoms they actually provide for individuals to choose the lives that they have reason to value' (Sen, 1992, in Walker, 2004, p. 2). For Sen, this choice amounts to an equality of capabilities.

Capabilities may involve life sustaining requirements, such as having access to fresh water, healthy food and shelter, as well as being educated, learning, enjoying friendships and feeling safe and respected. All these aspects of capabilities are central to the 'agency of freedom' and the 'agency of well-being freedom' (Sen, 1992, p. 57). For Sen, agency and wellbeing are intrinsically connected, making a lack of agency or freedom of genuine choice equal to disadvantage. It follows that if education or access to learning contributes to an individual's freedom and capabilities, then education and learning are key contributors to agency.

A case for some men's spaces

The proportion of older adults in the population of most Western counties is growing. Policymakers are paying more attention to the needs of this growing group of people. Since adults are living longer, governments are expected to develop strategies to assist them to live healthy and productive lives into their old age (Jenkins, 2011). Educationalists have also been paying attention to the growing number of older people who either access adult education programmes or who are isolated and disconnected from their communities and would benefit from connecting through education programmes. There is growing evidence that lifelong learning and informal learning opportunities impact in a positive way on self-esteem, self-confidence, life choices and resilience. Adults are more satisfied by learning which engages them, is non-threatening and, in the case of older men, is constructed in such a way that it maintains their sense of masculine identity, which is important for their health and wellbeing.

The circumstances where older men not in paid work benefit from connecting with a work-like community space that is enabling and develops their capabilities for life are of particular benefit, not only to the men themselves but to the broader community. For this particular group of men, the notion of work enables them to 'meet the social norms of masculine attitudes and behaviours' (Gradman, 1994, p. 105). The men's shed movement is an enabler of these characteristics through its capacity to provide a work-like environment for men from similar working backgrounds or with similar interests, allowing them to engage through a socially supportive environment that develops their independence and autonomy. The shed has been identified as a space where these enabling characteristics, previously connected to the workplace, can be created and experienced by men. Certainly, men's sheds have been identified as a site where positive, engaging and meaningful activities can occur (Ormsby *et al.*, 2010).

There is a growing argument (Golding, *et al.*, 2007; Foley *et al.*, 2008; Ballinger *et al.*, 2009; Ormsby *et al.*, 2010) in support of the benefits that sheds offer for particular groups of men. Sheds can provide a space that fosters social relationships that are meaningful for men's masculinity and male identity. For these men, a community-gendered space provides the environment to develop individual resources. These resources Nussbaum describes as a human right 'to develop a certain level of achieved wellbeing and the right to certain opportunities and capacities with which one may, in turn, make choices regarding one's life plan' (Nussbaum, 1997, p. 74). There is little doubt that men's sheds for particular groups of men, particularly those men not in paid work, can provide opportunities and capabilities to enable better life choices. These particular spaces are the enablers of agency for men through their masculinised and tailored approaches that afford men the opportunity to practise and experience masculine attitudes and masculine norms.

Conclusion

In this chapter I have put forward the case that in certain circumstances there is room and significant benefit for the existence and support for gendered, masculine, community spaces for men. They have the capacity to provide an informal learning environment where men can let down their (hegemonic) guard, feel safe to expose some of their fragility/vulnerabilities without feeling judged as a weak or 'lesser' male, and gather resources to develop capabilities for individual agency.

References

Ballinger, M., Talbot, L. and Verrinder, G. (2009) 'More than a place to do woodwork: A case study of a community-based men's shed', *Journal of Men's Health*, 6 (1), pp. 20–7.

Beckett, D. and Helme, S. (2001) *Engaging Older Learners*, Older Learners Project Final Report. Parkville: University of Melbourne.

Clark, D. (2007) *The Capability Approach: Its Development, Critiques and Recent Advances*. Oxford University and Manchester University: Global Poverty Research Group.

Connell, R. (1995) *Masculinities*. Cambridge: Polity Press.

Courtenay, W. (2000) 'Constructions of masculinity and their influence on men's well-being: A theory of gender and health', *Social Science and Medicine*, 50, pp. 1385–401.

Courtenay, B. and Truluck, J. (1997) 'The meaning of life and older learners: Addressing the fundamental issue through critical thinking and teaching', *Educational Gerontology*, 23 (2), pp. 175–95.

Donaldson, M. (1993) 'What is hegemonic masculinity?', *Theory and Society*, 22 (5), pp. 643–57.

Emslie, C., Ridge, D., Ziebland, S. and Hunt, K. (2006) 'Men's accounts of depression: Reconstructing or resisting hegemonic masculinity?', *Social Science and Medicine*, 62, pp. 2246–57.

Field, J. (2009) 'Good for the soul? Adult learning and mental well-being', *International Journal of Lifelong Education*, 28 (2), pp. 1–31.

Flood, M. (2003) 'Men's collective struggles for gender justice: The case of anti-violence activism', in M. Kimmel, J. Hearn and R. Connell (Eds.), *The Handbook of Studies on Men and Masculinities*. Thousand Oaks: Sage.

Foley, A. (2005) 'Searching for the C in ACE', Paper to AVETRA Conference, Brisbane, 13–15 April.

Foley, A. (2007) 'ACE working within/outside VET', Paper to AVETRA Conference, Melbourne, 11–13 April.

Foley, A., Golding, B. and Brown, M. (2008) 'Let the men speak: Health, friendship, community and shed therapy', Paper to AVETRA Conference, Adelaide, 3-4 April.

Fraser, M. (2002) 'What is the matter of feminist criticism?', *Economy and Society*, 31, pp. 606–25.

Golding, B. and Rogers, M. (2002) *Adult and Community Education in Small and Remote Towns in Victoria*, Report to Adult, Community and Further Education Board, Victoria. Bendigo: Bendigo Regional Institute of TAFE.

Golding, B., Brown, M., Foley, A., Harvey, J. and Gleeson, L. (2007) *Men's Sheds in Australia: Learning Through Community Contexts*. Adelaide: NCVER.

Golding, B., Foley, A. and Brown, M. (2008) 'Shedding school early: Insights from school and community shed collaboration in Australia', Paper to AVETRA Conference, Adelaide, 3–4 April.

Golding, B., Kimberley, H., Foley, A. and Brown, M. (2008) 'Houses and sheds: An exploration of the genesis and growth of neighbourhood houses and men's sheds in community settings', *Australian Journal of Adult Learning*, 48 (2), pp. 237–62.

Gradman, T. (1994) 'Masculine identity from work to retirement', in E. Thompson (Ed.) *Older Men's Lives*. Thousand Oaks: Sage Publications, pp. 104–21.

Hayes, R. and Williamson, S. (2006) *Evidence-based, Best-practice Guidelines for Victorian Men's Sheds*, Report for Office of Senior Victorians. Bundoora: School of Public Health, La Trobe University.

Jenkins, A. (2011) 'Participation in learning and wellbeing among older adults', *International Journal of Lifelong Education*, 30 (3), pp. 403–20.

Kimmel, M. (1994) 'Masculinity as homophobia: Fear, shame, and silence in the construction of gender identity', in H. Brod and M. Kaufman (Eds.), *Theorizing Masculinities*. Thousand Oaks: Sage, pp. 119–41.

Lattimore, R. (2007) *Men Not in Work: An Analysis of Men Outside the Labour Force*, Staff Working Paper. Canberra: Australian Government Productivity Commission.

Lewis, L. (2012) 'The capabilities approach, adult and community learning and mental health', *Community Development*, 47 (4), pp. 522–37.

McGivney, V. (1999) *Excluded Men: Men who are Missing from Education and Training*. Leicester: NIACE.

McGivney, V. (2006) *Adult Learning at a Glance*. Leicester: NIACE.

Messner, M. (1997) *Politics of Masculinity: Men in Movements*. Thousand Oaks: Sage.

NIACE (2010) *Response to the LSIS Consultation on Effective Community Development: A Strategic Framework*. Leicester: NIACE. Retrieved 8 April 2013 from www.niace.org.uk/sites/default/files/LSIS-community-development.pdf

Nussbaum, M. (1997) 'Capabilities and human rights', *Fordham Law Review* 66 (2), pp. 273–300.

Nussbaum, M. (2000) *Women and Human Development: The Capabilities Approach.* Cambridge: Cambridge University Press.

Nussbaum, M. (2003) 'Capabilities and fundamental entitlement: Sen and social justice', *Feminist Economics*, 9 (2–3), pp. 33–59.

Ormsby, J., Stanley, M. and Jaworski, K. (2010) 'Older men's participation in community-based men's sheds programmes', *Health and Social Care in the Community*, 18 (6), pp. 607–13.

Paechter, C. (2003) 'Masculinities and femininities as communities of practice', *Women's Studies International Forum*, 26 (1), pp. 69–77.

Phillips, A. (1992) 'Must feminists give up on liberal democracy?', *Political Studies*, XL, Special Issue.

Pugh, G. (2002) *Contemporary Issues in the Early Years: Working Collaboratively for Children.* London: Paul Chapman Publishing with the National Children's Bureau.

Rowan, L., Knobel, M., Bigum, C. and Lankshear, C. (2002) *Boys, Literacies and Schooling.* Buckingham: Open University Press.

Sen, A. (1992) *Inequality Re-examined.* Oxford: Clarendon Press.

Sen, A. (1997) 'Editorial: Human capital and human capability', *World Development*, 25 (12), pp. 1959–61.

Sen, A. (2010) *The Idea of Justice.* London: Penguin Books.

Tobias, R. and Bowl, M. (2012) 'Gender masculinities and lifelong learning', in M. Bowl, R. Tobias, J. Leahy, G. Ferguson and J. Gage (Eds.), *Gender, Masculinities and Lifelong Learning.* London: Routledge.

Walker, M. (2004) 'Human capabilities, education and "doing the public good": Towards a capability-based theory of social justice in education', Paper to the Australian Association for Research in Education Conference, Melbourne, 28 Nov–2 Dec.

CHAPTER SIX

Learning beyond the workplace

Barry Golding

Introduction

This chapter identifies a wide range of learning contexts where research has shown that the pedagogies are inclusive of men and enhance men's wellbeing. This includes informal community contexts that are seldom seriously considered as learning environments. It is not concerned with the workplace or vocational preparation undertaken through formal education providers. It includes a consideration of men's learning intentions and outcomes that are rarely considered in mainstream formal educational research. These include learning through sporting organisations, fire and emergency service organisations, men's special interest organisations, age-related organisation as well as religious, ethnic, Indigenous and cultural organisations. The chapter also discusses the characteristics that make these spaces attractive to men. These spaces beyond the workplace are often discounted in contemporary education and training research, and are notably absent in policies and other discourses about men. The chapter also examines how common (and different) places and spaces in diverse national contexts affect and enhance men's attitudes to learning. While men's sheds in community settings are given as one example, a fuller analysis of their implications for men's learning and wellbeing is provided in Chapter Eight.

A typology for men's learning formality

Most developed nations give privilege and attach status to formal learning. In general, learners exposed to more formal learning achieve higher qualifications and do higher status jobs. Academic 'higher education' typically leads to professional work, and vocational learning to lower status work. Formal learning is conventionally regarded as organised learning that involves curriculum, assessment and accreditation. By comparison, non-formal learning is organised, but with less emphasis on curriculum, little or no assessment and no accreditation. While informal learning is usually understood as all other types of learning, it should be remembered that much of what is learnt in formal education contexts and through work is informally acquired.

While much of this chapter is devoted to learning beyond formal training and paid work, it is important to acknowledge from the outset that work-embedded and vocational training are already effectively taught (in the UK) 'in the context of practical problem solving', and 'that high-quality vocational education and training almost always involves a blend of methods' (Lucas *et al.*, 2012, p. 9). On the other side of the globe, research into youth, literacy and new media in remote Indigenous Australia found that learning was:

> *variously self-directed, peer-based, observational, experimental and playful. [Young people] learned by observing, sometimes by trial and error and at other times from mentors and experts. Most importantly, they learned by doing.* (Kral and Schwab, 2012, p. 100)

The other diverse learning contexts focused on in this chapter work best for men for many of the same reasons that hands-on vocational learning and informal remote Indigenous learning are effective, in that they involve pedagogies that are:

> *broadly hands-on, practical, experiential, real-world as well as, often at the same time as, something which involves feedback, questioning, application and reflection, and when required theoretical models and explanations.* (*ibid.*, p. 100)

The fundamental and arguably radical differences can be seen to revolve around the greatly reduced role of the teacher/trainer and the learning

organisation, the relative invisibility of the learning processes and curriculum, the relative absence of assessment and the greatly enhanced
roles for the learner and the wider community. The paradox here is that
learning:

> is more likely to grow if [learning] itself is not over emphasised
> and people's life projects are the focus of the activity ... [This]
> call to emphasise learning over formal teaching and teaching raises
> some serious questions for policy makers. The successful learning we
> observed was often inconspicuous or invisible ... This suggests the
> need to acknowledge 'soft outcomes' such as gains in self-esteem,
> personal development, confidence, motivation, collaboration and
> problem solving. (Barton, 2009, p. 56, cited in Kral and Schwab,
> 2012, p. 101)

A typology about purposes for men's learning

As a consequence of recent and major learning and wellbeing studies,
such as *Mental Capital and Wellbeing* (Cooper *et al.*, 2010) and the rich
suite of studies underpinning the *Learning Through Life* study in the
UK (Schuller and Watson, 2009), 'we now know much more about the
impact of adult learning on health (including mental health), social participation, earnings and sense of agency' (Field, 2009, p. 10). Aside from
the value of learning for work and income, which is already built into
national policy settings in most nations, people 'also value their health,
their social connections (including family) and their ability to contribute to the wider community' (Field, 2009, p. 5), as well as their freedom
and ability to shape their own destinies (agency).

In the current era of relatively high unemployment in many nations,
where there are many more unemployed people than there are jobs available, even for those educated and trained, the rationale for sticking solely
to policy directed at learning for paid work is at odds with research that
confirms that lifelong and lifewide learning enhances wellbeing. While
there has been a tendency for some men to be missing from some forms
of adult learning, as McGivney (1999a) first suggested, and resistance
from Bowl and Tobias (2012, p. 3) to a discourse of 'failing boys', 'missing
men' and 'gender gaps' in education, all men arguably have much to gain
from actively being involved in learning. As Ruxton puts it:

> *The importance of what men do in their relationships with*
> *women, children and other men has led some to suggest that more*
> *emphasis should be placed in 'men's practices' rather than simply on*
> *masculinities.* (2002, p. 14)

The potential gains to men extend well beyond the individual to include family and community, though their relative importance to men is likely to be far from universal, nationally or culturally. Burke (2006, p. 719) observes that in the UK, the discourse of lifelong learning 'is one that favours instrumentalism embedded within structures that are themselves gendered, raced and classed'. Southern (2007, p. 336) suggests that Americans 'have learned to see [them]selves as separate individuals and have constructed [their] educational environments based on that notion. However we live in a world where understanding ourselves as always being in relationship is important', and where *instrumental learning* (learning facts and figures without full understandings of its meaningfulness) is becoming less important than *communicative learning* (Habermas, 1981). Teaching and learning at its best in an adult and community education environment is a relational act in which the learning environment and context invites us to want to be there, where we may possibly experience, learn and give back more than we expected (Southern, 2007, p. 332), including to the community.

While the response from most governments in the recent economic downturn has been to withdraw funding and support for community learning, the literature is clear. '[N]either public welfare nor market based models of provision [of lifelong learning] have been entirely successful in countering established patterns of exclusion' (Edwards *et al.*, 1998, p. 3). Nor is there is a 'simple linear connection between education and training and improved economic performance' (*ibid*, p. 2).

Third places and their particular importance for men

This section discusses the potential of what are sometimes referred to as 'third places' for engaging many men. In the process, men can and do experience significant learning and enhanced wellbeing, not by treating illness, but by enhancing factors such as the social determinants of health, referred to in Chapter Three, that help encourage men to socialise and keep well. In the field of medical sociology, Antonovsky (1979) coined the term 'salutogenesis' to focus on factors that support human health and wellbeing, rather than on factors that cause disease. Salutogenesis is particularly applicable to the informal community settings that are the focus of our book. Langworthy and Howard (no date, p. 27) consider that an adult's first place is normally home, the second place is usually the workplace and the 'third place' defines 'a social space where it is possible to have an informal meeting, chat to a friend or just hang out'.

Third places, as Oldenburg (1999) puts it, are usually public places that host the regular, voluntary, informal and happily anticipated gatherings beyond the realms of home and work. Importantly, for many older men not in regular paid work, the 'second place' has greatly diminished or gone, and for men living alone and/or estranged from partners or family, the first place can also be very limited and far from salutogenic or health promoting. Even for men still in paid work, there is a case for salutogenic community spaces where they can actively re-create a life and experiences in a community place or space apart from work, in the original sense of recreation, a word now seen to be more closely associated with sport. Given the growing proportion of workers in the 'worried well' category, often medicated for stress and chronic ill-health, sometimes associated with work and/or home (Bell, 2005), the case for a third place is even stronger.

There are several risks in arguing the case for a 'third place' model for men (where family and work are first and second places) to enhance men's learning and wellbeing by supporting community agency and capability. There is the risk that in a re-structured welfare state which governments have deliberately depleted and withdrawn from, 'community' might become both an alibi and a substitute for the hollowed out and depleted state (CRLL, 2009). Levitas gets to the core of the problem when she argues that there is a risk that the community might be become responsible for mopping up:

> *the ill effects of the market and ... provid[ing] the conditions for its continued operation, while the costs of this are borne by individuals rather than the state.* (Levitas, 2000, p. 194)

In other words, community is presented as both the problem and the solution.

It is pertinent here to identify the other key characteristics of 'third places' that men tend to meet and learn in: informally and frequently when not in paid work. In most developed countries, men's involvement in sporting organisations, recreational activities, service clubs, museums, woodwork clubs, engine and vehicle preservation societies, fire and emergency service organisations as well as, more recently, in community men's sheds could all be said to meet Oldenburg's (1999) third place definition. They often have inexpensive food and drink, are highly accessible and proximate (within walking or short driving distance), involve regulars who habitually congregate there, are welcoming and comfortable, and both new and old friends can be found there.

Unsurprisingly, several of these key characteristics of third places (including free WiFi) have been deliberately built into several 'fast food' chains and gambling venues in disadvantaged suburbs and communities to provide attractive vestiges of 'third place' communities, targeted at vulnerable adults with limited first and second options for gathering and socialising. These places, unlike other types of community owned learning spaces, often make a substantial profit and encourage dependency.

About learning through work

While our book deliberately avoids replicating findings from the extensive body of evidence about learning through paid work, it is important to briefly summarise previous discoveries before looking at learning by men beyond paid work. For people in work, the workplace 'learning community' is increasingly understood as the place where most adults learn. The principles of what makes for good workplace learning (NCVER, 2013) are now well known. Most research into workplace learning confirms the huge learning opportunities and advantages for those in paid work, compared with those available to people who are not working (unemployed, with a disability, in a caring role, withdrawn from the workforce prematurely) or retired. Fuller and Unwin, in an analysis of workplace learning, note that:

> the metaphor 'learning as participation' has become the dominant approach to understanding workplace learning. A central plank in this idea is that each workplace will offer distinctive opportunities, along qualitative and qualitative dimensions, for employees to learn. (2005, p. 24)

The key problem with extrapolating the same metaphor to learning through community organisations, despite its theoretical elegance and pedagogical power, is that it makes assumptions about participation that are taken as given but that do not necessarily apply to people not in paid work. Golding *et al.*'s (2009a; 2009b) suite of research into men's learning and wellbeing in Australia conclude that compared with men not in work (for any reason), men in work are generally coping, unless damaged through work. It is men who are not in work and without community connections who are potentially most at risk and least likely to keep learning or stay healthy, unless supported beyond work and in later life by connections through family, partner or friends.

A research study in Scotland by Cleary (2007) paints a somewhat different picture. Based on a study focused on men's low participation in post-compulsory education, it identified deep structural and attitudinal barriers for men who wanted to return to formal education. Social expectations that men would be the main 'breadwinner' were seen to prevent men from leaving employment and returning to education. Indeed, many men were more likely to return as a result of retirement or redundancy. Men who wanted to study and return to work were perceived as being more instrumental and vocationally oriented than women in terms of their expectations of the learning, and much less likely to engage in learning for pleasure in their leisure time.

The literature on what works for working men in Australia, particularly from studies of the learning preferences of farmers (who include many women) in rural and regional areas, provides some pointers towards what forms of learning might work for men with lower levels of formal education and literacy, who from Golding *et al.*'s research (2009a, 2009b) typically share a desire to learn hands-on, through learning by doing, and outdoors wherever possible.

Kilpatrick, with others (Kilpatrick and Williamson, 1996; Kilpatrick and Johns, 1999; Kilpatrick, 1999), undertook a series of field-based studies of rural farmer learning in Australia. The four main types of training examined were training (formal and non-formal activities including courses, seminars and workshops, farmer directed groups and field days) from 'people' not as part of a training activity (other farmers, acquaintances, employees, consultants and other experts), the media (print, audio, visual and electronic), as well as from experience and observation. In general, men's preferences were towards the latter, less formal end of the learning spectrum. Kilpatrick's suite of research identified that 'low actual or perceived literacy levels and lack of confidence as a learner are barriers to participation' (Kilpatrick and Johns, 1999, p. 4), particularly for formal, course-based training. Aside from the effects of a poorly educated workforce on farm productivity, Kilpatrick and Johns pointed to its 'compounding effect by inhibiting further training [and the] capacity to be flexible, adaptable and to respond to change' (p. 8).

Kilpatrick and Johns' study identified gendered differences 'in the amount and content of on-going learning undertaken by men and women, and in the learning sources selected' (1999, p. 153). Male farmers identified 'three specific barriers to participating in organised learning activities that were not mentioned by female farmers' (p. 164). These included their age, a disinclination to attend field days and seminars where private organisations were 'pushing their products' and previous negative experiences of inappropriate training. In general, men were more likely 'to prefer learning from their own experience and their fathers or family, while farming women preferred fee paying training' (Kilpatrick and Johns, 1999, p. 160). While there is insufficient space here to elaborate on the connection to men's learning, it is pertinent here to observe that boys in rural areas of Australia are approximately half as likely as rural girls to go on to tertiary study after completing school. Meanwhile, both rural boys and girls are around half as likely as their city counterparts to go on to tertiary study after completing school. The data suggest that gender issues can and do affect boys and men and can become intergenerational within families and communities in rural contexts.

Learning through sport and recreation

Sporting and recreational organisations have been important spaces in the community for many men in most world nations. Many such organisations exhibit the positive characteristics of third places referred to earlier. Most are salutogenic (health promoting) and men's involvement creates opportunities for them to learn by doing and contributing to the community at many ages and stages of life. McGinn noted, in a philosophical interview about sport, that:

> *Learning a sport ... is not something that lies outside of the realm of education. When you learn to play ... you acquire a specific sort of practical knowledge – of knowing how. You also acquire phenomenological knowledge ... of how something feels*

from the inside. … These experiences and the knowledge that goes with them are also in themselves valuable. (2008, p. 1)

Sage noted over three decades ago that 'Sport is one of the most ubiquitous activities in modern contemporary society' (1979, p. 10) and that in American society, 'sport and education are inexorably intertwined' (p. 5). Sporting research confirms that adult sport and exercise participants have multiple motives for participating in sport, with some gender differences. Studies of females in Western contexts suggest that women are more motivated by fitness, flexibility, health, affiliation and appearance (Gill and Williams, 1996).

There have been several studies of the relationship between sport and masculinities with connections to men's learning. Skelton noted that, in particular, football 'occupies a central place in many of the strategies aimed at counteracting boys' underachievement in Western schools' (Skelton, 2000, Abstract). However, football was also, in Skelton's study, 'central to the gender regime of the school, particularly to the construction of a dominant mode of masculinity' (Abstract). Efforts have recently been made in Europe to integrate football and learning with cultural integration, particularly for young migrant men (Hattrick, 2013). Its stated rationale is that:

Playing football in a team offers various opportunities of social learning and developing transversal competences – independent from cultural background. Sport can provide a useful function in reinforcing social inclusion. Many young migrant people show enthusiasm in (team) sports, with young men especially keen on football.

Australian rules football has similarly been integrated with schools (e.g. Clontarf, 2013) to engage Indigenous Australian young men in learning and at the same time train them to play at state and national level, with considerable success. Payne (2008) describes a study linking lifelong learning to cricket in South Africa through situated learning and community of practice theory.

There have been a number of studies in the past decade in Australia confirming the important role that sports play, including for situated learning and gender identity formation, such as through surf clubs (Light, 2006), and more broadly for young people through very diverse school, club and social environments involving sports (Light, 2008). Sport has also been strongly linked to localism (a need for roots, identity, belonging and solidarity) and social capital in field studies in Australia (Atherley, 2006). Tonts' study confirmed the value of sport in fostering social interaction, a sense of place and community and a range of physical and health benefits (2005, pp. 24–5).

Sport (particularly football and rugby) has the capacity internationally to involve a high proportion of men and boys in neighbourhoods and smaller rural communities, particularly for young men from diverse national and Indigenous backgrounds, building community networks and bonds. Tonts' study of competitive sport and social capital in rural Australia showed, however, that sport also 'acted to exclude certain citizens on the basis of race, class, gender and status' (2005, p. 24). Also, 'For those who are unwilling or unable to become involved in sport, the outcome is often a degree of social exclusion', not only 'from social networks, but also from popular notions of community identity' (Tonts, 2005, p. 25).

The fact that some games tend to be mainly for men, and that many (but not all sports) which include women involve gendered teams, means that men get to meet and enjoy the company of other men with generally complementary outcomes for partners, children and family. Many (but not all) sports are also streamed by age. Those that are also streamed by gender provide important opportunities for men and boys to interact with cross age mentoring through coaching and other forms of team and individual support. Some rugged, very physical team sports, like Irish hurling, Australian rules football, American gridiron and baseball and rugby, have become part of their respective national male psyche. The downside again is that men not interested or involved in sport can be excluded and judged to be less masculine.

Learning through fire and emergency services organisations

With some exceptions (e.g. Hayes *et al.*, 2004), the literature is remarkably silent on the critically important learning role played within fire and emergency service organisations, including the increasingly compulsory learning required of very large number of volunteers (mainly men) who are highly trained and ready for a wide variety of emergencies that may never happen. This is surprising given the ubiquity and essential services provided worldwide through volunteer organisations, mainly in fire services, but also in ambulance, mountain, ski or coastal rescue in many nations beyond the metropolis. While some emergency workers such as firefighters are full-time professionals in the larger cities of many nations, most communities and nations rely mainly on learning by trained volunteers. There is a high degree of discipline, regular (typically accredited) training and teamwork associated with these roles. The 'life and death' importance of their readiness and availability at short notice, along with their 'unambiguous and partisan roles' has earned voluntary firefighters 'widespread gratitude, status, and prestige in their communities' (Haski-Leventhal and McLeigh, 2010, p. 82), making fire-fighting 'the most admired and respected profession in the United States' (p. 82).

While previous studies of fire fighters confirm that 'almost all firefighters are male (between 96% and 98%)' (Haski-Leventhal and McLeigh, 2010, p. 84), this is changing. Lewis confirms that firefighting:

> *is one of the most sex-segregated professions … The highest proportion of women in firefighting is around 15 per cent in some United States brigades after affirmative action over a considerable period, but more usually under 5 per cent for fire services operating in western industrialised contexts.* (Lewis, 2004)

Learning through movements associated with adult and community education

The recent growth and spread of the men's shed movement internationally (discussed in Chapter Eight) raises questions about which other grassroots movements (from local associations to community based and adult learning groups) have started locally and spread nationally or globally in the past two centuries, why they have spread and (mostly) persisted, and what associations they have with theories of learning and wellbeing. They include:

- the *allotment garden* movement, that came out of searches for utopia associated with urbanisation in the nineteenth century, a movement that extended mainly across northern Europe, which has experienced a recent renewal;
- the *mechanics institute* movement, coming from Scotland in the 1820s and catering largely for working men. It later spread to

other Anglophone countries but is no longer an active movement;

- the *folk high school* movement, developed by Grundtvig in Denmark in the mid nineteenth century;
- the *community centre* movement that extended education beyond schools in the USA and many other countries from the early 1900s (related in some ways to the *neighbourhood house* movement driven by women in Australia from the 1970s);
- the *U3A (University of the Third Age)* movement coming out of France and proliferating rapidly and internationally from the 1970s.

As well as these movements that have crossed many national boundaries, other grassroots initiatives have contributed to transforming learning, such as the Landcare movement in Australia (Landcare, 2013), benefiting farmers and farming communities through the provision of information and learning to people 'on the land' in a form that is local, accessible and matched with adult and family needs.

While many of these movements have a person (typically a man) identified as a key initiator of the idea, the success of many have later attracted government support. All had their origins related in some way to parallel communitarian social movements that aimed to meet the needs of the 'common person' (in the case of the mechanics institute, mainly men) in ways that top down, institutional educational initiatives at that time could not. Most of these movements had particular benefits for disadvantaged groups, including families, children, women and men. The closest rough parallels to the community men's sheds movement elaborated in Chapter Eight are the folk high school and the mechanics institute movements, whose foci were less about formal education and more about popular education and 'enlightenment' of those previously not connected through learning.

Older men's learning through community settings

Research into how to ensure that older people, particularly men, can remain in paid work until, and sometimes beyond, the age of retirement (where such an age exists) has grown recently in volume and breadth, owing to a range of concerns. The main concern is that a premature loss of older men as workers is not beneficial for the national economy. While labour force participation remains higher for older men than older women, in some nations, including Australia, the proportion of men withdrawing from the workforce early (age 55–64 years) has generally increased over the past four decades, while the proportion of women similarly withdrawing has approximately halved (Dymock, 2008).

A growth in discouraged workers (defined by Australian Bureau of Statistics as someone who wants a job but is not actively looking: Ball *et al.*, 2000, p. 3) started in Australia during the 1990s and is age and gender related. Between age 30 and 60 discouraged workers are mostly women; at age 60 the numbers of discouraged men and women are close to equal; post age 60, it is mostly men. Discouragement is elevated in contexts and nations (such as Europe in 2013) in which unemployment is very high.

An examination of the Australian statistics on education and training participation by occupation and age group illustrates the nature of the problem, particularly for older people still in the workforce (Ryan and Sinning, 2009, p. 24, Table 4, based on 2006 data). Most (more than 50 per cent) of professional people in the workforce in Australia tend to participate in some form of education and training regardless of age. For labourers over the age of 40, participation drops off dramatically to around one-quarter. Beyond the age of 50 the drop off includes machinery operators and drivers. Beyond 60 it is only professional and community and personal service workers who are still in education and training. In summary, unsurprisingly, higher levels of education are associated with more professional jobs. Conversely the propensity to not learn while working is strongest amongst least educated workers. What is striking is the way younger workers access training much more than older workers.

Research into learning and ageing in Europe focuses on the 'whys and wherefores' of older learning (Aldridge and Tuckett, 2007), including how to get older people involved (EuBIA, 2010), and on ways in which learning might extend working life through improved worker retention, up-skilling and return to work (NIACE, 2006). This research has intensified recently in many European nations following foundational research from the 1990s by Jarvis (2001) including the formation of an ESREA Network on Education and Learning of Older Adults (from 2009), the *International Journal on Education and Ageing* (from 2010) and a recent handbook on older adult learning (Findsen and Formosa, 2011) as a follow up to Findsen's book, *Learning Later* (2005). With several exceptions (Aldridge and Tuckett, 2007; Mark, Montgomery and Graham, 2010), older men are seldom considered or researched separately or differently by researchers, despite exhibiting quite different observed patterns of work and learning.

The focus of the relatively recent older learner-related research in Australia provoked by the Australian Parliamentary *Age Counts* inquiry into issues specific to mature-age workers (*Age Counts*, 2000) has been more about older workers than learners (Lundberg and Marshallsay, 2007; Griffin and Beddie, 2011), and particularly how to get older men back into the workforce (including through education and re-training: Dymock, 2008; for older disadvantaged workers: BWA, 2004) than about what caused them to either leave or retire prematurely, or else not to work beyond the retirement or pension age. There were some early exceptions, including specific consideration of older men's learning (Hurworth, 1995).

Research from Asia is likely to provide somewhat different gendered older learning patterns. While Ohsako (1998, p. 7) suggested that 'Gender differences in patterns of learning and social participation are greater in Japan and Korea than in European countries and the United States', many of the examples cited are somewhat similar to trends in many other relatively developed nations.

The imperative to consider older men's work and learning has been prompted by a second concern, caused by advances in medical treatment, diagnosis and prevention and reduction in the birth rate: population ageing, which increasingly affects most world nations. The third and related concern is that national budgets for medical, welfare and aged care services, as well as for older learning (NIACE, 2006), are likely to be stretched in coming decades unless ways can be found to keep older men more independent and healthier, and contribute to the community for longer. In this way lifelong learning has come to be associated with the 'productive ageing' agenda, defined by the World Health Organization (WHO, 2002, p. 12) as the process of optimising opportunities for health, participation and security in order to enhance the quality of life as older men age and cope with change (Foskey and Avery, 2003). Productive ageing is also a key concern in Australia, with a number of commissioned research projects undertaken through the National Seniors Productive Ageing Centre, including about older men's learning and wellbeing (Golding *et al.*, 2009a).

The European Commission (EC, 2010, p. 2) notes that this definition of productive ageing includes the notion of continuing activity in the labour force as well as continuing participation in the community, as 'both older men and women face serious challenges as they seek to live active lives and age with dignity' (p. 3). Aside from recognising the importance of health promotion and services throughout the working life and ill health as a key factor in early retirement, the European Commission noted the particular importance in the current economic recession of active participation in voluntary activities following retirement (p. 5). Indeed, 16 per cent of older males were seen to be at risk from social isolation and poverty (p. 6).

Learning through community contexts

McGivney's (1999b) research into *Informal Learning in the Community*, though conducted in the UK independently of her parallel studies on men's learning (McGivney, 1999a, 2004), provides a strong and complementary framework for analysing men's learning and wellbeing in community settings. Some of the particular synergies with learning through community men's sheds are drawn out in Chapter Eight. McGivney (1999b, pp. v–vi) draws four main conclusions: first that 'Informal learning takes place in a huge variety of settings'; second that 'The location of learning is extremely important, often more so than its actual focus'; and third that 'Community-based learning plays a critical role in widening participation among people who are educationally, economically and socially disadvantaged.' The fourth conclusion relates to difficulties of measurement of informal learning in community settings, leading to related difficulties with estimating its impact. It is the second conclusion which most rings true in relation to findings about men's learning in adult and community education settings.

Thinking about informal learning has led to recent, widespread recognition in many formal international and national policy statements, as well as research findings, about the value of informal and adult learning. What is missing is a commitment to implement them. In the case of the Australian Prime Minister's visionary statement on *Transforming Learning and the Transmission of Knowledge*, there is recognition that 'Many of the assumptions regarding adult learning are consistent with the natural demands of informal learning' (PMSEIC, 2009, p. 29), and that:

> *much adult learning occurs at transitional stages in the lifespan,*
> *when new challenges such as entering the workforce, starting a family*

*or retirement, require a new set of skills and, in many cases, some
rethinking of a person's self concept.*

These statements are associated with an admission that 'these lessons
are not lost on those responsible for formal school education, even if
resources and other constraints limit their ability to implement them'
(p. 29).

Cleary's (2007) study of men's post-compulsory learning concluded that community learning centres 'may not be the main means by
which to attract more men'. Cleary suggested that men may be less
likely to need the 'warm' and 'cosy' atmosphere that the centres provide
and might be more comfortable in the company of other men (p.19).
McGivney's study came to a number of similar conclusions relating to
the effectiveness of community-based learning in the UK. Effectiveness
was enhanced when learning was targeted:

> *at specific groups, in informal community venues, offered at low cost
> or free of charge, provided in consultation with learners, tailored
> to individual or group needs and agendas, flexible, adaptable and
> provided with appropriate learner support.* (McGivney, 1999b,
> p. viii)

Conclusion

Formal, institutional, accredited learning through paid work has become
the foci of most national education and training policies. It is relatively
easy to quantify such learning and invoke causal relationships between
the quantum of accredited learning achieved by adults and the average economic benefits to individual workers and to national economies.
It is much harder, but equally important, to acknowledge and account
not only for the wider benefits of this formal work-related learning to
individuals, families and communities, but also the many benefits of
the diverse, less formal, other forms of lifelong and lifewide learning
which are not directly work-related. In the many world nations where
there are not enough jobs for the number of people already qualified to
fill them, the idea that learning is solely about work and the economy
breaks down. Learning beyond paid work and the many benefits associated with it has tended in the past to be seen as being for women.
While it is unsurprising that the trend towards many more women and

girls participating in formal education and paid work has been associated with the tendency for more men and boys not to participate, it is timely to think more about the wider and longer term implications and benefits for men of participating in learning beyond work.

References

Age Counts (2000) *Age Counts: An Inquiry into Issues Specific to Mature-age Workers*. House of Representatives Standing Committee on Employment, Education and Workplace Relations. Canberra: Commonwealth of Australia.

Aldridge, F. and Tuckett, A. (2007) *What Older People Learn: The Whys and Wherefores of Older People Learning*. Leicester: NIACE.

Antonovsky, A. (1979) *Health, Stress and Coping*. San Francisco: Jossey-Bass.

Atherley, K. (2006) 'Sport, localism and social capital in rural Western Australia', *Geographical Research*, 44 (4), pp. 348–60.

Ball, K., Misko, J. and Smith, A. (2000) 'The training needs of older workers', Paper to AVETRA Conference, 23–24 March, Canberra.

Barton, D. (2009) 'Researching adult learners' lives to understand engagement and progression in learning', *Literacy and Numeracy Studies*, 17, pp. 51–61.

Bell, G. (2005) 'The worried well: The depression epidemic and the medicalisation of our sorrows', *Quarterly Essay*, Issue 18. Melbourne: Schwartz.

Bowl, M. and Tobias, R. (2012) 'Gender, masculinities and lifelong learning: Entering the debate', in M. Bowl, R. Tobias, J. Leahy, G. Ferguson and J. Gage (Eds.), *Gender, Masculinities and Lifelong Learning*. Abingdon: Routledge, pp. 3–13.

Burke, P. (2006) 'Men accessing education: Gendered aspirations', *British Educational Research Journal*, 32 (5), pp. 719–33.

BWA: Business Working and Ageing (2004) *Furthering Success: Education, Training and Employment Transitions for Disadvantaged Older Workers*. BWA Group. Hawthorn: Swinburne University of Technology.

Cleary, P. (2007) *Motivation and Attainment in the Learner Experience (MALE): Final Report*, West of Scotland Wider Access Forum. Glasgow: CRLL.

Clontarf (2013) Clontarf Foundation. Retrieved 6 Febuary 2013 from www.clontarf.org.au

Cooper, C., Field, J., Goswami, U., Jenkins, R. and Sahakian, B. (Eds.) (2010) *Mental Capital and Wellbeing*. Chichester: Wiley-Blackwell.

CRLL: Centre for Research in Lifelong Learning (2009) *Scottish Forum on Lifelong Learning: Democratic Learning: Learning for Democracy*, Forum Report No. 20. Stirling: University of Stirling.

Dymock, D. (2008) *Sustaining Older Worker's Competence: Informing Policy and Practice*, Background Paper 3: Training and retraining older workers. Nathan: Griffith University.

EC: European Commission (2010) *Decision of the European Parliament and of the Council on the European Year of Active Ageing 2012,* Accompanying Document. Brussels: EC.

Edwards, R., Raggatt, P., Harrison, R., McCollum, A. and Calder, J. (1998) 'Recent thinking in lifelong learning: A review of the literature', *Research Brief No. 80,* London: Department for Education and Employment.

EuBIA: European Union Broadening People's Minds in Ageing (2010) *Getting Older People involved in Learning: The EuBIA Guide.* Leicester: University of Leicester.

Field, J. (2009) *Wellbeing and Happiness, Inquiry Into the Future of Lifelong Learning, Thematic Paper 4.* Leicester: NIACE.

Findsen, B. (2005) *Learning Later.* Malabar: Krieger.

Findsen, B. and Formosa, M. (2011) *Lifelong Learning in Later Life: A Handbook on Older Learning.* Rotterdam: Sense.

Foskey, R. and Avery, A. (2003) 'Older rural men: Learning for change', Paper to ALA Conference, Sydney, 27–30 November.

Fuller, A. and Unwin, L. (2005) 'Older and wiser? Workplace learning from the perspective of experienced employees', *International Journal of Lifelong Education,* 24 (1), pp. 21–39.

Gill, D. and Williams, D. (1996) 'Competitive orientations of adult sport and exercise participants', *Journal of Sport Behavior,* 19, pp. 307–18.

Golding, B., Foley, A., Brown, M. and Harvey, J. (2009a) *Senior Men's Learning and Wellbeing through Community Participation in Australia,* Report to National Seniors Productive Ageing Centre, University of Ballarat, October. Retrieved 22 May 2013 from http://archimedes.ballarat.edu.au:8080/vital/access/HandleResolver/1959.17/16450

Golding, B. Brown, M., Foley, A. and Harvey, J. (2009b) *Men's Learning and Wellbeing through Community Organizations in Western Australia,* Report to the Western Australia Department of Education and Training, University of Ballarat, October. Retrieved 22 May 2013 from http://archimedes.ballarat.edu.au:8080/vital/access/HandleResolver/1959.17/16443

Griffin, T. and Beddie, F. (2011) *Older Workers: Research Readings.* Adelaide: NCVER.

Habermas, J. (1981) *The Theory of Communicative Action, Vol. 1: Reason and the Rationalisation of Society.* Boston: Beacon Press.

Haski-Leventhal, D. and McLeigh, J. (2010) 'Firefighters volunteering beyond their duty: An essential asset in rural communities', *Journal of Rural Community Development,* 4 (2), pp. 80–92.

Hattrick (2013) Football-Learning-Integration, European Union. Retrieved 6 February 2013 from www.hattrick-project.eu

Hayes, C., Golding, B. and Harvey, J. (2004) *Adult Learning through Fire and Emergency Services Organizations in Small and Remote Australian Towns.*

Adelaide: NCVER. Retrieved 22 May 2013 from www.ncver.edu.au/publications/1497.html

Hurworth, R. (1995) *Living Longer: Learning Later: Assessing the Education Needs of Older Learners in Victoria*, Report for ACFE Board and Sport and Recreation. Parkville: University of Melbourne,

Jarvis, P. (2001) *Learning Later in Life: An Introduction for Educators and Carers*. London: Kogan Page.

Kral, I. and Schwab, R. (2012) *Learning Spaces: Youth, Remote Literacy and New Media in Remote Indigenous Australia*. Canberra: ANU Press.

Kilpatrick, S. (1999) 'Learning on the job: How do farm managers get the skills and knowledge to run their businesses?', *CRLA Discussion Paper Series* D3/1999. Launceston: University of Tasmania.

Kilpatrick, S. and Johns, S. (1999) *Managing Farming: How Farmers Learn*, RIRDC Publication N.99/31. Barton: RIRDC.

Kilpatrick, S. and Williamson, J. (1996) 'Farmer participation in training', *Rural Society*, 6 (4), pp. 3–12.

Landcare (2013) Retrieved 6 February 2013 from www.landcareonline.com.au

Langworthy, A. and Howard, J. (no date) *Where are the Third Places: Recreational Alternatives to Gambling?* Lilydale: Centre for Regional Development.

Levitas, R. (2000) 'What is social exclusion?', in D. Gordon and P. Townsend (Eds.), *Breadline Europe*. Bristol: Policy Press, pp. 357–83.

Lewis, S. (2004) *Gender and Firefighting*, Gender Equity Research Project 1. Melbourne: Metropolitan Fire Brigade.

Light, R. (2006) 'Situated learning in an Australian surf club', *Sport Education and Society*, 11 (2), pp. 155–72.

Light, R. (2008) *Sport in the Lives of Young Australians*. Sydney: Sydney University Press.

Lucas, B., Spencer, E. and Claxton, G. (2012) *How to Teach Vocational Education: A Theory of Vocational Pedagogy*. Winchester: Centre of Real-World Learning, University of Winchester.

Lundberg, D. and Marshallsay, A. (2007) *Older Workers' Perspectives on Training and Retention of Older Workers*. Adelaide: NCVER.

Mark, R., Montgomery, V. and Graham, H. (2010) *Beyond the Workplace: An Investigation into Older Men's Learning and Well-being in Northern Ireland*, Report for the Changing Ageing Partnership (CAP). Belfast: Queen's University Belfast.

McGinn, C. (2008) ABC Radio National, Interview, 14 November 2008. Retrieved 14 November 2008 from www.abc.net.au/rn/perspective/stories/2008/2415453.htm#transcript

McGivney, V. (1999a) *Missing Men: Men who are Missing from Education and Training*. Leicester: NIACE.

McGivney, V. (1999b) *Informal Learning in the Community: A Trigger for Change and Development*. Leicester: NIACE.

NCVER: National Centre for Vocational Education Research (2013) *What Makes for Good Workplace Learning?* Retrieved 26 March 2013 from www.ncver.edu.au/publications/1004.html

NIACE: National Institute for Adult and Continuing Education (2006) *Learning in Later Life: A Public Spending Challenge.* Leicester: NIACE.

Ohsako, T. (1998) 'Learning and social participation by senior citizens in Japan: Analysis of major issues from an international perspective', Paper to OECD and US Department of Education Conference, Washington DC, 6–8 April.

Oldenburg, R. (1999) *The Great Good Place: Cafés, Coffee Shops, Bookstores, Bars and other Hangouts at the Heart of a Community.* New York: Marlowe and Company.

Payne, G. (2008) *Case study: Creating Winners for Life: A Consortium between CSA (Cricket South Africa) and UNISA to Promote Lifelong Learning.* Rockhampton: Central Queensland University Press.

PMSEIC: Prime Minister's Science, Engineering and Innovation Council (2009) *Transforming Learning and the Transmission of Knowledge.* Canberra: Commonwealth of Australia.

Ruxton, S. (2002) *Men, Masculinities and Poverty in the UK.* London: Oxfam.

Ryan, C. and Sinning, M. (2009) *Job Requirements and Lifelong Learning for Older Workers.* Adelaide: NCVER.

Sage, G. (1979) 'Sport and the social sciences', *The ANNALS of the American Academy of Political and Social Science*, 454 (1).

Schuller, T. and Watson, D. (2009) *Learning Through Life: Inquiry into the Future of Lifelong Learning.* Leicester: NIACE.

Skelton, C. (2000) '"A passion for football": Dominant masculinities in primary school', *Sport Education and Society*, 5 (1), pp. 5–18.

Southern, N. (2007) *Journal of Transformative Education*, 5 (4), pp. 29–38.

Tonts, M. (2005) 'Competitive sport and social capital in rural Australia', *Journal of Rural Studies*, 21 (2), pp. 37–149.

WHO: World Health Organization (2002) *Active Ageing: A Policy Framework.* Geneva: WHO.

CHAPTER SEVEN

Men and boys: Ages and stages

Annette Foley and Barry Golding

Introduction

There has been considerable debate and research over the past decade examining the low educational achievement rates of boys, and the extent to which boys are at-risk or disengaged from schooling (Foster *et al.*, 2001; Martino and Berrill, 2003; Smyth *et al.*, 2013). In addition, issues associated with men's attitudes to formal learning and the impact that underachievement and low literacy levels have on men's lives have gained attention (McGivney, 1999; Lattimore, 2007; Jenkins, 2011). The intent of this chapter is to identify some of the pedagogies and practices that can involve men working alongside at-risk boys (and girls) to assist them to re-connect with learning and community participation through partnerships between schools and community men's sheds. The chapter makes use of research findings taken from two projects and uses a vignette to highlight the value of intergenerational learning for boys (and girls) in a community context. Finally, the chapter puts forward the case that for some boys, connecting with men through community organisations by means of mentoring relationships can engage and re-connect boys with learning and the community. There is also evidence that this form of intergenerational relationship, in the case of men's sheds, can be valuable for men with respect to their sense of identity through the sharing of knowledge and skills and be beneficial to their health and wellbeing.

The problem of disengaged youth

Over the past decade, there has been increasing concern and public debate about the proportion of young people who are disengaged from the school system. According to a longitudinal study survey of Australian youth commissioned by the National Centre for Vocational Education Research (NCVER), as many as one-quarter of young people between 15 and 24 years of age in Australia can be described as being disengaged, in that they are not in full-time work or study (Anlezark, 2009). Most of this group do not view this situation as being permanent, as most have plans to look for full-time work or enrol in study. Indeed, many young people, according to Dwyer and Wyn, are identified as having a paradoxical response to their circumstances:

> *Young people, whose opportunities to gain a livelihood are limited by high rates of regional unemployment, for example, tend to nonetheless have a strong belief in the capability of individuals to negotiate and shape a future for themselves.* (Dwyer and Wyn, 2001, p. 123)

Nonetheless, research in the US, Australia and the UK indicates that both gender and class are contributing factors that influence young people's aspirations for employment and help to explain why some young people disengage from schooling or work (Dwyer and Wyn, 2001). Some of these reasons involve poor academic performance, low self-esteem and a loss of a sense of control in their lives. Other reasons include feelings of alienation or experiences of bullying at school. Excessive out-of-school working hours can also have an impact on a young person's motivation to want to go to school (Audas and Willms, 2001), while others simply see school as being irrelevant (Reed, 1999).

This body of research indicates that cumulative effects of family circumstances can have profound impacts on an individual's educational attainment. These can include socio-economic circumstances, family structure and parental employment status (Audas and Willms, 2001). In addition, the role of peer networks and friendship groups plays a significant role in the decisions made by young people (Cohen, 1983; Ellenbogen and Chamberland, 1997; Maxwell, 2002; Smyth and Hattam, 2004). Ellenbogen and Chamberland examined the peer networks of young people to determine the factors that led to leaving school early in Canada. They identified three trends that influenced whether a young person might leave school.

> *First, actual dropouts and future dropouts have more friends who have dropped out of school. Second, future dropouts tend to be rejected by their school peers. Finally, at-risk individuals tend to lack integration into their schools social network* (1997, p. 18).

Smyth and Hattam identified a tension around doing schoolwork and maintaining friendships, and take up the argument that unless schools can be sensitive to the impact that friendships and academic performance can have on the success of young people, 'increasing numbers will become disaffected' (2004, p. 87).

> *Young people are going to school to be with their friends, but attending school is dependent on taking up, at least to some degree, an academic identity. That is young people are doing significant identity work between adopting the identity of the successful student and sustaining/nurturing an identity through intimate relationships.* (Smyth and Hattam, 2004, p. 87)

The effects of school on individual performance and success are of particular importance when considering the influences on students to leave the education system early. For this reason, significant expenditure and governmental attention has been directed at the school curriculum to broaden its focus to include vocational studies and establish pathways into work or training to engage young people more likely to be at-risk (Dwyer and Wyn, 2001).

The link between educational attainment and more success in obtaining employment is addressed in McMillan and Marks' (2003) Australian study that examined Year 12 completion rates. It concluded that completing Year 12 is associated with lower levels of unemployment and an increased earning capacity throughout life. In general, they concluded that completing Year 12 facilitates a smoother transition from school to work. Completing an academic Year 12, however, may not have an impact on the capacity to gain employment for those students who are not academically inclined. The development of vocational programmes in the upper school curriculum, such as the Victorian Certificate of Applied Learning (VCAL★) and Vocational Education and Training (VET) in Schools that incorporate an applied learning model have been established to cater for students on pathway to training, apprenticeships or other work-related opportunities (McMillan and Marks, 2003). Many of these VCAL and VET in school programmes have had success through a community VCAL model that involves schools delivering vocational programmes away from school settings.

The problem with boys' education

There is little doubt that leaving school early can adversely affect both boys and girls. However, for the purposes of this chapter we concentrate on boys' disengagement by examining what has been described as the 'crisis' of boys' education. Foster, Kimmel and Skelton (2001) highlight that as far back as the seventeenth century the English philosopher John Locke expressed a concern for boys' problems with language and literacy (Cohen, 1998, in Martino and Meyenn, 2001, p. 2). Again in the 1960s and 1970s, boys' issues with academic work and negative attitudes to schooling were identified. Subsequent studies have indicated that social class and race have a significant impact on boys' ability to succeed at school. In the 1990s, the problem with boys' underachievement was constructed as a consequence of 'boys being boys', resulting from the significant changes to the education system at the time. Back then, gender was the factor identified as having an impact on boys' educational success (Foster *et al.*, 2001, p. 2).

Despite the debates associated with boys' success at school, what we do know is that boys in the State of Victoria, Australia, are around 'one half as likely as girls to enrol in a tertiary course post Year 12' (Golding *et al.*, 2008). What we also know is that many men who participate in men's sheds have negative recollections of school that have prevented them from seeking to gain qualifications beyond their school years and that have affected their perceptions of formal education all their lives. With the current issue of boys withdrawing from school, at-risk and at odds with the school system, the potential for boys of today to face

★ The Victorian Certificate of Applied Learning (VCAL) is a 'hands-on' option for students in Years 11 and 12 in Victoria, Australia. Like the Victorian Certificate of Education (VCE), VCAL is an accredited secondary certification.

similarly negative perceptions which are carried throughout their lives is a significant issue for education policymakers.

The research methods

This chapter draws from two Australian research projects. The first study explored the attitudes of men involved in men's sheds across Australia, where there is a partnership between the men's shed and local schools. The study involved data from 24 community-based men's sheds in Australia (Golding *et al.*, 2007). The second study involved alternative school programmes, including some conducted through men's sheds, where boys are referred through the school or other agencies because of behavioural issues or school resistance. This study involved 15 boys between the ages of 14 and 17. In both studies a series of questions were asked related to perceptions of learning enjoyment and perceptions of formal learning and schooling. In both studies, programme co-ordinators were interviewed. In the case of the second study, both boys and co-ordinators were interviewed. In both studies that involved men's sheds, the men working alongside the boys were also interviewed.

The research data from both studies used the participant's narrative responses to identify themes in the data. Narrative research relates to interpretative qualitative studies in which stories are used to describe human actions. Narrative inquiry enables narrators to tell the stories of their lives and experiences. According to Chase, the narrative approach highlights narrators' 'identity work', 'as they construct selves within specific institutional, organisational, discursive and local cultural contexts' (2005, p. 658). A limitation to the findings of the studies involves the fact that only ten of approximately 200 organisations in Australia in 2007 had significant numbers of school-aged people involved in intergenerational programmes. Of the boys interviewed, 11 of the 15 were involved in some form of mentoring relationship with older men. In one case a men's shed was involved in a significant school-based vocational programme in partnership with the local school.

What the men and boys say

Community-based men's sheds, as elaborated in Chapter Eight, are grassroots organisations that involve men coming together to share friendship while involved in hands-on activities such as wood and metal work. What all sheds share is 'a commitment to the health and well-being of men through companionship, friendship and mentoring' (Golding *et al.*, 2008, p. 1). In some sheds across Australia, men are working alongside boys in partnership with local schools using a vocational curriculum in an applied learning delivery model. These programmes have demonstrated success regarding reconnecting boys with learning.

Data from the first study involved insights from co-ordinators and mentors involved in the shed-based programmes for at-risk students. One co-ordinator from a men's shed in Tasmania described the young people that came to the shed as 'kids who aren't necessarily interested in academic achievement but enjoyed building things'. Another explained that some of the boys get bored and angry with school, while others identified boys missing a significant male role model in their lives.

The shed environment was perceived as a key feature of the success with school-based partnership programmes, one co-ordinator noting that the kids were 'out of the school environment ... We are not like school teachers ... We like to have a little talk with them as well as a little project ... It gives them more confidence'. A co-ordinator in a shed in Western Australia commented on how the boys felt at home in the shed: 'It's like a workplace. Here we don't muck around. They come in and put on their overalls and start working alongside the men'.

The feeling of being treated as an adult by the men and feeling like the work the boys were doing is relevant to them was echoed time and again in the data. One shed in Victoria treated the boys as equal members of the shed and were proud of how the boys responded.

> *The kids come in, set up and start working on the projects they*
> *have going. It's great to see the men and boys working together*
> *and we even get the boys making coffee for us ... amazing,*
> *they really love being here.*

A co-ordinator of another shed closer to Melbourne commented on how proud the boys felt when they harvested, picked and sold their own vegetables.

*It shows them that their work can have benefits. They can see
that what they are doing is relevant to their life. We sell the
vegetables at the local farmers market and we donate the profits
back into the shed. They get a feel for managing money too.*

Another key finding in the data was the value that the men got back
from working and sharing their skills with the kids 'The older men ...
take on a different sort of stature almost. They are looking out for them,
trying to be a better example ... There is a bond that develops'.

The findings from the second study indicated that boys had disengaged from formal schooling for a number of reasons. These reasons
included bullying, feeling overwhelmed at school, 'feeling dumb' and
attitudes about school that involved school not being seen as relevant.
Other boys were removed from school because of incidents of violence
and intimidation towards peers.

A co-ordinator in an out-of-school programme in metropolitan Melbourne was asked how the programme tried to engage the boys. He
explained that:

*Well first of all I would have to say to be honest with them and tell
how it is and to engage them and try and make it fun and positive.
That's probably the main thing that I can think of, just to make sure
it is fun for them and to come up with ideas that they are going to
enjoy. Sometimes to have a chat to them and see if they have any
ideas that they can see in the programme that they would enjoy
better.*

In a programme delivered from a regional setting, another teacher and
co-ordinator explained that:

*[T]he way I engage them is simple: it comes down to trust. I really
love these kids and they know I do. I want them to be successful and
that develops trust.*

Respect and trust were also mentioned by another co-ordinator of a
programme for boys in metropolitan Melbourne. The boys that attended
this programme were all ex-offenders and had been removed from their
school and referred to this programme.

> *I would have to say certainly respect and trust is important, but
> also personal development, because that's probably the biggest thing
> I would have to say, the personal development.*

Taking time to build confidence was a key theme.

> *[E]ven though it takes six months for them to come out of their shell
> it takes all year to build up their confidence.*

Co-ordinators were asked why they thought boys stayed in these programmes. In most cases the co-ordinators emphasised that the programmes were not like school and the boys appreciated that. For
example, as one co-ordinator explained:

> *We are different from schools and basically what the reason is we are
> more hands-on. It is more like a work environment than a school
> environment, even though they still get paperwork.*

Co-ordinators were asked how important the space/environment was
for the boys. In all cases the spaces were described as very important
to the success of the programmes. One co-ordinator in a regional city
in Victoria explained the importance of having a space outside of the
school environment:

> *Being separate if you like, not that I like that word, but the
> guys know that they can come here and they are away from it all
> and it's like a safe haven or a safe house if you like ... They know
> they can come here and they know they can trust us and all the
> rest of it.*

In the study, boys were interviewed and also asked questions about why
they were not at school and how they felt about the programme they
were involved in. Boys who take part in the out-of-school programmes
often have an issue with the school structure and teachers. For this boy,
dealing with anger issues was a problem.

> *In High School I never really did get along with any of the teachers
> ... I had no money because I can't get youth study [allowance], so
> I thought I need something to do and coming back here gives me a*

chance to find a decent job ... So I have come back here and now I have my own place and am doing good for myself.

Other boys felt that the classroom restricted them, which caused frustration.

> *Sitting in the Maths classroom, I am not one who can normally sit in a room, whereas here we have some freedom and can walk around and that. I used to throw tables and chairs at the teacher ... and went a bit too far sometimes.*

Some boys expressed that they enjoyed the feelings of respect they felt they were afforded by their teachers in the programmes: 'I'm treated like an adult ... the teachers respect us.'

Other boys were bullied or felt isolated at school, which made them feel uncomfortable or angry with school, peers and teachers. For this boy, concentration in the school setting was also a problem:

> *Well I was never really good at school, can't really concentrate for long ... can't keep still and things like that, so never mixed.*

A significant theme in the responses involved boys being reasonably positive about their futures. One boy explained that he was looking forward to starting an apprenticeship in bricklaying, while another wanted to go to TAFE (public vocational education and training) and start a cooking course.

Another key theme coming from the boys' responses was the respect and trust they felt for their teacher/mentors. Finally, a key theme in the responses involved boys feeling like the programmes were relevant and work-like.

> *I do enjoy coming here because it is more my kind of my thing. I can't handle sitting down doing paperwork all day, every day, and here we get to use our hands with all the power tools and we can build stuff and right now we are doing stuff on my mini bike so we can ride a bike around the track for a long time ... It's more laid back and they basically ask us what we like to do and what we enjoy and what we have trouble with and they will try and help us with that as well.*

In both studies, the key themes coming from the data involved the pro-grammes assisting boys to build confidence in themselves. Respect was also a common theme in the responses. For both the boys and the men, respect was established through the development of relationships in an environment that the boys felt was 'more like work' and 'not like school'. Many of the respondents saw that the work-like environment, teamed with the mentor relationships the men provided for the boys, facilitated a space where they could learn skills from the men in an environment that held the boy's attention.

The data also pointed to themes relating to affection and caring from both the boys and the men working alongside them. This was indicated through comments from the boys such as 'I like it here ... I can relax and have a laugh with Bob without getting into trouble.' And from another boy, who enjoyed the feeling that he had a grandfather figure: 'Yes, he's like having a Pop ... we have a laugh. It's fun with him' And comments from the men ... 'I reckon they like it here. I kinda really sorta love them being here'... 'It's not hard working with the boys, in fact I love it when they come.'

Storying the 'View Dale Men's Shed'

This next section showcases the 'View Dale Men's Shed' by presenting a vignette: a narrative or story of the relationships between boys and men in a single shed. The vignette is used here deliberately to give a real sense of a men's shed and the relationships and benefits of boys working and learning from the men. We do this by compiling and distilling com-monly used discourses and described practices into a single representa-tion or story. Accordingly, what follows★ is an assemblage of commonly identified themes in the form of a 'snapshot' or vignette of a 'day in the life' of the View Dale Men's Shed.

View Dale Men's Shed is nestled in a valley in Central Victoria in Australia. It is quite a large men's shed as it consists of a particularly large and well-resourced workshop area, has its own kitchen area and boasts a large, functioning vegetable garden and greenhouse. View Dale Men's

---

★ The situation and setting depicted in the vignette is a 'snapshot' developed from actual case data looking at the commonly occurring themes coming from the interview data of men and boys from both studies. The story is compiled from actual sheds and programmes and enmeshed into a vignette to bring to life themes and practices identified in the data, though the men's shed name and people's names are not real.

Shed is funded and administered by the View Dale Community Health Centre, which also funds the local neighbourhood house. The men that participate in the shed range in age from 60 to 88 years old. Amongst the other programmes that are run from the shed, such as health and wellbeing programmes, the shed also has an agreement with the local secondary school. Once a week several of students identified as being at-risk attend the shed to work alongside the men, who mentor them and share their knowledge and skills in woodwork.

Dan is the men's shed co-ordinator. He is about 65 years old and before he retired he was the director of a regional Victorian men's prison. The local community health agency signed a memorandum of under-standing (MOU) with the local secondary college to work alongside the shed to facilitate an intergenerational learning opportunity for the students identified by the school as being 'at-risk'. The men were consulted about the initiative and most were supportive of the proposal. Those that did not feel they were able or supportive of such a programme were supported to opt out of any involvement in the MOU arrangement.

The shed co-ordinator, the school principal, some senior teachers and a representative from the community health agency worked with the VCAL curriculum co-ordinator to organise a VCAL programme extension to run out of the men's shed. This enabled the students to have curriculum outcomes attached to the intergenerational learning experience.

The initial group that commenced once a week at the shed involved mostly boys aged 14 to 16 years, though a few girls in the same age range also attended. Initially there were a few 'issues'. These issues involved the boys and girls not wanting to be involved in the programme and preferring to stand outside and smoke. After two weeks of students not stepping into the shed, Dan decided to make a stand. Essentially this involved Dan giving the students an ultimatum: either come in, meet the men and get involved, or else leave. Dan made it clear that none of the men were being paid for their efforts and none of them had to or wanted to share their knowledge with the students if the students were not committed.

The next week Dan saw a difference in the actions and attitudes of the students. Over several months students seemed to self-select the men they wanted to work alongside. The men started to share their skills and assisted the students to initially build small projects like bird boxes and letter boxes, then later got the boys involved in building a large shade house. The students also designed, built and tended a rather large and impressive vegetable garden that services the men's shed for lunches and the vegetables are sold at the local monthly farmer's market. This has been a huge success and allows the boys to give back to the local community through selling fresh, organically grown produce, with the profits contributed back to the shed by donating the takings.

By using this vignette we have showcased the themes coming from the data from both studies to emphasise the value and contribution that an intergenerational programme can have. There is clear evidence coming from the data that both the boys and the men benefited from the partnership.

Positive masculinities and intergenerational role modelling

There is a growing proportion of young people disengaging from school in Australia, Europe, Canada, the USA and New Zealand (Smyth *et al.*, 2013). Many of these students are boys. In the state of Victoria in Australia, for example, 81 per cent of females completed their schooling in 2009, whereas only 48 per cent of boys from low socio-economic areas completed their schooling (ACARA, 2009). These boys often come from low socio-economic backgrounds where their disengagement is often 'grounded in a masculinity politics that positions them in an antagonistic relationship with formal schooling' (Mills and Keddie, 2005, p. 5). As with many of the boys in the second study referred to earlier in the chapter, the data indicate that some boys can feel angry with the system and formal structures of school, making them feel voiceless and unable to see the relevance of an academic curriculum to their interests, lives and futures. The data in our studies shows that many of the boys who are involved in community VCAL or out-of-school programmes, where men share skills and knowledge with them, connect with hands-on work-like experience that is meaningful and relevant to the boy's lives and interests.

Strong and positive relationships with adults have been identified as being a key component for healthy psychological development of adolescence (Scales and Leffert, 1999, in Spencer, 2007, p. 185). Social influences are a significant factor in young people's success or failure at school. As children move into adolescence, they strive to create an integrated self-image (Erikson, 1963), which is influenced by significant people in their lives. To assist with this identity development, peer groups and role models supply children with their social understandings and help them form adult identities (Maxwell, 2002). The data from our studies indicates that meaningful mentor relationships between boys and men have positive influences that can engage boys with learning in meaningful ways that are promoted and encouraged by older men.

We suggest that making use of spaces other than school creates a climate of friendship and honesty that can capture the attention of boys who are disengaged from school. We support Smyth *et al.*, who call for 'radical thinking about the fixed notions of space and place within and through which learning occurs' (2013, p. 2). The data from our studies assists us to re-think the possibility of pedagogy and learning spaces that cater for intergenerational relationship building and expose boys to learning through authentic work-like spaces and provides an unscripted pedagogy that provides agency for the boys.

The findings from the data also lead us to consider the significant value of the mentoring relationship, not only to provide agency for the boys in relation to their developing skills for employment, but also to challenge some of the ways that culture and gender role norms shape boys' relational experiences. What we are suggesting is that the account of males' relationships that is often characterised as active rather than emotionally focused (Spencer, 2007) is challenged in these studies. The close nature of many mentoring relationships, such as those examined in our studies between boys and men, can have the potential to mitigate some of the culturally negative effects of conventional gender norms and expectations, what Connell (1995) describes as hegemonic masculinity. These norms restrict the emotional expression in males, which often compromises boys' relational experiences in school (Darling *et al.*, 2006). The data in our studies identifies the relationships that build up between the boys and men as displaying connections that promote positive forms of masculinity involving closeness, caring and affection for each other.

The intergenerational programmes examined in our studies showed that the mentoring relationships with the men can provide boys with positive emotional, social and cognitive benefits. For such benefits to be realised, according to Rhodes,

> close emotional bonds must be established between mentor and
> protégé. This contention is supported by recent research indicating
> that feelings of closeness and emotional support are key ingredients

of mentoring relationships that are associated with improvements of youth functioning for both boys and girls. (2002, p. 187)

We also recognise that the close emotional and social bonds developed between the boys and men have significant benefits for the men involved. Many of the men in men's sheds or community organisations are retired, and in some cases are experiencing issues associated with adjusting to a retired life where their identity is no longer enmeshed in their work roles. Other older men involved in these programmes are suffering with depression, loneliness, drug dependency and anger issues. The benefits the men get from intergenerational mentoring involve building strong meaningful relationships with boys, sharing skills that have been developed over many years and feeling valued and respected by the boys.

Conclusion

This chapter puts forward the case that a suitably structured vocational programme, delivered from a men's shed or similar community organisation that involves a partnership between the local school and adult men, is of significant value and provides innovative pedagogies and opportunities for the development of relationships that engage and develop agency for both men and boys.

References

ACARA: Australian Curriculum and Reporting Assessment Authority (2009) *National Report of Schooling in 2009.* Canberra: ACARA.

Anlezark, A. (2009) *At-risk Youth: A Transitory State? Longitudinal Surveys of Australian Youth.* Adelaide: NCVER.

Audas, R. and Willms, D. (2001) *Engagement and Dropping out of School: A Life-course Perspective,* Applied Research Branch, Human Resources Development Canada. Ottawa: Canadian Government.

Chase, S. (2005) 'Narrative inquiry: Multiple lenses, approaches, voices', in N. Denzin and Y. Lincoln (Eds.), *The Sage Handbook of Qualitative Research.* Thousand Oaks: Sage Publications, pp. 651–80.

Cohen, J. (1983) 'Commentary: The relationship between friendship selection and peer influence', in J. Epstein and N. Karweit (Eds.), *Friends in School.* New York: Academic Press, pp. 163–76.

Cohen, M. (1998) 'Healthy idleness: Boys' underachievement in historical perspective', in D. Epstein, J. Elwood, V. Hey and J. Maw (Eds.), *Failing Boys: Issues in Gender and Achievement*. Buckingham: Open University Press.

Connell, R. (1995) *Masculinities*. Cambridge: Polity Press.

Darling, N., Bogart, G., Cavell, T., Murphy, S. and Sanchez, B. (2006) 'Gender ethnicity, development and risk: Mentoring and the consideration of individual differences', *Journal of Community Psychology*, 34, pp. 765–79.

Dwyer, P. and Wyn, J. (2001) *Youth, Education and Risk: Facing the Future*. London: Routledge Falmer.

Ellenbogen, S. and Chamberland, C. (1997) 'The peer relations of dropouts: Comparative study of at-risk and not at-risk youths', *Journal of Adolescence*, 20, pp. 355–67.

Erikson, E. (1963) *Childhood and Society* (2nd ed.). New York: Norton.

Foster, V., Kimmel, M. and Skelton, C. (2001) 'What about the boys? An overview of the debates', in W. Martino and B. Meyenn (Eds.), *What About the Boys? Issues of Masculinity in Schools*. Buckingham: Open University Press.

Golding, B., Brown, M., Foley, A., Harvey, J. and Gleeson, L. (2007) *Men's Sheds in Australia: Learning through Community Contexts*. Adelaide: NCVER.

Golding, B., Foley A., and Brown, M. (2008) 'Shedding school early: Insights from school and community shed collaboration in Australia', Paper to AVETRA Conference, Adelaide, 3–4 April.

Jenkins, A. (2011) 'Participation in learning and well-being among older adults', *International Journal of Lifelong Learning Education*, 30 (3), pp. 403–20.

Lattimore, R. (2007) *Men Not in Work: An Analysis of Men Outside the Labour Force*, Staff Working Paper. Canberra: Australian Government Productivity Commission.

Martino, W. and Berrill, D. (2003) 'Boys, schooling and masculinities: Interrogating the "right" way to educate boys', *Educational Review*, 55 (2), pp. 99–117.

Martino, W. and Meyenn, B. (Eds.) (2001) *What about the Boys: Issues of Masculinity in Schools*. Buckingham: Open University Press.

Maxwell, K. (2002) 'Friends: The role of peer influence across risk behaviour', *Journal of Youth and Adolescence*, 31 (4), pp. 267–77.

McGivney, V. (1999) *Excluded Men: Men who are Missing from Education and Training*. Leicester: NIACE.

McIntyre, J., Freeland, J., Melville, B. and Schwenke, C. (1999) *Early School Leavers at-Risk*. Adelaide: NCVER.

McMillan, J. and Marks, G. (2003) 'School leavers in Australia: Profiles and pathways', *LSAY (Longitudinal Survey of Australian Youth) Research Report*, 31. Melbourne: Australian Council of Education Research (ACER).

Mills, M. and Keddie, A. (2005) 'Boys, productive pedagogies and social justice', Paper to AARE Conference, Sydney, 27 Nov–1 Dec.

Reed, L. (1999) 'Troubling boys and disturbing discourses on masculinity and schooling: A feminist exploration of current debates and interventions concerning boys in school', *Gender and Education*, 11 (1), pp. 93–110.

Rhodes, J. (2002) *Stand by Me: The Risks and Rewards of Mentoring Today's Youth.* Cambridge: Harvard University Press.

Scales, P. and Leffert, N. (1999) *Developmental Assets: A Synthesis of the Scientific Research on Adolescent Development.* Minneapolis: Search Institute.

Smyth, J. and Hattam, R. (2004) *'Dropping Out', 'Drifting Off', 'Being Excluded': Becoming Somebody Without School.* New York: Peter Lang.

Smyth, J., McInerney, P. and Fish, T. (2013) 'Blurring the boundaries: From relational learning towards a critical pedagogy of engagement for disengaged disadvantaged young people', *Pedagogy, Culture and Society*, 21 (2), pp. 1–22.

Spencer, R. (2007) '"I just feel safe with him": Emotional closeness in male youth mentoring relationships', *Psychology of Men and Masculinity*, 8 (3), pp. 185–98.

CHAPTER EIGHT

Men's sheds: A new movement for change

Barry Golding

Introduction

For those unfamiliar with community men's sheds and the rapidly growing movement associated with them, a stand-alone chapter in a book about men's learning through life might seem like a curious inclusion. Our rationale is that men's sheds in community settings integrate much of what we have already presented, and provide a neat fit between both men's learning and wellbeing. My intention in this chapter is to acknowledge that the pedagogies associated with men's sheds in community settings have the capacity to improve and radically change men's involvement in learning and promote their wellbeing, paradoxically and counter-intuitively without foregrounding either.

What underpins this thinking is research into those returning to adult education from nations such as Australia and Canada (Myers and Myles, 2005) that highlight that, while the least educated are least likely to participate, when they do participate they are most likely to benefit (Blundell *et al.*, 1999), and that training alone may represent an inefficient investment policy for the less skilled (Lefebvre and Merrigan, 2003). While this particularly applies to older men excluded in one or more dimensions (economic, social, spatial and institutional: Phillipson, 2011), it is important to note from the outset that sheds can and do accommodate the engagement of men of all ages in learning and that some sheds additionally focus on involving young men in their activities.

Community men's sheds are a good example of an international, community-based, grassroots movement that illustrates the thesis in

113

the rest of our book, particularly as it relates to men of any age not in the paid workforce. That is that both learning and wellbeing in community settings can be advanced by the collective action of men. The men's sheds movement has not only provided opportunities for men's informal community learning, but has also contributed substantially to their wellbeing. While the shed movement started slowly and from small beginnings in parts of Australia, its recent and rapid spread across and well beyond Australia to New Zealand, Ireland, England and Scotland is evidence of what can and does happen when men exercise human agency in social contexts (Bandura, 1989), and when governments listen to and work with men rather than problematising or patronising them. On one level, this chapter identifies, describes and evaluates several examples of good practice involving men's sheds, which now involve important learning elements in several countries beyond Australia. On another level, it provides insights into how new theories can and do emerge 'bottom up' by research which actively links theory to practice.

The timeliness of men's sheds as a concept

Personal men's sheds and similar workshop and garden shed-type spaces have been recognised by men for many decades as important and culturally iconic places for men to potter about, fix things and develop friendships in diverse situations. The development of men's sheds in community settings was an idea that began in Australia almost 20 years ago. Earle (1996), researching in South Australia, was the first to formally link participation in personal sheds as a compensatory strategy used by older men as they age, and also to extrapolate the idea from personal sheds to community sheds. This early theoretical breakthrough by Earle (a gerontologist) was consistent with the work by William Thomas in the field of gerontology from 1991 on the 'Eden Alternative' (EA: Eden Alternative, 2009). Like some men's sheds, EA addressed three perceived problems then evident in nursing homes (Brune, 2011, p. 508): loneliness, helplessness and boredom. EA tackled these problems by considering and positively working with people's individual needs, desires, life patterns, accomplishments, growth, contributions and connections to families and to the community (p. 509). While these principles have since begun to influence cultural change in long-term, aged care, some of the same ideologies apply and have been broadened to men's shed principles and practice. As with the men's sheds movement, 'the culture-change movement [spread] in advance of a solid research base to support its quality of life improvement claims' (Brune, 2011, p. 514).

One of the oldest continually operating men's sheds, and one of the most influential in terms of the movement's early development, is the Lane Cove Men's Shed in Sydney, Australia, ironically located in a former car park underneath an aged care centre. It was instigated in 1998 'to promote the health and wellbeing of older men in the community, and to provide a place to meet each other, network and make friends' (NSW *Hansard*, 2004). The Lane Cove Men's Shed was particularly aimed at men in the community aged over 55, 'men who are retired, outplaced or job redundant, those who have downsized living arrangements and those who feel isolated'. This transformation of the shed from an individual, mainly private place for men to make and fix things, typically in their own backyards, to a collective, community space for men, with underlying and powerful wellbeing, group participation and social learning purposes and outcomes is worthy of closer examination for four main reasons.

Firstly, it demonstrates the multiple social benefits of learning, including connecting with individuals who have similar interests (MacKean, 2009) through the creation of social networks outside of the workplace (Englebrecht and Skladzien, 2010). Secondly, it provides pointers to new ways of positively connecting learning with health and wellbeing. Thirdly, men's sheds incorporate alternative ways of perceiving and working with men as agents actively involved in transformation that goes well beyond themselves to include other men and communities, rather than seeking them as patients, clients, customers or students from deficit models of provision.

Fourthly, it demonstrates the need for less conventional services for the one-third of men not in paid work who fall outside the dominant discourse about work and productivity that regards men not in work, and older men in particular, as burdensome and problematic. Men's sheds took particular traction in Australia at the same time as early retirements were being described as endemic (Kinsella–Taylor, 2001) and as governments struggled to replace lost income tax. At the same time, Australia was preparing for a looming ageing population, seeing them, unfairly (VECCI, 2003), as an unsustainable cost item in care and partly responsible for the loss of national productivity and skills shortages. Over the following decade, as sheds spread across Australia, labour force participation of older men (aged 55 plus) has increased (to 42 per cent by 2009:

ABS, 2010, p. 2), though in 2009 two out of five people in Australia aged 55–69 who were not in the labour force (41 per cent of whom were men) listed their main activity as being retired or voluntarily inactive (ABS, 2010, p. 6).

Meanwhile, globally, the proportion of people aged 60 plus as a percentage of the total population trends upwards, from a low five to 12 per cent in all continents to a predicted 17 to 30 per cent by 2030 (with the exception of Africa) and 24 to 34 per cent (again with the exception of Africa at 11 per cent) by 2050 (UN, 2008). This trebling of people in older age cohorts in one century within most parts of the world is unprecedented in human history. It challenges notions about the nature and extent of post-retirement living and the age of retirement itself, originally set at the age of 65 in an era when most people who worked died soon after retirement. These challenges are particularly relevant to the significant proportion of the population which is unemployed in many European nations, approaching or exceeding 25 per cent in 2013, as well as the large additional pool of discouraged job seekers who have stopped looking for work.

In post-global-financial-crisis economies based around training for work, thinking about what men might do in Europe when not in paid work is extremely timely. Indeed, combating 'social exclusion among older people by encouraging them to actively participate in their communities as locals and at a regional level' and preventing 'dependency when people become old' were two of the three challenges (the third being helping 'people to stay at work longer') in the 2012 European Year of Active Ageing and Solidarity between Generations (EU, 2012). This thinking is also important beyond Europe, in nations like Australia whose economy has been more resilient but where ageing women, baby boomers, those on low incomes and in the poorest health have been most affected by the global financial crisis (Noone, 2012).

The research evidence

Given that the field of men's shed practice is very new, it is unsurprising that there is a limited body of rigorous, peer-reviewed research in this exploratory area of study, as summarised by Wilson and Cordier (2013). Multi-site, mixed method Australian studies include those by Golding *et al.* (2007), Hayes and Williamson (2007) and Misan *et al.* (2008). With over one thousand men's shed based organisations in the world, including approximately 900 in Australia, 100 in Ireland and 60 in the UK by early 2014, it is evident that they have achieved widespread and spontaneous take up at the level of community. One of the difficulties with scientifically proving impact is that men's sheds, even if they were very similar to each other (which they are not), do not neatly fit into one academic field or lend themselves to an easy study based around a positivistic scientific paradigm or the sort of quantitative inferential analysis sought by Wilson and Cordier on their questionable assumption that 'male health initiatives are a central part of the movement's ethos' (2013, p. 34). That said, there is sufficient evidence from a range of Australian studies reviewed by Wilson and Cordier (2013) and from research carried out in Ireland (Carragher, 2013) to confirm a wide range of benefits to the men who participate in men's sheds, their families and the wider community.

The serious mistake here would be to discuss sheds on the assumption that they have only one primary function premised on addressing deficit, namely targeting men's perceived need for learning, education, training or employment during issues with health, retirement, unemployment, depression or dementia; seeing them as a convenient place for 'tacking on' top-down services and professionals to address men's perceived need for socialisation, psychological support or nutrition; or for addressing some men's issues with drugs and alcohol or suicide, or as an alternative to community corrections. While all of these things are possible through sheds, there are many more obvious, positive intentions and outcomes, including activity, fun, relationships, friendship and giving back to the community. These other 'soft outcomes' are not premised on deficit and are not as amenable to efficient, standardised, cost-driven and regulation-compliant, hierarchical, departmentalised, top-down management provision of services typically found in hospitals, nursing homes and retirement communities (Brune, 2011). Nor are sheds amenable to meeting the associated expectations of hard, outcomes-based targets that increasingly go with government funding and performativity agendas.

A reminder here that while our common academic interest and bias in this book is on men's learning, there is now copious evidence that sheds produce many other outcomes for men's family and community wellbeing in ways that radically challenge many previous academic assumptions, particularly about age, masculinities, agency and community.

Why men's sheds work

Macdonald, Brown and Gethin note the tendency to falsely regard 'masculine deficiency' as the explanation for why some men do not use services. They note that, while men's sheds may not be necessary for today's young men as they age, the current generation of men from earlier eras, as well as many men from Indigenous and migrant backgrounds who are 'the issue now and for coming decades' (2009, p. 30), often play gender roles and exhibit 'masculine identities shaped by history, culture and dominant models of masculinity' (p. 27). These identities, which include placing a 'very high value on independence, managing themselves, competence, privacy and not asking for help — unless essential' (Macdonald, Brown and Gethin, 2009, p. 29), make such men much less likely to present for a wide range of conventional services, even when in crisis.

While personal men's sheds have been important and culturally iconic for men in Australia for a long time, the first men's shed in a community organisation started in Australia as recently as the mid 1990s. While backyard, house and garden sheds have been important for individual men, and shed-type places in workplaces, gardens and farms have been acknowledged in many nations as places in which much hands-on, workshop activity takes place, the term 'shed' had also been used for many decades to describe some important community places in Australia in which men have traditionally gathered. These include the fire brigade shed and the football and rugby sheds. Many nations have shed-based community organisations dedicated to keeping men's trade skills, traditions, tools and engines alive, such as in mining, agriculture and forestry museums. Hands-on activities and skills have been practised and passed down from father to son in sheds. Woodcrafts have been men's pursuits in most traditional cultures, and in several cultures, such as New Guinea, men's 'houses' formed an important part of community religion and ritual.

The global growth and influence of feminism from the 1960s has led to many men's places and spaces being seen as generally anachronistic, unnecessary and unhelpful to gender equality, and to women's equal participation in all aspects of society in particular. Most male-only community organisations and workplaces in developed nations have since been 'opened up' to women. These changes have met resistance in traditional and Indigenous cultures, as well as from older men who were socialised and educated in a pre-feminist era. In some ways, men's sheds organisations in the Western nations in which they have recently been established have something to do with some men 'answering back' by saying that some places for men are not necessarily out-dated, and indeed that for some men, families and communities, they are invaluable. While men's sheds are not attractive or necessary for all men, they have proved to be extremely positive for most men who participate, with positive flow-on effects for women, families and communities.

What are men's sheds in community settings?

The men's shed movement is comprised of a loose association of shed-based community organisations, mainly for and by men. It has very quickly become the largest community association in Australia, Ireland and New Zealand focused on the needs, interests health and wellbeing of men. Men's sheds provide a safe, regular, social space for informal voluntary activity and programmes with very diverse possibilities and outcomes matching the men and communities in which they are embedded. Unlike personal sheds, they are available to groups of men, organised independently or with auspice arrangements through a wide variety of other community organisations (including learning and health organisations). The activity usually (but not always) takes place in a group workshop-type space with tools and equipment in a public, shed-type setting. Because of these diverse settings, sheds are similarly as diverse as the men and communities they involve and spring from.

There are some important basics. Sheds work because the men involved typically actively participate, belong to and identify with the shed. Men enjoy and benefit from gathering socially, regularly, voluntarily, happily and safely to do hands-on 'stuff' together. What that 'stuff' is, is less important than the principles embedded in the men's shed concept. It works best when it is grassroots, by, for and about the local men. It is more about men helping each other and the community than men helping themselves or being 'serviced'. 'Shedders', as they call themselves, are active and equal participants in the activity. The irony is that by not naming the activity, the sheds provide the freedom and agency to talk informally, 'shoulder to shoulder' about other important things going on in their lives that would not otherwise be shared.

Beyond the diversity, Golding (2012, p. 129) has identified the key common attributes of men's sheds. They tend not to patronise participants as clients, customers or patients. They do not describe the activity or the participants in the shed (other than being men). They provide places for men to exercise agency over the shed activity as well as over their lives beyond work. They are radical in that they promote holistic learning in communities of practice (without the need for teachers, curriculum, teaching and assessment and without health workers). They are safe health- and wellbeing-promoting spaces deliberately inclusive of *all* men. Importantly and interestingly, they are successful because neither learning nor health is formalised or foregrounded in the name of the organisation. They work precisely because they are approached informally.

In 2014, men's sheds is an international movement with national associations in Australia, Ireland, New Zealand and the UK. Aside from the phenomenal numeric growth, several things are of interest here to researchers, as summarised below in a review of the findings from research on men's sheds.

The research literature on men's sheds

While there is a similar model underpinning all men's sheds, they have an ability to adapt to a very wide range of contexts, places, purposes, men, communities and scales. Because there are similarly diverse ways of analysing and making sense of them, community sheds can be seen as something of a chameleon. The underlying commonalities are that they are for *all* men and that they are low on hierarchy and formality, but high on agency and community engagement. While sheds can and should make all men feel empowered and included in the community and 'at home' in the shed, all sheds are different.

Researchers looking at and making sense of men's sheds will therefore see something different not only according to where they look, but also which lens they use to examine the phenomena. For example, for an adult learning professional, academic or organisation, a shed will tend to highlight sharing of skills and learning. By contrast, a health worker might emphasise health, a psychologist a site for changing behaviour, a gerontologist a place for the retired, an occupational therapist a therapeutic activity, a sociologist a place to get 'out of the house', a community service professional a site for community engagement and connection, and a drug and alcohol worker a place for intervention.

Men's shed practice reinforces the obvious, sometimes lost with the imposition of service and academic 'silos' on the complexity of people's lives. In this case, men's lives and needs beyond paid work, as well as men's sheds, are complex and diverse and do not fit into one neat box. What sheds paradoxically demonstrate is that learning and wellbeing work very well for some men when they are interconnected, not named up front and not provided in a typical individual, client-based, service delivery model pre-supposed on deficit.

Men's sheds have another important attribute. Being a grassroots, 'ground up', community movement they have tended to spring up and do best in locations where they are most needed. Sheds have done particularly well where the proportion of men not in paid work is relatively high. This includes post-industrial suburban areas and retirement locations with high proportions of retired men from trade backgrounds; rural and remote men who have moved to larger towns and regional cities; areas hit by crisis and change, after fire and flood in Australia, for example, or following the earthquakes around Christchurch in New Zealand; areas of lower socio-economic status, where local community action has identified a need; and very recently across Ireland where the proportion of men not in paid work includes significant numbers of younger, unemployed men.

While it is important in principle (and enforced by equal opportunity legislation in many nations) that *all* men are welcome, in reality, as in many community organisations, some men's sheds organisations involving older men from conservative backgrounds need reminding about the need for including other groups: of Indigenous, gay and bisexual men and men from diverse religions, countries and cultures. While discrimination on the basis of race, religion and sexual preference in most nations and organisations is illegal, so too is discrimination by gender. Men's sheds justification of their mainly or 'just men' stance has been endorsed by the Australian Equal Opportunity Commission, using the argument that this configuration is consistent with interventions that improve men's health and encourage social and community connection of men not in the workforce. This stance also has widespread support from partners, children and families of men involved, as well as women involved professionally in learning, health and welfare on the basis that many people (including women) benefit aside from the men themselves.

It is important here to acknowledge the active role of women in assisting the shed movement. Women have played major roles in developing and championing many sheds, and supporting the national and state associations. Almost all media stories about sheds (and there have been many) have been written and researched by women. Women have been behind many shed start-ups and the procurement of funds. Some sheds have a very successful female shed co-ordinator. That said, some shed organisations (and men) try to shift the work they see as 'women's roles', including compliance, budgeting, accountability and food preparation, onto women.

It is timely in the context of this very rapid growth of the shed movement to anticipate that shed-type models enhancing men's wellbeing will spring up in other national and cultural contexts, both in new and existing community sites, in some cases by another name in languages other than English. Some models will be supported by national and state governments, as part of national men's health and wellbeing, productive ageing or lifelong learning policies. For some nations, it might be that existing iconic and traditional locations for men to gather might be re-invented.

As identified later in the seven national chapters, men in most nations gather and benefit in terms of learning and wellbeing through voluntary involvement in sporting and fire and emergency services organisations. In some other nations, such as Samoa, men's participation was traditionally around the 'kava bowl', involving men's ritualised group drinking of the mild intoxicant, kava. In Scandinavia, men tend to continue the tradition of gathering around fishing and hunting, which in some Nordic nations also extends to men's saunas. In Portugal, pigeon racing and fishing clubs have been important sites for men to gather. In the Maldives, it tends to be the place near the beach where men fix their fishing nets. In many Mediterranean nations, the custom has been for men to meet and drink coffee, a tradition that is followed by older, culturally diasporic migrant men in some Australian cities, and also goes on in the USA, as summarised by the following recent, first hand account from the internet.

> *You know the guys who sit around and talk shit all morning in a designated location, while drinking coffee? If you go to a gas station or a diner that opens early enough in the morning you've probably seen them ... about four or five grizzled old guys that just hang out there all morning. There's no designated meeting time — it's sort of an unspoken thing that everyone just shows up around the same time, like they drive by looking for each other's cars in the parking lot.*
> (Neogaf, 2013)

The idea of men 'talking shit' and 'playing' in sheds is not unimportant as a starting point to deeper and more meaningful conversations and shared activities. Tse (2005) extracted three main themes from research into older people's needs for activity and companionship through adult day activity groups in Australia. The importance of companionship, including being and talking with others, was one of the themes, as was keeping occupied and 'getting out of the house'. Other research confirms the importance also to women of having places, spaces and opportunities to 'natter' (known as having a 'chinwag' in England; and a 'bit of craic' in Ireland). Talking socially without exchanging too much information is an important way of people making contact, an activity that now extends to internet-enhanced conversations, including for men in 'virtual sheds' (ShedOnLine, 2013).

Men's sheds and learning

Golding's suite of research summarised in Golding (2012) tends to analyse men's sheds from a learning and wellbeing ontological perspective. Because this book is fundamentally about men's learning and wellbeing, and authored mainly by learning-oriented researchers, the main emphasis in the rest of this chapter is about learning. What is learned through men's sheds, often from and by previously poorly connected men, is far from unimportant. Men learn hands-on skills through practical, productive activity. They learn the positive value of leisure activity and friendships with other men. They gain new insights into the importance and ways to enhance fitness, relationships, healthy eating, identities as men and emotional wellbeing. They learn to cope with changes associated with not being in paid work, ageing, disability and retirement. Most importantly, men develop, share and enjoy lives and new identities in a third place beyond paid work and home, bestowed through and by association with the shed.

Learning which happens in men's sheds works largely because the pedagogies positively accommodate groups of men of all ages with a sometimes long-standing aversion to formal education and provision that is organised top-down. As Cully (2004, p. 227) notes, in Australia 'the formal VET system remains strongly biased towards provision of training for people aged 15 to 25'. Unlike U3A (University of the Third Age), which tends to provide programmes for already committed learners (Neilsen, 2003, p. 56), and OM:NI (Older Men: New Ideas), which is based around men sharing stories in supportive men-only contexts, men's sheds were recognised as early as 2004 by Morrison (2004) as providing something quite different for men. Morrison particularly picked out men whose 'identity and culture have been shaped in the unique and highly gendered experiences of war and post-war Australia' (2004, p. 2), and accurately predicted their capacity of 'multiplying across Australia' (p. 5). They encourage mentoring and sharing of leisure, trade, craft, health and safety skills, teaching men that they have something to give back to other men and the community at any age.

The absence of training, teachers and assessment matches the specific informal learning needs of the men who participate in sheds, making them feel at home, valued and valuable. Men learn through communities of practice in a way that does not involve the 'shame' associated with failure. Men's sheds develop and share what they do know rather than emphasising what men cannot do or do not know. The focus is on the needs of men as equal and joint participants in the activity, using and expanding on the (sometimes limited) formal literacies, skills and interests they do have. Men's sheds provide positive role models for other men. In some cases, where young people including school resisters are involved in men's shed activity, as discussed in Chapter Six, men provide critically important cross-age mentoring.

In the process, men of any age learn many new things, without 'enrolling' in any 'course'. Some men learn how to break social, family or work isolation, and the depression that can often be associated with this. For men at home with a partner for the rest of the week, sheds can relieve 'underfoot syndrome' for both parties. This phenomenon has also been described in Japan (Faiola, 2005). From a workplace and skills perspective, sheds are very much about transition to 'a third place' (aside from work and home, see Chapter Six) during the third age and well into the fourth age postulated by Soulsby (2000). From a productive ageing perspective, men's sheds tick most boxes for many older men. Where and how the learning takes place is also important. Hands-on learning is typically enjoyable where the tasks are real, with obvious, practical and transferable benefits. For some men, working with an open door or with views of the outside is also important.

Men's sheds and the learning associated with participation for the types of men who take part in them can perhaps be best understood from a sociological perspective in terms of cohort experiences (McNair, 2009). While much research and government policy effort goes into postulated, smooth transitions or pathways for young people through education and training to adulthood and work, 'the current pattern is of a much more complex and unpredictable phase of life, for young people entering it, as for older people leaving it' (McNair, 2009, p. 38). As McNair (2009, p. 38) presciently stressed in 2009, as the global financial crisis was continuing to unfold in the UK, 'Qualifications do not provide protection against this turbulence, although social class and networks do'.

Learning, as McNair stresses, has three broad purposes in relation to three forms of capital: identity, human and social (2009, p. 41). It helps people 'to find meaning in their lives; to support themselves and their dependents; to engage in a wider society; and to manage and adapt to change' (p. 41). Each of these purposes are arguably achieved through men's sheds, driven by a more mobile male population subject to new circumstances, less predictable labour market entry and exit, a much longer third age in healthy and active retirement and a longer fourth age living in some kind of dependency (McNair, 2009, p. 51). In the bigger picture, and using Sen's (1980) capability framework, men's sheds accommodate affiliation with other men; play, through working enjoyably 'shoulder to shoulder'; bodily health (Golding, 2011), as well as senses, imagination and thought.

Conclusion

This chapter examines the 'grassroots' shed model and movement and challenges preconceptions about the difficulty of enabling men's agency and learning in community settings, including for older men. The chapter presents an analysis of the movement that confirms the ability of diverse men, particularly those beyond the paid workforce, to take responsibility for several of the key social determinants of health, including their learning and wellbeing. They are also flexible and diverse as a bottom up, 'grassroots' movement to work in very diverse cultural and community contexts, and informally connect otherwise very disconnected men (unemployed, retired, disabled, withdrawn from the paid workforce) to a range of services without problematising and patronising them.

This includes some men with ambivalence and significant negativity towards formal learning. On the one hand, sheds are conservative in that they reinforce and celebrate some traditional ways of being a man and doing things together, 'shoulder to shoulder'. On the other hand, they are radical in that they are based on models of community involvement that are democratic and inclusive, which eschew negative and hegemonic masculinities, are respectful of women, promote salutogenic (health promoting) behaviour and encourage learner autonomy. This final condition is consistent with meta-analyses into research across all forms of learning which states:

> *that emphasis should be placed on practices, in both individual and collaborative contexts, that seem to have the potential to promote pupils' autonomy in learning. This would seem to be the most secure foundation for lifelong learning.* (Black *et al.*, 2006, p. 130)

References

ABS: Australian Bureau of Statistics (2010) *Australia Social Trends, September 2010: Older People and the Labour Market*, Cat. No. 4102.0. Canberra: ABS.

Bandura, A. (1989) 'Human agency in social cognitive theory', *American Psychologist*, September 1989, pp. 1174–84.

Black, P., McCormick, R., James, M. and Pedder, D. (2006) 'Learning how to learn and assessment for learning: A theoretical inquiry', *Research Papers in Education*, 21 (2), pp. 119–32.

Blundell, R., Dearden, C., Meghir, C. and Sianesi, B. (1999) 'Human capital investment: The returns from education and training to the individual, the firm and the economy', *Fiscal Studies*, 20, pp. 1–23.

Brune, K. (2011) 'Culture change in long-term care services: Eden-greenhouse-aging in the community', *Educational Gerontology*, 37 (6), pp. 506–25.

Carragher, L. (2013) *Men's Sheds in Ireland: Learning through Community Contexts*. Dundalk: Dundalk Institute of Technology.

Cully, M. (2004) 'Older workers', in K. Bowman (Ed.), *Equity in Vocational Education and Training: Research Readings*. Adelaide: NCVER, pp. 206–24.

Earle, L. (1996) *Successful Ageing in Australian Society: A Community Development Challenge*. Adelaide: Recreation for Older Adults Inc.

Eden Alternative (2009) 'The Eden alternative: Improving the lives of elders and their care partners'. Retrieved 21 March 2013 from www.edenalt.org

Englebrecht, C. and Skladzien, E. (2010) *Later Life Learning: Unlocking the Potential for Productive Ageing*. Canberra: National Seniors Australia Productive Ageing Centre.

EU (2012) *European Year for Active Ageing and Solidarity between Generations 2012: Everyone has a role to play*. Brussels: AGE Platform Europe.

Faiola, A. (2005) 'A painful homecoming', *The Age*, Review, 29 October, p. 4 (originally in the *Washington Post*).

Golding, B. (2011) 'Older men's wellbeing through community participation in Australia', *International Journal of Men's Health*, 10 (1), pp. 26–44.

Golding, B. (2012) 'Men's sheds, community learning and public policy', in M. Bowl, R. Tobias, J. Leahy, G. Ferguson and J. Gage (Eds.), *Gender, Masculinities and Lifelong Learning*. Abingdon: Routledge, pp. 122–33.

Golding, B., Brown, M., Foley, A., Harvey, J. and Gleeson, L. (2007) *Men's Sheds in Australia: Learning through Community Contexts*. Adelaide: NCVER.

Hayes, R. and Williamson, M. (2007) *Men's Sheds: Exploring the Evidence Base for Best Practice*. Bundoora: La Trobe University.

Kinsella-Taylor, L. (2001) *Retirement in an Era of Ageing: The Cost and Impact of the Early Displacement of People from Work*. Report for Australian Employers Convention.

Lefebvre, P. and Merrigan, P. (2003) 'Assessing family policy in Canada: A new deal for families and children', *Choices*, 9.

Macdonald, J., Brown, A. and Gethin, A. (2009) *Older Men and Home and Community Care Services: Barriers to Access and Effective Models of Care*. Sydney: Men's Health Information and Resource Centre, University of Western Sydney.

MacKean, R. (2009) 'Ageing well: An inquiry into older people's experiences of community-based learning', Unpublished Masters Thesis. Hobart: University of Tasmania.

McNair, S. (2009) *Demography and Adult Learning: A Discussion Paper for the NIACE Commission of Inquiry*. Leicester: NIACE.

Misan, G., Haren, M. and Ledo, V. (2008) *Men's Sheds: A Strategy to Improve Men's Health*, Parramatta: Mensheds Australia.

Morrison, R. (2004) 'The wellbeing of older men', Submission No. 189 to House of Representatives Standing Committee on Ageing, 31 March 2004.

Myers, K. and Miles, J. (2005) *Self-assessed Returns to Adult Education: Life-long Learning and the Educationally Disadvantaged*, Research Network W35.

Neilsen (2003) *AC Neilsen Research, National Evaluation of Adult Learners' Week 2001 and 2002*. Adelaide: NCVER.

Neogaf (2013) 'Indoctrinated by an old men's coffee club'. Retrieved 21 February 2013 from www.neogaf.com/forum/showthread.php?t=381343

Noone, J. (2012) *Ageing Baby Boomers in Australia: Understanding the Effects of the Global Financial Crisis*. Canberra: National Seniors Productive Ageing Centre.

NSW *Hansard* (2004) *NSW Legislative Assembly Hansard*, 5.15pm, 17 March 2004, Speech by Mr Anthony Roberts.

Phillipson, C. (2011) 'Challenging social exclusion in old age: National policies and global pressures', Presentation 11 February 2011, Keele University, Keele. Retrieved 21 February 2013 from www.crsi.mq.edu.au/public/download. jsp?id=10628

ShedOnLine (2013) Retrieved 21 February 2013 from www.theshedonline.

org.au/discussions/

Soulsby, J. (2000) *4th Age Learning Report*. Leicester: NIACE.

Tse, T. (2005) 'Adult day groups: Addressing older people's need for activity and companionship', *Australasian Journal of Ageing*, 24 (3), pp. 134–40.

UN: United Nations Secretariat (2008) *World Population Prospects: 2008 Revision*. New York City: UN.

VECCI: Victorian Employers' Chamber of Commerce and Industry (2003) *Older Workers: Myths and Realities*. Melbourne: VECCI.

Wilson, N. and Cordier, R. (2013) 'A narrative review of men's sheds literature: Reducing social isolation and promoting men's health and wellbeing', *Health and Social Care in the Community*, pp. 1–40.

Part Two

CHAPTER NINE

Men's learning in the UK

Rob Mark and Jim Soulsby

Summary

In this chapter we begin by examining the impact that an ageing society is having on learning and trace the development of men's learning in the UK with some illustrative examples from the past. We then look at findings from recent research in the UK on participation in learning and associated policy developments, which show that we have known for a long time about the issues that militate against men's learning in the UK, but have done little to alleviate them. Finally we look at some examples of projects that engage men in learning in the UK and draw some conclusions on key issues around men and learning in the UK.

Introduction

McGivney's (1999) first major research work on men in the UK accurately concluded that, while men's participation in education is often quantitatively different, what is more striking is men's quite different learning priorities and interests and their participation in fewer education settings. McGivney in some senses anticipated some of the informal, community-based pedagogies that have developed in the past decade and that are discussed in this chapter. She observed that:

Men who are not attracted to learning programmes and that seem

131

> *to replicate the worst aspects of their schooling can be drawn into*
> *those that are based directly on their existing interests and skills.*
> (McGivney, 2004, p. 125)

McGivney's (2004) conclusion, that it is the combination of most men's narrow focus on employment related learning, in combination with an increasingly instrumentally focused UK education policy, that has led us to this difficult place, is perhaps even more relevant 15 years on. In the context of the continuing, difficult, downstream effects of the global financial crisis, McGivney's plea to seriously focus on male groups who are not participating in education or training, outside or on the margins of the labour market, redundant or prematurely retired (pp. 131–2) remain highly relevant for the UK in 2014.

What has changed since McGivney's inspiring catalogue of research in the UK in 2004, aside from the now very high proportion of men of working age not in the paid workforce, is the recognition of the rapidly growing proportion of older men in their third and fourth ages as a consequence of increased longevity and rapid population ageing. These issues are elaborated in the section that follows.

An ageing society

In the UK, average life expectancy is expected to increase from 78.3 years in 2010 to 85.2 years in 2060. In 2010, 4.7 per cent of the total population was aged 80 or over. This is forecast to virtually double to 9.3 per cent by 2060 (European Commission, 2012). While the number of older people is increasing in society, many are asking whether more focused planning is required to meet the ever-increasing needs of older people and the implications for provision of services, including education services. In an ageing society such as the UK, there is a growing interest in factors that can contribute to the wellbeing of older adults. Most research on the wider benefits of learning has tended to focus on young people or those in mid-life, with very little evidence on the impact of learning on the wellbeing of older adults.

A recent report entitled *Learning and Wellbeing Trajectories Among Older*

Adults in England has found evidence to support the view that learning can contribute to an individual's overall wellbeing (Jenkins and Mostafa, 2012). The research considered adults who were aged 50 to 69 years living in private households in England. Their research distinguished between formal and informal learning, and found that informal learning was associated with boosts to wellbeing. There was also some evidence that obtaining qualifications was linked to higher wellbeing, but no evidence was found that formal education/training courses were associated with higher wellbeing. Informal learning consisted of participation in education, music and arts groups and evening classes as well as participation in sports clubs, gyms and exercise classes. The level of prior qualifications was found to have a significant impact on both formal and informal learning participation. Those with more education were more likely to participate. The research found that many variables have small effects on measured wellbeing, suggesting that learning participation may have a useful role to play as a contributor to the wellbeing of older adults. Men were found to be less likely to engage in both formal and informal learning activities than females.

This research is one of a small number of studies providing quantitative evidence that participation in learning can have beneficial effects. The study used data from the English Longitudinal Study of Ageing (ELSA), a large-scale, ongoing survey of older adults that includes a broad range of information about their mental and physical health, wellbeing, quality of life and economic and social circumstances.

Men in an ageing society

McGivney's pioneering studies at the National Institute of Adult Continuing Education (NIACE) during the 1990s into the relative absence of men from adult education, commencing with *Excluded Men: Men Who are Missing from Education and Training* (McGivney, 1999), highlights the evidence from the field that 'manual workers, men with poor literacy and no or few qualifications, ex-offenders and African Caribbean men' (p. 12), as well as disaffected young men and men aged over 40, are largely under-represented in most areas of education and training, and that information on what has been successful in attracting male learners is scarce.

Lifelong Learning in Later Life (Findsen and Formosa, 2011), as well as referring to McGivney's work, draws readers' attention to research around gender and health. It considers that some men's behaviours mitigate against men's propensity not to take on board health promotion messages because of self-perceptions about their masculinity (Courtenay, 2000). In recent years, research evidence has been brought forward which looks at the wider benefits of learning – health and wellbeing, social capital, mental capital and combating ageism and negative stereotyping (Findsen and Formosa, 2011, pp. 162–3).

McGivney (1999, 2004) refers to 'masculine identity' and 'a culture that encourages men to cling to traditional roles and patterns of behaviour in which learning does not figure as hugely important' (pp. 88–89) as being barriers to participation in learning. Work by Ford and Soulsby in the East Midlands of England saw this sort of behaviour defined as 'third age laddishness' which had the potential to affect younger male members of the family (Soulsby and Ford, 2000; Ford and Soulsby, 2001). Other research suggests that men who experience higher levels of frustration are less likely to persist with learning if the outcomes are not immediately evident (King and O'Driscoll, 2002).

The 2012 Grundtvig Learning Partnership, Older Men as Active Learners (OMAL, 2012), acknowledged that older people (age 60 plus), especially those who are educated to a low level and socially deprived, are very often vulnerable, marginalised and also socially excluded, passive and lonely. The project focused on organisations and programmes at local/regional/national levels that are offering social and educational activities for older men.

The UK government's *National Adult Learner Survey* (NALS), completed in 2010 (NALS, 2010), reinforces the assumption that social class is a barrier to learning. Using the current Index of Multiple Deprivation (IMD) and a composite measure of deprivation encompassing six domains – income; employment; health and disability; education, skills and training; housing; and geographical access to services (with the fifth quintile representing the most deprived and first quintile the least deprived) – the survey suggested that only 59 per cent of fifth quintile respondents in England (age 16–69) reported any learning, compared with 76 per cent of the first quintile (least deprived group). The survey is also consistent with NIACE's findings on the impact of age on learning (at age 50–59, 69 per cent reported undertaking any learning; at age 60–69, 48 per cent; and beyond age 70, only 24 per cent: McNair, 2012). The NALS research also indicates a closing of the gap between the genders in reporting any learning, but suggests that gender differences persist for some types of learning. Men are somewhat more likely than women to take part in informal learning (47 per cent of men compared to 40 per cent of women) and vocational learning (66 per cent of men compared with 62 per cent of women).

These findings appear to contradict the findings of Jenkins and Mostafa (2012, p. 5) who suggest that males were less likely to engage in both formal and informal learning activities than females. This may be due to current confusion over definitions of learning. While Jenkins and Mostafa define formal learning as involving attendance at a formal education/training course or working towards a qualification, informal learning is defined as membership of a learning group such as a music or arts groups or evening class, or membership of a sports club, gym or exercise class (Jenkins and Mostafa, 2012, p. 10). The National Adult Learning Survey (NALS, 2010) breaks down learning into non-formal and informal dimensions. Formal learning is defined as learning that is intended to lead to a nationally recognised qualification, even if the qualification is not achieved. Non-formal learning is defined as a course or taught class that does not lead to a nationally recognised qualification. Informal learning is regarded as learning that involves self-study to improve knowledge of a subject, not involving taught classes or qualifications. This might include reading books, manuals, journals or attending seminars.

However, in 2009, the UK government launched its own discussion paper, attempting to redefine formal and informal learning, *Welcome to the Learning Revolution* (DIUS, 2009). This 'revolution' emphasised the importance of informal learning (previously defined as non-formal learning), thus changing definitions of learning and ultimately affecting its measurement. In this discussion paper, the UK Government recognised:

> *the profound importance of informal adult learning to people's lives and our nation's well-being. Informal learning can help people gain*

> *personal satisfaction, development and fulfilment. For the low skilled and with poor experiences of formal education, informal learning can be an important stepping stone to further learning, qualifications and more rewarding work. It can help keep people mentally and physically active and independent into old age. It can also bring people and communities together. This strategy reaffirms cross-government commitment to informal learning and sets out how the Government will act as an enabler, capacity builder and connector to maximise the potential benefits.* (DIUS, 2009, p. 1)

The concept of non-formal learning has since disappeared off the agenda, precipitated by the 'learning revolution', which suggests that much learning and adult education takes place outside the traditional adult learning environments and is well established among local communities. The government wants to encourage this form of learning and has provided short-term funding for initiatives, but at the same time is changing funding for adult education providers which shifts provision (particularly the participation of older adults) away from state-funded, 'formal' education systems.

As recently as May 2013 the UK Government launched its new guidance on funding for adult and community learning in England, providing yet another definition of community learning:

> *Community learning is just one of many names that have been used to describe non-formal adult education during its long history. Back in the early 19th century adults often took part in learning organised through a wide range of family, community, social and religious organisations. Those trades unions, cooperative societies, independent lending libraries and movements for the vote all offered opportunities for people to improve their chances in life. BIS-funded community learning is faithful to its roots. One of its most important roles is still to inspire people, particularly those who have had the fewest chances in life, to take up learning and progress — whether to employment, further learning, better health or more confident parenting.*
> (Spotlight, 2013, p. 1)

In this paper the Government indicated that its annual funding for community learning must focus on 'securing additional funding over and above the public subsidy, e.g. through fee income, sponsorship, grants, funding from other government departments and/or commercial sales' and 'maximising value for money by pooling resources, sharing services, attracting contributions in kind and training/supporting volunteers' (Spotlight, 2013, p. 7).

This strategy is supported, according to government, by the work of the fifteen Community Learning Pilots which preceded it. In these there are attempts to create local planning structures to better reach across communities and to reach those disadvantaged in terms of skills, income and quality of life.

Men's learning organisations

A glance back at developments in adult education over the past century in the UK shows that the involvement of men in education is not a new phenomenon. Historically men have, until relatively recently, populated most adult education provision, perhaps because the kind of provision which developed was largely aimed at providing vocational skills for areas of work which were male dominated. The following are some examples of provision aimed specifically at skills development in work areas dominated by men.

Mechanics' Institutes

The Mechanics' Institutes were educational establishments formed to provide adult education, particularly in technical subjects, to working men. As such, local industrialists often funded them on the grounds that industry would ultimately benefit from having more knowledgeable and skilled employees. The world's first Mechanics' Institute was established in Edinburgh in October 1821 as the School of Arts of Edinburgh (later Heriot Watt University) with the provision of technical education for working people and professionals (Mechanics' Institute, 2013a, 2013b). Its purpose was to address societal needs by incorporating fundamental scientific thinking and research into engineering solutions. The school revolutionised access to education in science and technology for ordinary people. Following its success in Edinburgh, it later spread to Liverpool, Glasgow and London in 1823 and later across the world, including right across Australia.

Working Men's Clubs

The Working Men's Clubs and the Institute Union (CIU) were also examples of provision orientated towards the educational needs of men. Their aims and philosophies were similar to the Mechanics' Institutes, and they also encouraged educational activity. On her club historians' website, Cherrington (2013) looks at the issues behind the reduction in the number of Working Men's Clubs nationwide.

> *Largely set up by working men themselves as a form of mutual self help, they were mostly left to their own devices. Nowadays many clubs are struggling to keep their doors open and there is very little help forthcoming. In fact, it seems that legislation passed over the past few years seems intent on helping to shut those doors firmly and thus hasten the decline of clubs throughout the country. Excessive regulation and a refusal to look at the bigger picture of what clubs do for their local communities are part of the problem for many clubs as fewer members volunteer to take on the ever-more time consuming management tasks.* (Cherrington, 2013)

U3A (University of the Third Age)

Now over 30 years old, in the UK the University of the Third Age (U3A) has accumulated nearly 300,000 members (U3A, 2013). A web search of some of the biggest and longest established U3As in England reveals very satisfying stories of growth but does not provide a recent gender breakdown of membership. Research undertaken by Soulsby (1989, 1998) suggests that historically the distribution has been approximately one-third men, two-thirds women. There is little to suggest that the situation in 2013 has changed significantly. Looking at the websites does not suggest either that this gender 'disparity' is viewed in any way as an issue. Yet, recent email correspondence within the membership of the Association for Education and Ageing has highlighted at least one London U3A where there is concern about the continuing low rate of male membership, and research is underway to investigate the reasons. So, whilst the U3A movement is very successful and continues to grow, it is as yet uncertain how the movement might help to engage older men, not only those who have been identified as being from backgrounds with poor educational levels, relatively low skills levels and employment histories, but also those from other social classes who have benefited from some higher education.

The concepts of community and localness have been the subject of much political debate in the last 30 years, with many attempts through community programmes and National Lottery funding to re-create communities. Despite the political encouragement to succeed, these 'top-down' approaches have always been blighted by short-term funding and prescribed and pre-determined ideas of success and aspiration. The concepts of working class have also been redefined because of these societal changes, with the creation of an underclass viewed by some sections of the media and politicians as too dependent on state support. Owing to very recent changes to the way Big Lottery funding is accessed locally and the recommendations of the Heseltine Review (Heseltine, 2012) on 'localism', new local action groups or committees are not necessarily geared to fulfilling the skills and learning needs of disengaged members of those local communities – particularly older unskilled men.

What history may tell us is that the successes of the past in being able to reach workers to encourage them to 'improve' themselves were down to the very localness of the activity, the high employment levels (albeit much work being low or unskilled) and the peer support on offer for those embarrassed by their poor educational levels. The removal of all those underpinning key components of society has reduced any prospect of meaningful action for and by older working class men.

Men's sheds as learning centres

In recent years there has been a growth in community men's sheds as an alternate way of meeting the non-formal educational needs of older men. Following the successful growth of men's sheds in Australia, Ireland and New Zealand, there is renewed interest in the development of similar activities in various parts of the UK, with sheds already established in

Wales, Scotland and England and national associations established in the UK and Wales during 2013. Men's sheds have grown from the idea that some men like and benefit from spending time tinkering, repairing and making things while socialising with others who have similar interests. Many too are interested in working on projects that will aid the community and be of use to other people.

The Men's Sheds Network has been established in the UK following the first national conference on men's sheds in the UK by a group of people involved in running men's sheds and supporting their development. The network aims to encourage the growth of sheds so that they are available to anyone who wants to use them (Men's Sheds Network, 2013).

One of the first men's sheds in the UK was created in Cheshire, in the north-west of England, led by Age Concern Cheshire (now Age UK Cheshire). Following the launch, the Age UK national office obtained charitable funds to create similar initiatives in other parts of England, and sheds were created in Blidworth (Age UK Nottingham), south London (Age UK Bromley and Greenwich), Camden Town, London and South Lakeland in the north-west. In the Isle of Man the Southern Community Initiative has opened a Manx shed.

There was an expectation in 2011 that Age UK would take a lead in helping the men's sheds concept to develop across the country, but this has not yet happened. Part of the original Age UK philosophy was to create items for sale that would then raise money for charities. This same philosophy has also been behind the support of 'Tools for Self Reliance', which has encouraged sheds in the UK to create useful resources for people living in Africa. The men's sheds movement is providing innovative responses to male isolation and is contributing to enhancing good health using National Lottery funding. There is no one model for development, the emphasis being on the local context. There are new and planned initiatives involving local Age UKs, as well as some being supported by the Peabody Trust (in the London area), and local agreements (Men's Sheds Network, 2013).

In Northern Ireland, men's sheds have developed in several areas of the Province including South Armagh, Armagh City, Antrim and Hollywood. The sheds are drawing on local regeneration funding and are supported by the Irish Men's Sheds Association (Irish Men's Sheds, 2013) as an 'island of Ireland' initiative.

The first men's shed in Scotland opened in 2011 in an old library building in the Westhill district of Aberdeen. Earlier, Aberdeenshire council produced a community plan (2010–2014), which recognised that people are living and staying healthy for longer after retirement, meaning that older men need to socialise and stay active. As a result, a group of men came together to make the men's shed a reality. The shed encourages retired men looking for a new interest in life to come along. The men want to keep active, have company and continue to contribute to their community. While their families have built up a circle of friends and interests, they have not, but would like to do so and to help others at the same time. The project has a range of activities, including upholstery, a stationary engine and water pump project, building a model railway and a tools for self-reliance project which refurbishes tools to ship to workers in Africa, giving them the tools of their trade and enabling them to make a living (Westhills, 2013).

The men's sheds movement in the UK is still relatively small, but is clearly gathering momentum, with around 50 sheds open or to be opened by early 2014. However, there is a danger that models created by external, well-meaning agencies will impose activities and emphasise the 'charitable' aspects of their work which, while laudable, could pre-vent men from becoming autonomous and ultimately able to decide the kind of activities they want to develop. The current negative ideological approach in the UK towards localism does not lend itself to local own-ership. Although there is a very welcome move towards single budgets, with pooling of resources from differing UK government departments, local, regional and national, there is no sign that there will be 'real' local ownership, with perhaps too many strings attached to the available money.

Innovative approaches to engaging men in learning

A number of other projects have been developed in Scotland, aimed at encouraging men to get involved in their own learning. Most notable of these is the GalGael project, a community project based in Govan, a former shipbuilding area of Glasgow. Since 1997, the project has been building and sailing traditional boats in celebration of Scotland's boat building heritage in this area of Glasgow, which was formerly one of the greatest shipbuilding areas in the world (GalGael, 2013). Gal-Gael might best be described as a learning community more like the shed model than a training programme. The community of people come together to meet the needs of those who come, through co-operation and sharing and by recognising the need for belonging, to learn, to work, to contribute creativity and to connect meaningfully with others.

The project offers learning journeys which seek to reconnect people with themselves and with the significance of the places around them through offering positive learning journeys grounded on practical activities such as working on producing wooden products, handcrafting furniture, cooking, processing Scottish timber or helping out at a range of public events. The learning journeys are enriched by wider activities like boatbuilding, rowing, rural skills and community and creative projects. The workplace offered by GalGael is said to challenge and inspire, with conditions that are conducive to learning and transformation. Staff and peers guide new participants in designing their own development plan according to their needs and goals.

The project works in partnership with other local bodies, including staff at the local college, the open museum and community artists, who provide the most opportunities for development of relevant and timely skills, capabilities and confidence. Each individual develops a learning plan which is a journey through the various opportunities which GalGael can offer. The project does not offer formal training programmes, but rather an opportunity to learn in an informal environment through providing tools, a workplace and support to allow the individual to grow by taking a leading role in their own progression and development.

The learning journey provides a chance to pick up on new skills and develop good life habits, creating numerous opportunities for developing strengths through the use of traditional skills as a vehicle and through working with natural materials such as wood, stone and metal. The journey develops practical skills as well as the opportunity for personal transformation on a deeper personal level, which may include improved motivation and resilience. The GalGael community seeks to challenge, inspire and empower each individual, and when individuals leave they are said to have better life chances and a better outlook. For some finding paid work will be the end of the journey, while for others regaining a positive sense of self and community will make the journey worthwhile.

Participants are mostly men of all ages and include the unemployed, some of whom are experiencing mental illness and drug addiction, while some participants have spent time in prison. For most, being part of a group or family of people who nurture and care for each other is an important success factor. A strong band of dedicated volunteers is key to making these programmes happen; these include ex-participants and local people, some retired craftsmen and women who want to keep traditional skills alive. Many of the volunteers are people who have finished work and are keen to pass on the skills that they have learnt through their careers.

Underwood and Soulsby (2011) undertook a mapping exercise to highlight what similar activities existed for older men in the East Midlands of England that might contain some practical and useful learning and stimulating activities. The list included employment sector related organisations for ex-employees, including Corby Steel Pensioners, retired fire fighters and ex-military (Soldiers', Sailors' and Airmen's Family Association: SSAFA). It also included a wide range of recycling and renovation organisations including bicycle repair, garden and house maintenance (by ex-offenders), groundwork renovation, furniture renovation and railway preservation. Other organisations that are particularly inclusive of men are garden allotments, mountain rescue teams, angling clubs and Sealed Knot historical re-enactment groups.

This list could be replicated for every part of the United Kingdom, and it does reveal the range of activities that can be accessed by (older) men. What is missing in the UK is a systematic local strategy to link these opportunities (and others) to men when they are seeking (or in need of) guidance, direction and advice. In Australia, Golding's work (Findsen and Formosa, 2011, pp. 165–6) has revealed the place of men in many local community initiatives. What is not known in the UK is the degree to which that applies. What is known is that there are no systemised local approaches through the relevant rescue agencies, such as fire, ambulance, mountain rescue and lifeboat rescue, to target and recruit men as volunteers. The UK government's new focus on community learning may create such opportunities to better link to existing opportunities for the engagement of men in community life (Spotlight, 2013).

Fathers' learning

Another way in which men are getting involved in education is through informal education of their children. A number of organisations and groups have developed to provide support for fathers who are enhancing skills and attitudes to support their children. One example is the 'Scotland's fathers and their children project', which seeks to create an environment where children who experience severe poverty and disadvantage can attempt to reach their full life potential through support from fathers or those who take on a fathering role (Fathers' Network Scotland, 2013).

The project seeks to better equip fathers to provide for their children, practically, mentally and emotionally, to improve relationships between children and fathers, to enrich children's experiences through a variety of social opportunities and to promote recognition by the wider community and family of the importance of the role of the father and his equal status. The project organises and delivers a programme of family activities which include one-to-one support, personalised advocacy, signposting fathers in different directions and small group work activities for men who wish to develop their parenting skills.

Conclusion

In this chapter we have examined and illustrated how non-formal adult education provision in the UK is beginning to acknowledge and respond to the needs of men, particularly older men. However, government policy concerning adult learning does not lend itself to activities that better include disengaged older men. There is little evidence of a sense of understanding, awareness or recognition of the needs of disengaged older men and there would not seem to be any political will to take up the issue. While there are many initiatives in the UK around young people who are not engaged in education or training, to date there is no such focus on older men.

In her ground-breaking research, McGivney (1999, 2004) recognised that the learning needs of older men were not well served by adult education. Unfortunately, a decade on, very little has changed and there is little evidence to suggest that governments and communities have taken advantage of that knowledge. The volatile employment situation in 2013 and government programmes to enhance employability suggest that the situation for disengaged older men needs to improve. Furthermore, developments in men's learning in the UK are, to date, not based on any policy imperative from government or from any sound theoretical or evidential base. Like so many current and recent initiatives around later life learning and engagement, practice is well ahead of the necessary research and policy. The need to develop policy and practice based on internationally informed research into men's learning remains an ongoing challenge for the UK government.

References

Cherrington, R. (2013) Retrieved 21 May 2013 from www.clubhistorians.co.uk/html/what_is_the_ciu.html

Courtenay, W. (2000) 'Constructions of masculinity and their influence on men's well-being: A theory of gender and health', *Social Science and Medicine*, 50 (10), pp. 1385–401.

DIUS: Department for Innovation, Universities and Skills (March 2009) *Informal Adult Learning White Paper: The Learning Revolution*. Retrieved 28 May 2013 from http://webarchive.nationalarchives.gov.uk/+/http://www.dius.gov.uk/skills/engaging_learners/informal_adult_learning/white_paper.

European Commission (2012) *The 2012 Ageing Report. Economic and Budgetary Projections for the 27 EU Member States (2010–2060)*, Brussels: European Commission. Retrieved 21 May 2013 from http://ec.europa.eu/economy_finance/publications/european_economy/2012/2012-ageing-report_en.htm

Ford, G. and Soulsby, J. (2001) *Mature Workforce Development East Midlands 2000*,

Research and Report, NIACE for East Midlands Development Agency (EMDA). Leicester: NIACE.

Findsen, B. and Formosa, M. (2011) *Lifelong Learning in Later Life: A Handbook on Older Adult Learning*. International Issues in Adult Education, 7. Rotterdam: Sense.

GalGael (2013) Retrieved 28 May 2013 from www.galgael.org/

Heseltine (2012) Retrieved 29 May 2013 from www.independentaction. net/2012/12/14/what-the-lottery-has-got-in-mind-for-us-all http://news. bis.gov.uk/Press-Releases/Heseltine-Review-A-new-partnership-for-growth-68278.aspx

Irish Men's Sheds (2013) Retrieved 28 May 2013 from www.menssheds.ie/

Jenkins, A. and Mostafa, T. (2012) *Learning and Well-being Trajectories Among Older Adults in England*, Research Paper 92. Leicester: NIACE. Retrieved 21 May 2013 from www.bis.gov.uk/assets/biscore/further-education-skills/docs/ l/12-1242-learning-and-wellbeing-trajectories-among-older-adults.pdf

King, P. and O'Driscoll, S. with Holden, S. (2002) *A Study of the Learning Styles of Women and Men and their Implications for Further Education and Training*. Dublin: AONTAS.

McGivney, V. (1999) *Excluded Men: Men who are Missing from Education and Training*. Leicester: NIACE.

McGivney, V. (2004) *Men Earn, Women Learn*. Leicester: NIACE.

McNair, S. (2009) *Older People's Learning: An Action Plan*, NIACE Policy Paper. Leicester: NIACE.

McNair, S. (2012) *Older Peoples' Learning in 2012: A Survey*. Leicester: NIACE.

Mechanics' Institute (2013a) Retrieved 29 May 2013 from http://en.wikipedia. org/wiki/Mechanic%27s_Institutes

Mechanics' Institute (2013b) Retrieved 29 May 2013 from www. mechanicsinstitute.co.uk/index.php?option=com_content&view=article&i d=48&Itemid=27

Men's Sheds Network (2013) Retrieved 27 June 2013 from http://menssheds. org.uk/

NALS: National Adult Learner Survey (2010) *National Adult Learner Survey*, BIS Research Paper No. 63, October. NIACE: London.

OMAL (2012) Retrieved 28 May 2013 from http://omal.si/

Soulsby, J. (1989) 'Developing a model for the creation and support of self-help education groups for the retired, non-waged and older adult'. Unpublished dissertation towards a Master of Education. Manchester: University of Manchester.

Soulsby, J. (1998) 'Mapping the world of Older Learners', *Older and Bolder Newsletter*, (6). November 1998. Leicester: NIACE.

Soulsby, J. and Ford, G. (2000) *Northamptonshire Third Age Employment and Learning Project*. Northampton Chamber.

Spotlight (2013) *Spotlight on Community Learning May 2013*. Retrieved 28 May 2013 from www.gov.uk/government/uploads/system/uploads/attachment_data/file/193955/13-p167a-spotlight-on-community-learning.pdf

Underwood, L. and Soulsby, J. (2011) Background paper for the joint Age UK, NIACE, Mental Health Foundation and University of Leicester Conference, September 2011, Discovering Men's Sheds.

U3A (2013) Retrieved 29 May 2013 from www.u3a.org.uk/

Westhills (2013) Retrieved 28 May 2013 from www.westhillmensshed.co.uk/

CHAPTER TEN

Men's learning in Ireland

Lucia Carragher, John Evoy and Rob Mark

Introduction

While the percentage of Ireland's population participating in education for greater lengths of time has increased significantly over the last 20 years (Higgins *et al.*, 2008), men in Ireland continue to be more disadvantaged educationally than other groups in the population. The barriers to male participation in education and training in Ireland were identified by Owens (2000). Owens identified marginalised men – men experiencing long-term unemployment, social exclusion, poverty and isolation because of race, disability, poor health, sexuality, age or social class – as particularly hard to reach and engage in adult education. There is growing recognition that men in these circumstances can be overlooked because men in general are recognised as a dominant group (Connell, 1995; Evoy and Hanlon, 2010).

From the mid 1970s, gender equality policy in Ireland understandably focused on women as an excluded and marginalised group. Notwithstanding the importance of gender equality and inclusion policies continuing to address the inequalities experienced by women (CSO, 2008), gender conscious policy is now beginning to recognise the differences and specific needs of diverse marginalised men (Ferguson and Hogan, 2004; Evoy, 2007; McAleese, 2007). There is also a growing international awareness, as this book explains, that many men benefit in important ways from specific community work and educational approaches (Golding *et al.*, 2007).

In this chapter, we begin by looking at the context of adult learning in both the Republic of Ireland and Northern Ireland. Educational approaches in recent years have become increasingly focused around a neo-liberal discourse that emphasises skills for employment. Public policies have also been driven by a need to widen access to education for people from excluded groups and, in this respect, the issue of gender equality has come to the forefront, with the focus largely on the need to provide access and up-skill women to enter the workforce. Until recently, there has been very little emphasis on the educational needs of some men as an excluded sub-group. This has changed somewhat with the growth in the evidence base around the absence of men from both mainstream and community education in Ireland and as the movement to establish men's sheds as one way of meeting the social and educational needs of older men not in the workforce has taken hold. We trace the recent and rapid growth of men's sheds in Ireland and show how informal learning is providing new opportunities for engaging men beyond the workplace on both sides of the Irish border. In particular, we draw attention to the contribution that men's informal learning is making towards rebuilding shattered communities, and in helping to heal the psycho-social wounds left by decades of civil unrest in Northern Ireland.

Contextual background

Ireland is made up of two countries – the Republic of Ireland and Northern Ireland (which is part of the UK). From 1968 to 1998, a long campaign was waged by opposing communities in Northern Ireland over the country's constitutional status. The mainly Protestant Unionist community argued that Northern Ireland should remain part of the UK, while the mainly Catholic Nationalist community argued it should leave the UK and become part of the Republic of Ireland. Throughout the 1970s, 1980s and into the mid 1990s opposing paramilitary groups waged violent campaigns to advance their causes. The death toll from this period was borne largely by men, particularly young men in socially disadvantaged areas. The *Cost of the Troubles Study* found that over the course of the 'troubles', 40,000 people were injured in the civil unrest and at least 3,585 people were killed (Fay *et al.*, 1999). Of those killed, 91 per cent were male; 37 per cent were under the age of 24, 53 per cent were under the age of 29 and 74 per cent were under the age of 39 (*ibid*).

In 1998, after over three decades of violence, a peace agreement was finally reached over the future of Northern Ireland. Under the terms of the Good Friday Agreement, devolved powers in key policy areas, including education, were returned to the Northern Ireland government and special arrangements were put in place to facilitate North–South co-operation in specific areas, education being one of these. Today, both governments enjoy relatively good relations and there have been many hundreds of cross-border projects funded by the International Fund for Ireland and EU PEACE and INTERREG programmes. However, as Pollak (2012) points out, North–South co-operation arising from the Belfast Agreement has been largely government-led and funded by generous EU grants. He adds that, now that such funding is running out and given the Irish government's huge economic challenges, North–South co-operation in non-governmental sectors, and particularly in the community and voluntary sectors, has largely run out of steam.

In addition, Northern Ireland, as recent events have shown, remains a deeply divided society and sectarianism continues to be a major problem, especially near the 'peace walls' that separate unionist and nationalist communities in Belfast. These areas experience considerable social problems, including high unemployment and limited economic opportunities, particularly for men.

Policy context

Adult education and social policies across Ireland share many similarities as well as some important differences. In particular, Northern Ireland is deeply divided along religious lines, underpinned and reinforced by the duplication of services such as schools and housing. A significant number of people in Northern Ireland have grown up in segregated areas, where education in schools is segregated on religious grounds and on ability and class, as decided by the 11 plus transfer test (abolished in 2008).* For many, the first opportunities for sustained contact with 'the other side' only come about when at third level education or when they have their first employment experiences (McGrellis, 2004).

In 2005, the government's Shared Future Policy warned that 'Separate but equal is not an option. Parallel living and the provision of parallel services are unsustainable both morally and economically' (Community Relations Unit, 2005, p. 20). However, in practice, almost half of all

---

* The transfer test was used to stream children to particular types of post-primary schools based on their ability. It was officially discontinued in Northern Ireland in 2008, but has re-emerged as a different selective process.

school children continue to be taught in schools where 95 per cent of pupils are of the same religion (Hansson *et al.*, 2013). In addition, government's capacity to get to grips with segregation and inequality has been challenged by the wider issues linked to the impact of the global recession and the economic downturn.

Within both jurisdictions, attention is increasingly focused on promoting the skills agenda as a way of addressing high levels of unemployment and social disadvantage. In 2002, Northern Ireland's Department for Employment and Learning (DEL) introduced its policy for lifelong learning, *Further Education Means Business* (DEL, 2002), to align adult learning to the skills needs of the local economy (Nolan, 2007). This was subsequently reinforced in *Success through Skills* (DEL, 2009) and strengthened again in the updated and revised ten-year strategy, *Success through Skills: Transforming Futures* (DEL, 2012). For government, an important aim is to encourage employers to become more involved in determining what training state funding supports. Organisational structures have been tightened with the withdrawal of government funding from the two main providers of community education, the Workers' Educational Association and the Ulster People's College. In addition, the six large further education colleges have been given a clear mission to focus their efforts on the needs of the local economy, ensuring that state-sponsored lifelong learning will, for the foreseeable future, have a narrowly utilitarian function (Nolan, 2007).

Similarly, within the Republic of Ireland, Grummell (2007) argues that educational policymaking is increasingly shaped by neo-liberal discourses that adapt adult education principles, such as lifelong learning and emancipation, for their own economic and political logic. She notes that while Ireland's *Learning for Life: White Paper on Adult Education* (DES, 2000) moved the focus of attention from the primacy of economic factors and the labour market to encompass a broader range of political, community and social aims, it limited its understanding of community development to marginalised people who share common problems and aim to become actively involved in solving their problems, negating any sense of state or societal responsibility for social exclusion and disadvantage (Grummell, 2007, p. 5).

The focus on the skills agenda has been given added urgency by the global economic crisis, with thousands of jobs being lost, many of them in the building sector. In the south, unemployment increased from four per cent in 2006 to 14.6 per cent in December 2012, the fourth highest unemployment rate in Europe (CSO, 2012). In the north, the economy has been less affected, though at 8.5 per cent in 2012 (Department of Finance and Personnel, 2013a), unemployment is the highest it has been since 1998. The economic downturn has affected different occupations and groups in very different ways, with men in the construction sector and those with low skills and limited education disproportionally affected. The unemployment rate for men in Ireland as a whole stood at 18.8 per cent in 2011, while for women it was considerably less at 10.4 per cent (CSO, 2012). Within Northern Ireland, the male unemployment rate (10.6 per cent) has risen by 5.1 percentage points during the last ten years, whilst the female rate (5.4 per cent) increased by 0.4 percentage points during the same period, and over three-fifths of unemployed men (64.3 per cent) are long-term unemployed (Department of Finance and Personnel, 2013b). For older men and men with low skills, the loss of employment can be devastating, in some cases forcing men into early retirement or resulting in long-term unemployment, as skills become devalued by employers and options for retraining are limited either by a lack of suitable opportunities or negative attitudes toward formal learning situations, both of which are linked to culturally constructed gender identity.

Men's learning in Ireland

O'Connor's (2007) evaluation of gender and education in Ireland confirms that boys are significantly more likely than girls to leave school early and to demonstrate low levels of attainment in education. He notes that each year more boys are born in Ireland than girls, with the result that there are approximately 1,800 more 17-year-old boys than 17-year-old girls in Ireland, yet girls outnumber boys by between 2,400 and 3,300 among candidates for the Leaving Certificate each year. Similarly, women outnumber men within the full range of adult and community education programmes funded by the Department of Education and Science. O'Connor identifies classic gender stereotypes in the choice of education programme made by both men and women, with men's participation largely confined to vocationally-oriented training, especially construction-related training, and women's dispersed across areas from business and office skills to caring, arts and crafts (*ibid*).

While no single theory can satisfactorily explain men's participation and non-participation in learning (McGivney, 1990), educational achievement is strongly influenced by socio-economic status, and attitudes to learning start to develop from an early stage. Horgan's (2007) research with children in Northern Ireland identifies boys as young as nine or ten becoming disenchanted with school and starting to disengage. She draws attention to the interaction of educational disadvantage faced by children growing up in poverty, the difficulties faced by teachers in disadvantaged schools and differences in the way boys and girls are socialised, leading to boys being particularly failed by the school education system. Horgan found that children attending disadvantaged schools complained of being 'shouted at' by teachers and, for boys in particular, she notes, this led to a loathing of school, with older boys the only children to talk in a positive manner about truanting.

Research by the National Adult Literacy Agency (NALA), conducted by Lalor *et al.* (2009), identifies the lasting effect negative school experiences can have on educational decisions in adulthood. The authors provide evidence from men who experienced difficulties with illiteracy that stem back to childhood and school experiences. The men reported difficulties at work due to an ever-increasing emphasis on functional literacies, including computer literacy, in the workplace. The effects of low levels of literacy, as found in the NALA study, are discussed in Chapter Four.

Men's sheds in Ireland: Learning through immersion in the community

Based on the Australian model, the Irish men's sheds movement has flourished since it took root in 2009. The first men's shed in Ireland was set up in August 2009 in Tipperary Town. By early 2014 there were approximately 200 men's sheds in operation and registered with the Irish Men's Sheds Association. The Irish Men's Sheds Association was set up in 2011 to support the development and sustainability of men's sheds across both jurisdictions of Ireland. Prior to the emergence of the men's sheds movement, and in the context of European and Irish national policies, the strategies that addressed men's learning in the community were underpinned by three main policy documents: *Learning for Life: White Paper on Adult Education* (DES, 2000); *Strategic Framework for European Cooperation in Education and Training: European Commission Document* (CEU, 2009) and *National Men's Health Policy* (DoHC, 2008).

A national study linked to men's sheds in Ireland found that few men participating in sheds (19 per cent) had attended a formal learning pro-gramme in the past year and just one-third reported having had a posi-tive educational experience in school (Carragher, 2013). Many of the men placed little value on what was taught in school. As one man stated, 'I think school teaches you basics. We can all say that we left school early ... but when we were there we got the basics, as I say, the reading, writing and arithmetic'. Another added, 'So far as school is concerned, it never taught me very much at all'. One man considered the source of his learning in life and commented, 'I left school at 14 and what I know now I learnt it along the road'. Reflecting on the value of life's lessons learned through the 'school of hard knocks', another man commented, 'You have so many knocks in life as you came along that you were taught by your knocks, you were taught by experience. If you walked along and you fell down that road, you won't do it again'.

In terms of the learning opportunities available to participants in men's sheds to develop skills, respondents particularly identified hobby and leisure skills (75 per cent), technical trades and craft skills (68 per cent), computer and internet learning (67 per cent), health and safety skills (49 per cent), team and leadership skills (37 per cent) and horticul-tural skills (37 per cent). Over a quarter (28 per cent) of sheds offered participants opportunities to advance their communication and literacy skills.

To identify preferred ways of learning, participants were asked: 'If more learning opportunities were available in the men's sheds, would you be interested in taking part?' Just over three-quarters of respond-ents (76 per cent) were keen to access more learning and, of those who answered affirmatively, the majority expressed a preference for hands-on learning (71 per cent). However, more than half (57 per cent) of men surveyed also expressed a preference for learning either through special interest courses or where they could meet other people (56 per cent). Half of respondents (50 per cent) said that they would prefer to learn through observation on field days or demonstrations. Just under half (46 per cent) expressed a preference to learn in a small group, 42 per cent said they would be interested in enrolling in a course in order to get a qualification, just over one-third (34 per cent) said that they would like to learn via the internet, one quarter (25 per cent) would prefer individual tuition, over one quarter (29 per cent) 'in a class', the same proportion (29 per cent) by 'taking on responsibility' and 20 per cent as 'preparation for further study' (*ibid*).

Those men who expressed a preference for more learning opportunities were also asked: 'How and where would you prefer these learning opportunities be provided?' Nearly half (47 per cent) of the respondents indicated that their preference would be for a member of the men's shed with the appropriate skills to teach them. The next most popular choice was to bring in a local tutor/trainer from outside of the shed (40 per cent), and a small proportion opted for a tutor/trainer from outside their town or county (nine per cent), via the internet (one per cent) or 'a organisation elsewhere in a larger centre' (one per cent). In terms of preferences for where learning opportunities should be provided, the most popular choice was to keep it in the shed (88 per cent), with very small numbers indicating a preference to go to another local community organisation (three per cent), a local community learning centre or neighbourhood house (three per cent), an adult or vocational education provider (three per cent), some other venue outside the local area (two per cent) or at home (one per cent). All things considered, the results suggest that community-based men's sheds are recognised by men as an effective and strongly preferred site for informal learning and skills development.

Case studies of different sheds

That the concept of men's sheds has been inserted into the policy discourse in the differing disciplines is a reflection of how, in practice, each men's shed is different from the next. The men who participate and the outcomes are equally diverse. In order to develop an understanding of this diversity we will explore the realities of four men's sheds from across Ireland by offering short, qualitative case studies of each. The sheds described here vary considerably in a number of ways, such as the age demographic of the participating men, the location, urban or rural, Northern Ireland or the Republic and funded or not funded.

The self-reliant, non-funded, rural men's shed in the Republic of Ireland

The idea for a men's shed for Bannow, a small rural community in County Wexford, was first discussed in June 2011 when a local community development worker set up a public open information meeting in the village hall. Even though the meeting was poorly attended, some of the attendees liked the concept and commenced setting up their shed.

They visited a number of neighbouring sheds and went about finding premises. They found an unused filling station belonging to one of the men who was to become a key participant in their shed, who offered it rent free. They have since gone on to successfully develop their shed in line with the low-cost, sustainable model that the Irish Men's Sheds Association advocates in most cases. Having a rent-free building is key to sustainability of low-cost, self-reliant sheds.

The men's shed at Bannow is typical from the point of view that the men who participate are not involved in other types of adult learning. Their shed has developed some characteristics which are worthy of note and which contribute to its unique character. Their shed opens in the evenings, as opposed to earlier in the day when most other sheds open. Many men who attend sheds which open during the day say it 'gives them a reason to get up in the morning' and goes some way to replace their experience of work. The shed at Bannow plays a different role in the men's lives, perhaps for some as a positive alternative to drinking alcohol in a pub. They have developed a great sense of community in their shed, as some comments from their members describe: 'Whenever you come down, the lads always welcome you; it's a very friendly place' (Joe) and 'Everything we do is to help someone else' (Peter). The men of the shed at Bannow are very proud of their inclusive ethos; men of all backgrounds and abilities are welcomed. Their shed plays an important role in the community because of the lack of alternative activities for men in the surrounding areas.

A non-funded men's Shed in Dublin supported by a local social inclusion agency

The men's shed at Blanchardstown, in the northern part of Dublin, Ireland's capital, started in a similar way to many of the sheds in Ireland since 2011, by accessing the basic start up support of the Irish Men's Sheds Association. They held an information morning in April 2012 and, following a number of challenges, they were given access to an unused building developer's site. Since then, the men have transformed the site into a very active men's shed. It was set up with the support of the Blanchardstown Area Partnership (BAP), an agency that aims to address poverty and social exclusion and to support the unemployed back into the workforce.

There are some important characteristics of the shed at Blanchardstown that make it stand out from other sheds in Ireland. Most notably, the men in this shed are a younger age group – men in their 20s, 30s and 40s who have suffered as a result of the recession, many of whom are under severe financial stress. Jean, who works with BAP, gives an insight into why the men's shed is important in their area:

> Youth unemployment is so high compared to other parts of Ireland, and what's frightening is [that] the highest rate of suicide is in young men. The guys can lose hope if there is no jobs or if they don't have money at the end of the week. It is not making them feel very good about themselves.

The following wisdom comes from one of the men who participate in the shed:

> We have this kind a thing in life that big boys don't cry and all that stuff, ya know, we hold in our problems and we hold in our troubles, and you try and deal with them yourself. I find the men's shed is medicine for depression. It's my medicine for depression basically, this is what gets me out of the house.

A border shed

The Dundalk men's shed is situated close to the border with Northern Ireland. It opened in 2011 with a deliberate cross-border remit to support the peace and reconciliation in the border region, funded by a grant from the International Fund for Ireland (IFI), set up under the Anglo–Irish Agreement. The grant from the IFI provided funding for three sheds in County Louth, one in the south of the county (in the town of Drogheda) one in the rural northeast of the county in the Cooley Peninsula and one in the border town of Dundalk. Dundalk in particular was identified for funding because of its proximity to Northern Ireland and concerns that political tensions in Northern Ireland could stir up dissident support in Republican strongholds in the town. The grant from the IFI enabled the recruitment of a co-ordinator and to rent a large shed kitted out with workbenches and tools and a kitchen and recreation area.

Initially, the shed opened two or three days per week but over time this was increased to five days a week to meet demand. The age profile of men ranges from 50 to 90 years and each day there are around 25 to 30 men pottering about the shed, working on a range of projects from woodturning to painting and pottery, and in-between sitting around chatting and enjoying each other's company. There is an eagerness to learn and many of the men have undertaken learning programmes in the shed, supported by the local Vocational Educational Centre. The Dundalk shed has played an important role in fostering positive relations between sheds across the border and in supporting fledgling sheds to get established. They regularly play host to and make visits to sheds across the border in both Unionist and Nationalist communities. As one man from the Dundalk shed commented:

> *In the shed you don't talk about politics. It's not that we don't know about it, it's that it doesn't matter. In this here shed you have ex-Republican prisoners, men who ended up moving to Dundalk from the North because of the Troubles – probably some of them 'on the run' – you have former Garda, Irish soldiers, and men from all walks of life, people who would never, ever have got together and sat in the one room, never mind worked together, but for the men's shed. What I'm sayin is, if we can come together and bury our difference, surely everyone else can.*

Armagh Men's Shed (Northern Ireland)
The Armagh Men's Shed received initial funding from the European Union's INTERREG IVA programme, a European Union supported Structural Funds Programme which seeks to address the economic and social problems which result from the existence of borders. The men in the Armagh shed witnessed the achievements of their counterparts across the border in the Dundalk shed and were eager to replicate their successes. In turn, men from the Dundalk shed supported their northern counterparts to get their shed up and running; sharing furniture as well as exchanging information and experiences. The Dundalk shed, for example, donated a leather suite of furniture to the Armagh shed that it had received from a business that closed in Dundalk. The men from the Armagh and Dundalk sheds continue to enjoy a natural comradeship and genuine interest in each other. As one man said, 'we wanted the relationship'. On visits to the Dundalk shed, the men cooked and sat around together discussing ideas for their sheds. As one man said:

People in Ireland would have funny ideas of what people on the other side of the great divide are like, so meetin each other and seein that we are the same and interested in the same things is real important.

The men in the Dundalk shed carved out a wooden picture consisting of four doves which depict the four historical provinces of Ireland and the linkages between them. They invited the men from Armagh and other visiting sheds to sign their names on the frame. The large wooden carving in now full of signatures and currently hangs in a central place in the Dundalk shed.

Men's learning in Northern Ireland

Within Northern Ireland, Mark *et al.* (2010) provide unique insights into older men's learning experiences from the perspective of those who have lived in polarised districts of Belfast during a time of civil unrest and societal danger and uncertainty. Many of the men participating in the study were emerging from paramilitary activity and fear of this, as well as alcoholism, social exclusion, major health crises, depression and other mental health problems, political and cultural suppression and environments where education was not regarded as worthwhile or valuable. The findings revealed that many of the men were experiencing an awakening to the benefits of learning, especially regarding history and heritage. The authors identify evidence of the capacity of community-based organisations to provide contexts that have the ability to address disadvantage, particularly social exclusion, unemployment, stress, substance abuse and underdeveloped literacy skills. Through informal learning environments, all aspects of lifelong and lifewide learning were being practised and enhanced, with the added benefit of having a positive impact on older men's health and wellbeing.

Mark *et al.* (2010) show that informal learning can be used as a strategy to avoid social problems such as excessive drinking and gambling. Community-based organisations provide unique and powerful contexts in which older men can express all aspects of communication not available elsewhere in their everyday lives, to practice and develop their masculine identities, improve skills, socialise, support and mentor one another, interact in groups and seek further help when needed.

The study also shows that enjoyment, belonging, friendship and mental stimulation are highly valued aspects of informal learning for older men. These outcomes typically come about by following a hobby or interest rather than through formal training. Within these organisations men find a place where they can have an input on the design and content of learning, achieve a 'qualification' by receiving a certificate and aspire to leadership amongst their peers, all of which provide a sense of empowerment and achievement. Several men took pride in realising the valuable influence they had on others in their community by taking up positions as peer tutors.

Many research participants referred affectionately to the close connection and friendship amongst male group members, uniquely found in informal learning. One key finding of the Mark *et al.* (2010) research is that informal learning environments provide men with involvement in a closely-knit group with an interactive style of teaching and learning. This facilitates mental stimulation and is attractive because the men have a say in the course content and activities that are locally situated. Moreover, the holistic approach allows for peer support to deal with personal problems, and this is found to be helpful to the men, especially for those dealing with literacy difficulties. The men took part for a range of social reasons such as having a hobby, a social outlet, sense of belonging, leadership skills and comradeship, rather than just vocational development and training. Within the informal learning environment, the men found it acceptable to reveal vulnerabilities and to ask for help, which allowed 'curiosity' to flourish as well as bringing a routine and structure to their day. The men gained a sense of control, personal discipline, accountability, achievement, purpose, hope, increased confidence and a 'feel good' factor. In the new post-conflict Northern Ireland, the authors identified an openness amongst Loyalist men to use community-based learning to become 'armed with information' rather than weapons. They argued that men were realising the positive influence on the identity of male peers emerging from oppressive cultural and political norms.

Conclusion

This chapter outlined the context for men's learning across Ireland and discussed the factors influencing men's participation in learning. In both jurisdictions, men with low skills, or with skills that are no longer relevant to the labour market, find themselves grappling with a much-changed world of work. Within Northern Ireland, men are living with the legacy left by decades of civil unrest in which communities continue to live parallel lives. Against this background, governments on both sides of the border have developed skills strategies that place most emphasis on the needs of the economy and on raising formal skill levels to deliver higher productivity and increased economic competitiveness. However, as this chapter demonstrates, men's participation in formal learning environments remains limited in both jurisdictions. Barriers to men's learning are related to lack of accessible educational structures, individual attitudes to learning and funding obstacles. Providers require a greater understanding and moves towards resolving these issues. This will require a better balance between the current emphasis placed on the economic benefits of formal education and recognition of the positive impact of learning on wellbeing. The dramatic growth of the men's sheds movement in Ireland and the success of sheds in engaging hard-to-reach men in learning have demonstrated that learning can become an integral part of men's lives at any age. Evidence from the island of Ireland suggests that community men's sheds are making learning accessible to older men in a way that has not happened previously. In essence, the men's shed movement in Ireland is providing a space where men not only engage in practical hands-on activities, which they find socially and culturally acceptable, but can rebuild shattered communities, helping to heal the psychosocial wounds left by decades of civil unrest in Northern Ireland. This type of learning model has much to teach our educational institutions and us all.

References

Carragher, L. (2013) *Men's Sheds in Ireland: Learning through Community Contexts.* Dundalk: Netwell Centre. Retrieved 22 January 2014 www.netwellcentre. org

Connell, R. (1995) *Masculinities.* Cambridge: Polity Press.

CEU: Council of the European Union (2009) 'Strategic framework for European cooperation in education and training, – Europe 2020', *Official Journal of the European Union*, Conclusions No. 119/02, 12 May.

CSO: Central Statistics Office (2008) *Women and Men in Ireland.* Dublin: Central Statistics Office.

CSO: Central Statistics Office (2012) *This is Ireland: Highlights from Census 2011.* Dublin: Stationery Office.

Community Relations Unit (CRU) (2005) *'A Shared Future' – Improving Relations in Northern Ireland: The policy and strategic framework for good relations in Northern Ireland*, (21 March 2005), Belfast: CRU, Office of the First Minister and Deputy First Minister (OFMDFM).

DEL: Department for Employment and Learning (2002) *Further Education Means Business*. HMSO.

DEL: Department for Employment and Learning (2009) *Success through Skills*: HMSO.

DEL: Department for Employment and Learning (2012) *Success through Skills: Transforming Futures*. HMSO.

DES: Department of Education and Science (2000) *Learning for Life: White Paper on Adult Education*. Dublin: Stationery Office.

Department of Finance and Personnel (2013a) *Northern Ireland Labour Force Survey: January–March 2013*. Belfast: DFP, Economic and Labour Market Statistics Branch.

Department of Finance and Personnel (2013b) *Statistical Press Release*. Belfast: Economic and Labour Market Statistics Branch.

DoHC: Department of Health and Children (2008) *National Men's Health Policy*. Dublin: Department of Health and Children.

Evoy, J. (2007) *Developing Strategies to Engage Traveller Men in County Wexford*. Wexford: Co. Wexford Development Board.

Evoy, J. and Hanlon, N. (2010) *Report on the Engage Programme Review 2010*. Wexford: County Wexford Vocational Educational Committee.

Fay, M., Morrisey, M., Smyth, M. and Wong, T. (1999) *The Cost of the Troubles Study: Report on the Northern Ireland Survey – The Experience and Impact of the Troubles*. Derry, Northern Ireland: INCORE.

Ferguson, H. and Hogan, F. (2004) *Strengthening Families through Fathers: Developing Policy and Practice in Relation to Vulnerable Fathers and their Families*. Waterford: Centre for Social and Family Research.

Golding, B., Brown, M., Foley, A., Harvey, J. and Gleeson, L. (2007) *Men's Sheds in Australia: Learning through Community Contexts*. Adelaide: NCVER.

Grummell, B. (2007) 'The "second chance" myth: Equality of opportunity in Irish adult education policies', *British Journal of Educational Studies*, 55 (2), pp. 182–201.

Hansson, U., O'Connor-Bones, U. and McCord, J. (2013) 'Whatever happened to Integrated Education?', *Shared Space*, 15, pp. 47–62.

Higgins, C., Lavin, T. and Metcalfe, O. (2008) *Health Impacts of Education: A Review*. Dublin: Institute of Public Health in Ireland.

Horgan, G. (2007) *The Impact of Poverty on Young Children's Experience of School*. York: Joseph Rowntree Foundation and York Publishing.

Lalor, T., McKenna, A., Doyle, G. and Fitzsimons, A. (2009) *Men and Literacy: A Study of Attitude and Experience of Learning*. Dublin: National Adult

Literacy Agency (NALA).

Mark, R., Montgomery, V. and Graham, H. (2010) *Beyond the Workplace: An Investigation into Older Men's Learning and Well-being in Northern Ireland.* Report for the Changing Ageing Partnership (CAP). Belfast: Queen's University Belfast.

McAleese, M. (2007) 'Encouraging the social engagement of older men in our communities', *Áras an Uachtaráin*, 16 October.

McGivney, V. (1990) *Education's for Other People: Access to Education for Non-participant Adults.* Leicester: NIACE.

McGrellis, S. (2004) *Pushing the Boundaries in Northern Ireland: Young People, Violence and Sectarianism*, Social Capital ESRC Research Group Working Paper No. 8. London: London South Bank University.

Nolan, P. (2007) *Inquiry into the Future for Lifelong Learning: The Northern Ireland Perspective.* Belfast: Queen's University Belfast.

O'Connor, M. (2007) *Sé Sí: Gender in Irish Education.* Dublin: Department of Education and Science.

Owens, T. (2000) *Men on the Move: A Study of Barriers to Male Participation in Education and Training Initiatives.* Dublin: AONTAS.

Pollak, A. (2012) *Little Community Sector Interest in North–South Cooperation.* Centre for Cross Border Studies. Retrieved 2 September 2013 from www.crossborder.ie/?p=3229

CHAPTER ELEVEN

Men's learning in Portugal

António Fragoso, João Filipe Marques and Milene Lança

Introduction

In the last three decades, rapid changes in Portuguese society have affected almost all dimensions of life in Portugal. The Portuguese population recognises a mix of traditional and modern in their normative cultural and social systems, which both operate simultaneously. Medeiros (1988) argues that there are no solutions of continuity between these normative systems, indicative of hybridisations that potentially lead to tensions. This hybrid mix includes Portuguese approaches to gender and masculinities. In this chapter, we examine different theoretical positions on gender, masculinities and men's learning in contemporary Portuguese society, informed by a European learning partnership study of men learning in the community. We include some initial results of the Portuguese strand of this study, including some provisional conclusions which guide our ongoing research based around a case study of men involved in a Portuguese fishing club. Portugal is a society in transition, where gender roles are currently being redefined. As this process unfolds, we conclude from our research that some men seek out spaces in which to learn from each other, whether informally or through self-directed learning.

Gender and masculinity in contemporary Portuguese society

The aspects of social reproduction frequently connected to the social construction of gender are sexual dichotomy, social stratification, work division and the social construction of emotions. The processes whereby sex differences are used to construct different gender identities depend on cultural contexts, and often stem from sets of stereotypes about the expected behaviour of men and women.

Gender stereotypes linked to masculinity generally include traits that have a more instrumental dimension. Stereotypically, men more often exhibit characteristics such as independence, confidence, decision-making or violence. Women are often stereotypically associated with more emotional or expressive traits, such as dependence, passivity, instability, care-taking and orientation towards others (Connell, 1987). Socialisation for male social roles varies between cultural contexts and plays an important role in men's attitudes towards formal and informal education and lifelong learning (Chodorow, 1978, 1989; Jackson and Scott, 2002).

Critical studies that focus on men are a new field of study which first appeared in the 1990s in the Anglo-Saxon academic world in the wake of feminist sociology and gender studies (e.g. Badinter, 1993). The dissemination and popularisation of studies on masculinity followed the work of Connell (2005), who played a central role in defining key concepts such as 'gender order' and 'gender regime'. 'Hegemonic masculinity' is one of Connell's central concepts for the analysis of the social and cultural construction of diverse masculinities and the role that power plays in shaping them (Connell, 2005).

Largely inspired by the Gramscian notion of hegemony, 'hegemonic masculinity' refers to a pervasive cultural model dictating how men are supposed to act, feel and express their emotions. This model is the dominant form of performing and living masculinity. According to Connell (2005), hegemonic masculinity can be defined as the configuration of gender practice that embodies the currently accepted answer to the problem of the legitimacy of patriarchy, which guarantees the dominant position of men and the subordination of women. For instance, this positioning supposes activity in opposition to women's passivity and implies constant performances, discourses, gestures and body postures by which men make explicit their position in the dominant model. Deeply anchored in power relations, namely in male domination, hegemonic masculinity subordinates all other alternative masculinities, including complicit and subordinated masculinities (Connell, 1987, 2005). Therefore, hegemonic masculinity is intrinsically monogamous, heterosexual and, depending on the context, racist and homophobic.

In Portugal's past, men and women have been strictly differentiated by gender roles. Men were expected to protect their family and provide resources, while women would stay at home to take care of the children. The revolutionary period beginning in 1974 marked the end of a dictatorial regime, and Portugal now has a higher number of women in full-time jobs than many European countries. Today, women constitute more than half of the economically active population in Portugal and constitute the majority of students in higher education. Women are currently represented in all areas of social life, including institutions, companies, professions, schools and universities. This inclusion had enormous consequences at the level of values and attitudes surrounding gender roles, gender relationships and family life.

The rapid transformation in Portuguese society was accompanied by a rapid transition from a traditional model of 'man as breadwinner' and 'woman as caretaker' to a more democratic and egalitarian division of work and social roles. This transition has led to important changes in the understanding of masculinity. For this reason, some authors discuss 'masculinity in crisis'. MacInnes (1998) argued that masculinity has always been in crisis. MacInnes suggested that crises arise from the fundamental incompatibility between the core principle of modernity, which states that all human beings are essentially equal (regardless of their sex), and the core tenet of patriarchy, that men are naturally superior to women and women are naturally subordinate to men. Gender inequalities, as well as some traits of hegemonic masculinity, still exist in many aspects of social life in Portugal (Aboim, 2010) and arguably affect significant aspects of learning and training.

In Portugal, initial themes in gender studies were largely studies of female roles, oppression and discrimination, as well as the asymmetric distribution of power between men and women. Gradually, however, other dimensions, such as class, ethnicity and sexual orientation, entered the field and widened its scope of analysis (Amâncio, 2004). Issues around masculinity entered the agenda in the 1990s via the discipline of social anthropology. Almeida used Connell's concept of hegemonic masculinity to study the (re)production of masculinity in a small rural village in southern Portugal. This study showed that masculinity among young Portuguese peasants is a fragile condition that is always in danger and subject to vigilance and affirmation through discourse and performance (Almeida, 1995). This research was followed by a sociological study about gender and masculinity in the Portuguese army which concluded that certain hegemonic features still play very important roles in the definition of the military identity (Carreiras, 2004).

More recently, a research team composed of sociologists and social psychologists published three different studies in a book suggestively entitled *Learning How to be a Man: Constructing Masculinities* (Amâncio, 2004). The first study defined an 'occupational culture' to be the system of values, signs, beliefs, ideologies, languages, gestures and rituals shared by the members of a given profession that structures interpersonal and intergroup relations. Cultures (re)produced by the jobs that require education are clearly gendered and still include important traits of the traditional hegemonic masculinity, even if these professions are now open to women. The ideal type of these professionals – surgeon, judge, typographer, taxi driver – as described by the professionals themselves, virtually overlaps the ideal of traditional masculinity, as defined in a stereotypical, rigid and emphatic way (Marques, 2004). Language is largely used as a domination tool that is not only directed at women, but also at alternative masculinities (Connell, 2005).

The other set of studies analysed the attitudes of young Portuguese males towards behaviours involving some type of risk: alcohol consumption, sexuality and driving. In contemporary Portugal, a 'normative' way of being a man strongly pressures youngsters to adopt behaviour that is directly linked with ill health, accidents and reduction of average life expectancy. Alcohol consumption, often in excess during adolescence, contributes to the establishment of a difference between boys and girls, and simultaneously reinforces masculinity. A stronger identification with traditional masculinity leads to more frequent and greater alcohol consumption (Laranjeira, 2004). The same relationship is found in sex-related behaviours. Sexually compulsive behaviour, as well as compulsive heterosexuality and negligence of sexually transmitted disease prevention, are consequences of the embodied social norms regulating dominant male sexuality (Santos, 2004). Aggressive driving, regardless of the risks involved, constitutes another attribute of this 'normative' way of being a man (Martinho, 2004) that shapes the concept of hegemonic masculinity.

These studies clearly relate men's and boys' physical and psychological vulnerability to conformity with traditional masculinity models. The adoption of certain ways of 'being a man', such as the consumption of alcoholic drinks, risk-regardless driving or compulsive, non–protected sexuality, are idealised behaviours of hegemonic masculinity that are too often lethal (Laranjeira, 2004).

Masculinities in Portugal have been studied from the perspective of family values and attitudes towards family life (Perista, 2002; Aboim, 2010; Wall *et al.*, 2010). Recent research uses the interesting concepts of 'old masculinity' and 'new masculinities' to refer to transitional gender relations and male family roles experienced in contemporary Portugal (Wall *et al.*, 2010). Despite the popularity of modernist values defending equality, freedom of choice or a more relational-based family, gender role differentiation persists in Portuguese society.

Despite the change in the woman–nature association to woman–individual, and progressive deconstruction of hegemonic masculinity, this movement has not erased the social force of gender inequalities in Portugal (Aboim, 2010). The gendered regime of the family still illustrates the very limited participation of men in family life, especially in certain classes. The results of several studies on the distribution of domestic work between men and women clearly show that the time dedicated to these tasks is marked by asymmetry (e.g., Perista, 2002; Wall *et al.*, 2010). Although very high female participation in the labour market is observed in Portugal, this participation has not been counter-balanced by greater male participation in tasks within the domestic sphere. Greater feminine workload in housework and family care is evident. Male participation in household tasks is a little higher in house-holds with more children and in families with higher levels of education and income (Perista, 2002).

It is undeniable that masculinities, male identity and male lifestyles are changing in contemporary Portuguese society. However, the direction of these changes is not always clear. Recent research testifies that young men adopt the sexuality attitudes in 'old masculinity' and older men simultaneously adopt 'new masculinities' towards family life and other areas. The directions and dynamics of these changes will certainly have implications for attitudes towards formal and informal education. Therefore, it is time to look at men's learning.

Men's learning in Portugal and the importance of informal learning

The Portuguese learning situation can be succinctly summarised using data from the last national survey of education and adult training (INE, 2009). The data show an overall high participation in diverse types of education, training or learning among individuals who are younger, students, economically active, more academically qualified and competent in foreign languages and ICT (information and communications technologies). The proportion of those participating in formal education, non-formal education and informal learning is strongly determined by age. The survey does not consider learning after the age of 65 years. The group between 55 and 64 years of age has the lowest proportion of participation in every category (11 per cent in lifelong learning activities, one per cent in formal education, ten per cent in non-formal education and 26 per cent in informal learning).

There is a strong correlation between participation in learning and income level, as illustrated in Table 11.1. Greater monthly income indicates a greater percentage of participation in lifelong learning and non-formal learning. Finally, there is an apparent great divide between women and men's learning, although this fact is not stressed in any part of the survey results or conclusions.

Table 11.1 shows that participation of men, when compared with women, is lower for every income stratum. If women are considered a preferred target of adult education and training for historical and social reasons, current differences between women's and men's attitudes towards learning demonstrate the importance of clearly understanding why men are not engaged in learning. We should not forget that the highest proportion of participation is in informal learning, in which one-quarter of adults were engaged. It is evident that little attention has been given to these gender-related differences. We argue that prevailing gender differences and women's struggle to attain a more egalitarian position in Portuguese society have masked the somewhat worrisome situation of Portuguese male learning. Prior to the current study, we know of no Portuguese research concerned with this topic.

Clearly, there is good reason to focus on men's informal learning in Portugal. However, a first step is to define the meaning of informal learning, which represents most significant lifetime learning. Traditionally, we have defined three forms of learning – formal, non-formal and informal. Informal learning has always been the most blurred concept of the three. If we look at research, it is difficult to identify learning beyond basic institutional frames, formal participation or vocational training. However, researchers do recognise the importance of socialisation, and the difficulties of accessing and measuring information on informal learning, in addition to basic philosophical reasons, can explain the lack of research in the field (Gorard et al., 1999).

Table 11.1 Individuals in Portugal between 18 and 64 years of age who participated in lifelong learning and non-formal education (percentage) by gender and monthly income

	Lifelong learning			Non-formal education		
Monthly income bands	Totals (%)	Men (%)	Women (%)	Totals (%)	Men (%)	Women (%)
Less than €500	19.2	19.2	19.2	14.9	15.6	14.5
Between €500 and €750	27.4	22.6	35.4	23.5	19.3	30.4
Between €750 and €1000	40.5	36.4	49.5	35.9	32.2	43.9
Between €1000 and €1500	53.5	48.9	61.2	50.1	45.4	58.0
Between €1500 and €2000	60.2	55.0	67.4	58.3	52.2	66.9
Between €2000 and €3000	72.0	71.5	73.1	68.4	67.8	69.7
More than €3000	75.0	68.8	91.4	72.4	68.8	82.0

Source: INE, 2009.

Informal learning can be defined as education occurring outside the typical institutions and settings that provide structural education (such as schools or universities) or meet well-defined (sometimes instrumental) objectives. McGivney (1999) argues that informal learning arises from the activities and interests particular to individuals and groups which occur in people's everyday lives, and covers a wide range of contexts. According to Schugurensky (2000), informal learning includes self-directed learning, incidental learning and socialisation. While self-directed learning is intentional and conscious, incidental learning is unintentional but conscious, and learning acquired through socialisation is unintentional and unconscious.

Our desire to study the informal learning of men in Portugal was strengthened by Golding's work in Australia (Golding, 2011a, 2011b) which is suggestive of the relationship between older men's learning and their wellbeing, as well as the impact of informal learning over a number of dimensions, including policy. In 2012, we decided to start a modest learning partnership to obtain exploratory data in collaboration with other European colleagues, as briefly described in the next section.

The OMAL learning partnership and its Portuguese strand

The OMAL (Older Men as Active Learners in the Community) project is a four-nation (Portugal, Slovenia, Estonia and Malta), EU-funded, learning partnership focused on older men's learning. The project acknowledges that:

> In most countries, the share of the older people (60+) who participate in organised education is rather limited ... The focus of the research is the state of knowledge about the organisations and programmes on the community level, offering activities (social and educational) for older men ... [The project] will analyse the possibilities older men have at the level of local community to be actively involved in social exchange and learning ... The Partnership team will map the current situation about possibilities of older men's learning in the chosen communities in the participating countries ... [based] upon the idea that older adults should be the subjects of the social transformation process. (OMAL, 2013)

The specific aim of the project is to investigate the problems of vulnerable men who are marginalised, defined as less-educated men with lower socio-economic status and with low paying jobs prior to retirement. The project focuses on community organisations where older men predominate and tries to understand how the initiatives in which

171

they are involved have an impact on their subjective wellbeing without disturbing the natural contexts in which events occur. The selected case studies anticipate that older men's learning in different countries will involve diverse, contextually situated cases, ranging from religious fraternities in Malta, bowling clubs in Slovenia, fishing clubs in Portugal and informal learning in day centres in Estonia. These initial case studies are providing early insights that are being used to refine research methods and to craft more precise research questions to be tackled in subsequent deeper research.

In Portugal, there are a large number of informal groups and community organisations where men (or mostly men) gather to occupy a community public space. This characteristic entails a gender distinction. As we showed in Fragoso and Ollagnier (2011), women tend to be confined to domestic spaces organised around care (children/older people) and family property. This traditional gender segmentation has been reinforced by labour market differences because women primarily worked at home and men had easier access to paid work.

Despite the causes, it is a fact that numerous groups of men occupy many public spaces and community organisations in Portugal. These community organisations include pigeon racing clubs, fishing and hunting groups, petanque clubs and volunteer fire brigades. Some community groups, such as fire brigades, are well organised and formally managed, with accredited training. Other groups are informal in all respects. In the context of the OMAL project, we selected three case studies with which to start: one pigeon racing club and one fishing club in the city of Faro and one petanque club in the city of Portimão. The following section presents a brief description of the amateur fishing club of Faro and the consequent data interpretation.

Case study of an amateur fishing club in Faro

The amateur fishing club in Faro, southern Portugal, was created in 1956 by a group of 11 friends. Over the first years of the club's existence, men joined to participate in fishing competitions and it grew to approximately 650 members at one point. Today, the club has 278 members, most of whom (85 per cent) are men. It still encourages strong face-to-face socialisation and is tightly integrated into the Faro community: four out of five of its members (81 per cent) live in the city.

Today, the club is skewed towards older age groups. Only seven per cent of the members are younger than 25 years old, 12 per cent are between 26 and 39 years old, 51 per cent are between 40 and 64 years and 29 per cent are between 65 and 82 years. Around one-quarter (24 per cent) of members are retired. Around two-thirds are either blue-collar workers (37 per cent) or white-collar workers (34 per cent). The balance of members comprises students and those who work at home or are retired.

Current fishing club activities include fishing competitions at various levels, social fishing and indoor activities. The club's teams that perform well at regional competitions are allowed to compete in national competitions; if the teams rank in the first group at the national level, they have access to worldwide competitions. Social fishing is a central activity in which fishing appears to be a pretext for socialisation, and competition is neither important nor official. These activities usually end with a common lunch or dinner at the club bar. A number of indoor activities, including playing cards, dominos, darts, snooker, drinking and talking, take place in the club's bar.

This case was studied using document analysis, informal conversations during initial contacts, observation in the natural spaces of the club and during some outdoor activities, and ten non-structured interviews (Ruiz, 1999). Although our research is unfinished, our case study allows us to report some early findings and generate some provisional, wider conclusions of relevance to the four-nation study.

Older men's participation and intergenerational dynamics
The older fishing club members participate in local or social competitions because their physical limitations exclude them from national or worldwide competitions. However, older members primarily use the club spaces for social gatherings, and they notably establish social relationships with people of various ages.

> *People here are very friendly and always willing to help … we have very strong ties. It's curious that these bonds do not have a definite age. It's funny how people can meet and have a good relationship, even at completely different ages. Here I see kids who are ten or 11 years old. I see people who are 70 and I find that very interesting.* (Male, 42)

The club appears to be an important source of intergenerational informal learning. Aside from its encouragement of strong personal friendships, it also has a surprisingly family-oriented structure that operates to unite the men involved. It is very common to see whole families at the beach fishing or having lunch or dinner together. Sometimes, three different generations are fishing at the same time. The sense of belonging extends beyond family ties. As a 63-year-old male says, 'Let me put it this way. There are men who don't have a family and *this is* a family'. It is important to note that the club is open to non-members, including people from the community, whether they fish or not, and they may use the club bar. For instance, there is a group of unemployed young adults who are in the club every day, and a group of friends retired from the police force that use the club as a main space for social life after retirement. Our data indicate that club activities are fundamental to the fight against isolation among men (especially older men), creating strong face-to-face ties of friendship. Strong feelings of belonging and the creation of a common identity make these ties possible.

Gender relationships
Although the club members are primarily men, women participate at three different levels. Firstly, men respect women who participate in the fishing competitions due to their fishing abilities, and some women have participated and won individual and team events at all levels, including world cups. During the interviews, the men who want to have more women at the club identify fishing competitions as the women's key way of entering the club. Secondly, some women do very traditional female tasks to help the club, such as cooking lunches, managing the bar or organising raffles. In this sense, the club reproduces traditional gender roles. Thirdly, there are women who use the club spaces as a means of socialisation, similar to any other person. However, the patterns of socialisation are different for men and women. Women primarily like to talk in groups, easily share their feelings and do not stay for extended amounts of time; men mainly express themselves through involvement in different games and frequent the club for longer periods of time.

Learning informally from the collective
The amateur fishing club of Faro is recognised as one of the best clubs in the country; over the years, they have won a large number of individual and team trophies at events that include worldwide competitions.

Therefore, it seems logical to inquire whether the club has organised some type of structure to support the technical aspects of fishing. Surprisingly, this is not the case. The club has no financial support, no coaches, no organised training, nor any type of planned training structure. Its club members simply go on frequent fishing trips together, mostly on weekends, and informally learn together from each other. Again, friendship and family ties are the most important components in the social networks that support this type of learning.

Conclusion

Because our research on men's learning is at an early stage, our conclusions, while provisional and based on an intensive study of only one club, provide clues to our future research. Our first conclusion concerns transitions between Portuguese gender roles. The transition from the traditional model of 'man as breadwinner' and 'woman as caretaker' to a more egalitarian division of social roles is far from secured. Family life is still marked by asymmetries that are passed on and visible in club life. Women are the ones who cook and manage the bar. The characteristic informality of specific roles creates a certain dilution of these asymmetries, but that does not mean that asymmetries are absent.

Our second conclusion has to do with the gender differences that clearly appear in male and female socialisation within the club. For men, the club is a safe space, free of pressures, where they can spend long hours engaged in games and minor competitions, which are not regarded as important activities by women. Women tend to regard these male activities as 'doing nothing'. These typical, male, 'doing nothing' activities and ways of socialisation in the fishing club are seldom possible in formal or non-formal learning contexts, which primarily attract women, and which are typically framed by clear intentions and instrumental objectives. This informal context and the associated informal learning that the club provides happens in a 'safe', male-friendly space that some men highly value. Even if this need might seem unimportant, the club may be a way to relieve some everyday social and family pressures. This argument leads us to our third conclusion, regarding hegemonic masculinities.

We were unable to identify typical characteristics of hegemonic masculinities among fishing club members. Here it is important to recall Almeida's (1995) research that depicts Portuguese masculinity as being in a fragile condition that is permanently subjected to vigilance and affirmation. This informal fishing club context may represent a space where men do not feel strongly compelled to demonstrate all of the key components from which their masculinity is composed. Most of the men are already retired and are generally not burdened by professional pressures. For men who do still work, social actors from their paid employment are not present. While the place and space of the club is constructed and experienced as 'a family', in the sense of the safety and social support it provides, at the same time, traditional family structures are not operative. As a working hypothesis, we question whether such informal contexts serve as free spaces that are devoid of the typical social actors and practices that promote the building of hegemonic masculinities. We argue that this possibility is worthy of further investigation.

Fourth, we find it unwise to speak of men without speaking of women. The construction of both types of social roles is interdependent; masculinities cannot be built only among men. For the purposes of our research, it will be important to know more female opinions of these types of mostly male spaces and activities.

Fifth, our analysis of the types of informal learning (as defended by Schugurensky, 2000) indicates that, apart from the very specific fishing techniques that are seemingly learned by collective yet self-directed learning, most of the club activities appear to represent incidental learning. However, there is a considerable component of socialisation, unintentional and unconscious, that is fundamental to the men who use this club.

Finally, we want to acknowledge that much research is still needed in order to identify the connections between informal learning and men's subjective wellbeing. Although we can identify some provisional clues, more time is needed to obtain robust answers.

Acknowledgements

Our sincere thanks to Rute Ricardo, who undertook most of the fieldwork in the case study of the amateur fishing club in Faro. This text was possible partially due to support from the Portuguese Foundation for Science and Technology (FCT).

References

Aboim, S. (2010) 'Género, família e mudança em Portugal', in K. Wall, S. Aboim and V. Cunha (Eds.), *Vida Familiar no Masculino: Negociando Velhas e Novas Masculinidades*. Lisboa: Comissão para a Igualdade no Trabalho e no Emprego, pp. 39–66.

Almeida, M. (1995) *Senhores de Si: Uma Interpretação Antropológica da Masculinidade*. Lisboa: Fim de Século.

Amâncio, L. (Ed.) (2004) *Aprender a ser Homem: Construindo Masculinidades*. Lisboa: Livros Horizonte.

Badinter, E. (1993) *X e y a Identidade Masculina*. Lisboa: Asa Editora.

Carreiras, H. (2004) 'Gender and the military: A comparative study of the participation of women in the armed forces of Western democracies', PhD Thesis (unpublished). Florence: European University Institute.

Chodorow, N. (1978) *The Reproduction of Mothering: Psychoanalysis and the Sociology of Gender*. California: University of California Press.

Chodorow, N. (1989) *Feminism and Psychoanalytic Theory*. USA: Yale University Press.

Connell, R. (1987) *Gender and Power*. California: Stanford University Press.

Connell, R. (2005) *Masculinities*. California: University of California Press.

Fragoso, A. and Ollagnier, E. (2011) 'The involvement of women in training as a step towards an emancipatory community development process', in O. Unluhisarcikli, G. Guvercin, O. Secki and I. Sabirli (Eds.), *Positioning and Conceptualizing Adult Education and Learning within Local Development*. Istanbul: Bogaziçi University Press, pp. 32–40.

Golding, B. (2011a) 'Not just petrol heads: Men's learning in the community through participation in motor sports', *European Journal for Research on the Education and Learning of Adults*, 2 (2), pp. 165–80.

Golding, B. (2011b) 'Social, local, and situated: Recent findings about the effectiveness of older men's informal learning in the community contexts', *Adult Education Quarterly*, 61 (2), pp. 103–20.

Gorard, S., Fevre, R. and Rees, G. (1999) 'The apparent decline of informal learning', *Oxford Review of Education*, 25 (4), pp. 437–54.

INE (2009) *Aprendizagem ao Longo da Vida: Inquérito à Educação e Formação de Adultos 2007*. Lisboa: INE.

Jackson, S. and Scott, S. (2002) *Gender: A Sociological Reader*. London: Routledge.

Laranjeira, A. (2004) 'Não és homem não és nada: Masculinidade e comportamentos de risco', in L. Amâncio (Ed.), *Aprender a ser Homem, Construindo Masculinidades*. Lisboa: Livros Horizonte, pp. 51–73.

MacInnes, J. (1998) *The End of Masculinity: The Confusion of Sexual Genesis and Sexual Difference in Modern Society*. Philadelphia: Open University Press.

Marques, A. (2004) 'Os trabalhos da masculinidade: Culturas ocupacionais sob hegemonia masculina', in L. Amâncio (Ed.), *Aprender a ser Homem: Construindo Masculinidades*. Lisboa: Livros Horizonte, pp. 29–50.

Martinho,T. (2004) 'Viver jovem, morrer depressa: Masculinidade e condução de risco', in L. Amâncio (Ed.), *Aprender a ser Homem: Construindo Masculinidades*. Lisboa: Livros Horizonte, pp. 51–90.

McGivney,V. (1999) *Informal Learning in the Community: A Trigger for Change and Development*. Leicester: NIACE.

Medeiros, F. (1988) 'Um Sistema Social de Espaços Múltiplos – a autonomia do local na sociedade portuguesa', *Revista Crítica de Ciências Sociais*, No. 25/26, pp. 143–62.

OMAL: Older Men as Active Learners (2013) Retrieved 23 January 2013 from http://omal.si

Perista, H. (2002) 'Género e trabalho não pago: Os tempos das mulheres e os tempos dos homens', *Análise Social*,Vol. XXXVII (163), pp. 447–74.

Ruiz, J. (1999) *Metodología de la investigación cualitativa*. Bilbao: Universidad de Deusto.

Santos, H. (2004) 'Sexo para o que der e vier: Masculinidade e comportamentos preventivos face à SIDA', in L. Amâncio, (Ed.), *Aprender a ser Homem: Construindo Masculinidades*. Lisboa: Livros Horizonte, pp. 91–120.

Schugurensky, D. (2000) *The Forms of Informal Learning: Towards a Conceptualization of the Field*. NALL working paper. Toronto: OISE, University of Toronto.

Wall, K., Aboim, S. and Cunha, V. (Eds.) (2010) *Vida Familiar no Masculino: Negociando Velhas e Novas Masculinidades*. Lisboa: Comissão para a Igualdade no Trabalho e no Emprego.

CHAPTER TWELVE

Men's learning in Greece

Georgios K. Zarifis

Introduction

This chapter looks at different aspects of learning among younger and older men in Greece in a time of social and economic crisis. It reflects particularly on research findings from the PALADIN (Promoting Active Learning and Ageing of Disadvantaged Seniors) project funded under the European Lifelong Learning Programme (PALADIN, 2009) and from evidence on youth unemployment in Greece. It considers two important and intertwining factors that relate to identifying older men (over 50 years) and younger men (between 18 and 30 years) who can be described as socially and economically disadvantaged in Greece. These factors include access to and participation in meaningful learning, as well as guidance and counselling for participation in learning. The chapter will examine the conditions that enable or empower men to lead diverse and productive lives through 'learning for change'. Based on empirical research findings, the chapter describes and explains some factors that prevent younger and older men in Greece from engaging in various learning activities. The chapter concludes that, while much of the literature on successful and productive ageing focuses on personal characteristics of individuals as determinants of the types and amounts of learning activities in which they engage, there is no particular formula for empowering men (younger and older) to take responsibility for their own learning. Rather, there is a multiplicity of interacting factors that can vary depending on the way these men view themselves and their situation.

There is a large amount of social research in Greece that focuses on the role of gender, most with specific reference to women rather than to men (Deligianni-Kouimtzi *et al.*, 2000). This is largely because Greece has often been considered a patriarchal society, in which women have typically occupied subordinate positions as well as sometimes being socially invisible. Contested as this perception might be, especially during the current economic crisis, it is not surprising that much of the Greek research on gender is primarily focused on and undertaken by women. It is a fact that since the 1970s, with the end of dictatorship and accession to the European Union, women's status and social image have dramatically changed in Greece. Much of the research on gender explores, amongst other issues, those of equality in education and the work domain, identity building, family roles and power relations with particular reference to women (Ziogou-Karastergiou, 2006). A small fraction of this research investigates the extent to which a space for women's leisure-based learning has evolved in Greece in recent decades. Leisure time, in particular, has been widely seen as an aspect of social modernity where processes of individuation, cultural participation and appropriation intersect (Koronaiou, 2010).

Research focused on women's discretionary learning provides evidence of the growing importance for Greek women of leisure time as an opportunity for more autonomy and independence in the midst of a range of social, economic and familial constraints. Leisure-time learning activities, especially in the public sphere, are increasingly demanded by women as part of a right to 'a time of one's own', distinct from family leisure time. Within this framework, leisure-based learning activities become a source of transformation, especially in family life, as new values and lifestyles emerge from the sphere of free time, forming new identities. Thus, discretionary learning provides many Greek women with the space to think over and overpass traditional stereotypes and roles, daring to confront a male-dominated society in economic, political, informational and scientific spheres.

In this chapter, I examine the conditions under which disadvantaged younger (18 to 30 years) and older (50 plus years) men in Greece can be empowered to lead diverse and productive lives at a time of significant financial and social crisis for the country. It is important at the outset to note that the term 'disadvantaged' is case specific (referring to those in a disadvantaged, needy or deprived state or position) and needs to be approached within a specific context (such as social, economic, cultural, educational or medical). In general terms, 'disadvantaged' refers, in the European social policy context, to a particular group of people with inadequate learning resources due to limited or restricted access to learning provision (European Commission, 2007, p. 87). It refers to people (in the context of this chapter, specifically to men) who are unemployed, education dropouts or non-participants in learning, such as migrants (unskilled or low skilled), people with disabilities (mental or physical), those who have taken early retirement and third age learners (50 plus).

This chapter focuses on arguably the most pressing problem that Greece faces today (as a result of the long standing debt crisis and lack of economic development), namely a very high level of unemployment. Unemployment may lead to severe poverty and social exclusion as a result of a reduction in welfare provision. According to EUROSTAT (2012), the highest proportion of people at risk of poverty or social exclusion in 2011 was recorded in Bulgaria (49 per cent), Romania and Latvia (both 40 per cent), Lithuania (33 per cent) and Greece and Hungary (both 31 per cent). Conversely, the lowest levels were in the Czech Republic (15 per cent), the Netherlands and Sweden (both 16 per cent) and Luxembourg and Austria (both 17 per cent). Figure 12.1 shows the relevant percentage of men at risk of poverty in Greece and across the European Union.

At the time of writing, unemployment in Greece had reached 27 per cent of the total active population (Europe's highest level, with 59.4 per cent unemployment among young people and 24 per cent among men of all ages: EUROSTAT (2013a) report on unemployment, 1 March 2013). A series of short-term actions were announced in January 2013 to attempt to address this phenomenon, especially among young men, such as the 'National Youth Action' with a budget of €517 million, for example. However, the situation at the moment is very difficult, particularly if the rising numbers of younger and older men being out of work are factored in. The male unemployment data in Tables 12.1 and 12.2 summarise Greece's position in the current European context (2013 data).

This growing phenomenon has immediate repercussions on men's living standards as well as on their orientation in life in general. The distress caused by the effects of unemployment and an inability to re-enter the labour market is so immense for some that the level of disorientation, lack of self-esteem, anxiety and insecurity can lead to extreme reactions, such as committing suicide. There is, therefore, a need for intervention

Figure 12.1 Men at risk of poverty (percentage of total male population)

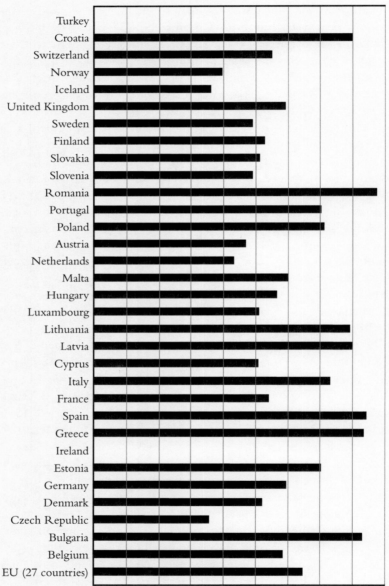

Source of data: Eurostat. Last update: 18 March 2013. Hyperlink to the table: http://epp. eurostat.ec.europa.eu/tgm/table.do?tab=table&init=1&plugin=0&language=en&pcode=tsdsc350

Table 12.1 Unemployment rate among men age 15–34 (2012, Q4)

Period	2010 Q3	2010 Q4	2011 Q1	2011 Q2	2011 Q3	2011 Q4	2012 Q1	2012 Q2	2012 Q3	2012 Q4
Geographical region										
EU (27 countries)	11.9	12.2	12.8	12.0	12.1	12.9	13.9	13.5	13.3	
Euro area (17 countries)	12.5	12.7	13.3	12.5	12.5	13.6	14.9	14.6	14.5	
Greece	13.6	16.1	18.5	19.2	20.6	24.3	26.6	28.0	29.3	31.4★

Source: Data extracted from EUROSTAT, 2013 (last updated 15 March 2013).
★ The rate is 41.2 per cent in urban regions.

Table 12.2 Unemployment rate among men age 55–64 (2012, Q4)

Period	2010 Q3	2010 Q4	2011 Q1	2011 Q2	2011 Q3	2011 Q4	2012 Q1	2012 Q2	2012 Q3	2012 Q4
Geographical region										
EU (27 countries)	6.7	6.9	7.1	6.7	6.5	6.9	7.5	7.3	7.0	
Euro area (17 countries)	7.1	7.4	7.6	7.1	7.0	7.4	8.0	7.0	7.8	
Greece	5.9	6.9	7.8	7.8	8.4	10.1	11.9	13.1	14.1	15.3

Source: Data extracted from EUROSTAT, 2013 (last updated 15 March 2013).

strategies, not only to alleviate the effects of unemployment, but also to find new ways of engaging men in employment.

While the intention in this chapter is not to elaborate on the Greek crisis, it is essential to stress the class of events that can be clearly defined as 'crisis'. While one would expect people to react intensely to these confronting life-events, there is a need for a more sophisticated means for understanding the 'nature of crisis' in Greece, and the ways in which people (men in this case) react to them (see Greenwald, 2011). Many men, for example, who lose access to paid work make meaning of the crisis as a state of disempowerment or 'losing voice'. It can produce a deep state of shock that literally defeats many men, leaving them without voice and often deprived of their social identities. This appreciation of the crisis is not much documented in the literature, probably because the relevant literature often sits above the individual and his/her personal life, instead emphasising the global financial system and its major players and markets. But, as this crisis of historically unprecedented magnitude and scope unfolds, attention rightfully turns to its implications, particularly for disadvantaged men. Most men give meaning to the events that happen in their lives and are essentially empowered to do so when they feel socially adequate and 'safe' and have a positive orientation to life. Each person witnessing or participating in the same event will experience it differently.

To a large extent, these differences are attributable to each person's unique life history. We understand the new and the novel or the highly emotionally charged in terms of what we have already experienced. We find ways of fitting new experiences into what we already know and that allow a sense of both familiarity and comfort. This prospect, however, is not always achievable, especially if the effects of the crisis are longitudinal. Some men will need outside support and empowerment, not only to maintain what they have, but also to rise above their disadvantage and create a new and preferably sustainable orientation for their future lives (Greenwald, 2011).

The main argument here is that there are evidently two important factors that relate to identifying men as being disadvantaged or disempowered. Firstly, there may be an inability to access education because men are either not informed or aware of educational opportunities, or because existing educational opportunities are not appropriate to this particular group of men. Secondly, men may be unable to participate in learning because they do not consider it important or because they think it is irrelevant to their development (Bettio *et al.*, 2012). It is of critical importance in addressing these two conditions (providing educational opportunities and strengthening or increasing the motive for participation) that men are enabled or empowered to make their way in, and actively take part in a productive way through participation in lifelong and lifewide education and learning activities. These fundamentally intertwining factors can help make meaning of the *modus operandi* for empowering men who are financially and socially, as well as emotionally and psychologically, affected by the crisis in Greece.

Reflecting on qualitative data from the PALADIN project, as well as data I have collected from unemployed and low skilled younger men (18–30) with 15 in-depth interviews that were conducted for the purpose of this chapter, I explain the different ways in which younger and older disadvantaged men experience learning during crisis, and focus on actions intended to raise their efficacy level, provide access to self-directed learning or orientate them towards meaningful learning, as well as towards useful guidance and counselling.

Empowering disadvantaged senior men through learning: The PALADIN experience

According to Page and Czuba (1999), who adopt a Freirean approach, empowerment is essentially a process that challenges our assumptions about the way things are and can be. It challenges our basic assumptions about power, helping, achieving and succeeding. To begin to demystify the concept of empowerment, we need to understand the concept broadly in order to be clear about how and why we narrow our focus of empowerment for specific programmes and projects (to a specific dimension or level, for example) and to allow discussion of empowerment across disciplinary and practice lines. In this chapter I adopt a more technical approach, as presented by the World Bank (2013). According to this approach, empowerment is the process of increasing the capacity of individuals or groups to make choices and to transform those choices into desired actions and outcomes. Central to this process are actions that build individual and collective assets, and improve the efficiency and fairness of the organisational and institutional context that governs the use of these assets. Empowered people have freedom of choice and action. This in turn enables them to better influence the course of their lives and the decisions that affect them. However, perceptions of being empowered vary across time, culture and domains of a person's life.

The impact of demographic ageing within the European Union (EU) is likely to be of major significance in the coming decades. Greece, as in most European societies, is an ageing society. The population aged 64 years and over was 19 per cent in 2010. For a variety of reasons a large number of older men in Greece have been experiencing the impact of the financial and economic crisis on a daily basis. The circumstances giving rise to this are many and varied, including unemployment and struggling to find a new job; losing a lifetime of savings; paying more for basic goods and vital services; and in some cases simply withdrawing from social or cultural participation. While other age groups also face similar difficulties, no one should underestimate the particular vulnerability amongst men aged 50 and over who are experiencing the debilitating effects of social exclusion in old age.

The crisis has affected both the psychological and physical condition of older people in Greece. At an age when they should be able to enjoy their retirement, many older people today have to deal with excessive responsibilities, such as continuing to care for other older people, for example their own parents, or permanently looking after grandchildren in order to support their children who are in employment. Financial difficulties also push older people to distress and depression and, in the most extreme cases, to suicide. In Greece, data from an emergency suicide prevention helpline showed that in 2010, 46 per cent of calls were from people aged 50 years and over, with an estimated 25–30 per cent increase in people seeking help from psychiatric services during the crisis. In 2008, data for completed suicides showed a very low overall rate of 2.8 per 100,000 population. Rates for 2007 to 2009 showed an 18 per cent increase, with figures for January to May 2011 showing a 40 per cent rise over the same period in 2010. Suicide rates for men are consistently much higher than for women. Mortality rates for suicide by age group are highest in over-80 year olds for both men and women (see Age Platform Europe, 2012, p. 11).

Problems faced by older men are growing, and include difficulties in accessing affordable health services and long-term care, as well as a shortage of adequate housing to support a dignified life. High energy costs are also a concern for a growing number of older men, and poverty as a result of changing circumstances amongst older people, particularly in pre-retirement age cohorts, is increasingly common. The persisting gloomy economic outlook and consecutive losses of life-earnings and savings through failed investments in real estate or financial products, has exposed this expanding population group to a higher risk of poverty. Most disadvantaged men represent the lower middle class which, until recently, was not confronted with such risk. Providing support to this vulnerable social group is a challenge. Philanthropic solutions are being increasingly used for basic problems of survival. Non-government organisations (NGOs) and other bodies, together with the Orthodox Church NGO *Apostoli*, have an extensive and growing system of free food collection and free meal distribution, along with a scheme for pharmaceutical collection and distribution for those unable to pay for essential medication. This situation in many respects reflects that experienced in Greece 30 years ago, when many older people had no effective health insurance or access to free primary health care. In essence, the current situation seems to be so pressing for older adults that their new priorities have completely changed their daily routines and hence the way they learn.

Existing initiatives are focused on the more immediate relief of those in need of basic health services and food, and are not concerned about access to and participation in different types of learning. Since life is an endless process of learning, change and adaptation to various challenges and conditions, it is of crucial importance to cultivate and develop an ability to make the most of the situations, so that disadvantaged men become empowered to access and participate in learning activities designed for them, learn more and adapt better.

The objectives of the PALADIN project (2009) were to develop and test psychometric instruments (readiness scales) to facilitate self-learning processes of seniors seen to be disadvantaged (over 50 years old with low qualifications), and to set up a network of innovative activities, focused on self-training and learning approaches at community level. The project was designed to contribute to the empowerment of disadvantaged older men in Greece (as well as other countries, including Portugal, Spain, Malta and Hungary) through the development and application of a methodology that promotes self-directed activity in five fields: activity (employment or voluntary), health, finances, citizenship, and education (formal, non-formal and informal).

Empirical studies of self-directed learning show that people with high self-directedness have personal initiative, perseverance, self-discipline and tend to be goal oriented (Candy, 1991; Courtney and Rahe, 1992;

Foucher and Gousselin, 1995; Carré, 2002). They also tend to manifest self-confidence, to have high levels of self-esteem and life satisfaction (McCune, Guglielmino and Garcia, 1990; Jones, 1994). Based on a methodology (available at PALADIN, 2009) that deployed a series of readiness scales and instruments for efficacy measurement (Oliveira *et al.*, 2011), 103 seniors (men and women) were contacted in ten 'Day Care Centres' (*Kentra Anihtis Prostasias Ilikiomenon – KAPI*) in the city of Thessalonika and its greater area, as well as in houses for the elderly and in rural areas in the region (house tenants), ranging from 51 to 91 years old with a mean age of 68. Among these respondents, 45 were men.

From our research, conducted with Greek men aged 50 or over, conclusions were generated on promotion of self-directed learning for disadvantaged older men. In summary, in order to empower men to access and participate in meaningful learning initiatives, two distinct aspects were identified (Oliveira *et al.*, 2011). The first and most profound aspect is associated with men giving a higher value to educational activities as a way of providing the tools necessary to improve their quality of life. The second, perhaps less evident, aspect is that some of the men expressed doubts about the efficacy of education and training activities as a way of changing the life circumstances of older men. Participants generally believed that people only participated in such activities when they were available for work or when they needed to learn for professional reasons. However, the importance attributed by many men to training in the area of information and communication technologies should be noted.

Significantly, most participants considered that meaningful and effective learning takes place in a safe and familiar environment. Many men stressed the importance of the traditional Greek coffee shops (*kafeneia*) that were shaped by influences from the great Greek cafes in Constantinople. The majority of men noted that these places are essentially empowering 'learning spaces' for assembly and dialogue, exchanging views, sharing information and engaging in political analysis. Besides coffee shops, another aspect they considered relevant to meaningful learning was travelling. Group travel was the main reason why the majority of the men who participated in these 'Day Care Centres' (*KAPI*) found the experiences so attractive.

In terms of providing guidance and counselling for participation in learning, most men believed that counselling was important for their self-esteem to be reinstated and for an awareness of their usefulness to be restored. They further pointed out that societal attitudes should be changed towards senior men in order to positively change their self-image, and that assistance should be provided for men above age 50 in acquiring modern skills and knowledge for life. This would require that adult training should not only be focused on the labour market; all other forms of lifelong learning should similarly be supported, and all types of self-directed learning should be encouraged in order to allow senior men, who are effectively crisis survivors, to acquire new and essential life skills. Health, activity, citizenship and finances were additionally confirmed as key learning domains for the majority of older men in Greece. Reinforcing their skills in these domains could immediately and positively contribute to their everyday life.

Another finding highlighted by men who had moved to Thessalonika from Athens when the financial crisis emerged was the role of the 'Friendship Clubs' (*Lesches Filias*), an initiative of the city of Athens, as a way of supporting individuals to use an informal approach to guidance and counselling. These clubs operate in various city districts and neighbourhoods and offer guidance services to older men. They are places that allow elderly Athenians to seek warmth, contact with peers, social support and entertainment. The Friendship Club programme also provides creative opportunities, occupational therapy, physiotherapy, day trips and visits to cultural venues. Overall, the majority of men who participated in our research stressed that engaging in organised learning activities wrongly presupposes already established social ties and also some homogeneity among participants (sharing the same goals, being from similar social backgrounds and reciprocally sharing trust among participants).

Young men learning from the crisis: Focusing on 'what really matters'

There has been a recent destruction of many jobs and increased duration of joblessness in Greece. Unemployment across the country is likely to continue to rise and stay stubbornly high for some time to come, well after the economy has begun to recover, especially among young adults. Beyond this generalisation, this downturn has more adverse implications for vulnerable segments of the population such as young men aged 18 to 30. According to Malkoutzis (2011), Greece has a valuable untapped resource in its youth. Roughly one tenth of the population (1.1 million people) is under 25 and another 1.5 million are aged between 25 and 34.

189

They tend to be relatively well educated, well travelled and politically aware compared with older Greek people. But it appears that opportunities for them to make a positive contribution to Greek society in the years to come are going to be severely limited. The latest unemployment figures show that 40 per cent of Greeks under 25 years old are out of work.

According to EUROSTAT (2013b), the unemployment rate for men aged 15 to 24 years in Greece was 53 per cent in December 2012. In the wake of the continuing economic downturn, young men have been particularly affected by a range of factors, including a high proportion in heavily affected male employment sectors such as construction. In response to this situation, appropriate policies might utilise targeted crisis interventions that aim to keep youth employed wherever possible, while also assisting new entrants and those who have lost jobs in finding employment (or, at a minimum, staying attached to the labour force with learning interventions), particularly as the economy recovers.

However, despite high rates of unemployment, many young men in Greece are developing a different set of priorities for making meaning and coping with the current economic crisis. Based on the information collected from research interviews, 15 low-skilled young men (aged 18 to 30) were contacted and interviewed in December 2012. All men were unemployed or working in part-time employment, with very low incomes (less than €300 per month) and with low and middle educational backgrounds (they had completed either compulsory education or upper secondary education). At the time of the interviews they were participating as volunteers in supporting Thessalonika's bid as the 'European Youth Capital' for 2014. The issues that these young men brought forward were primarily related to access to meaningful learning and participation in activities that favoured group work and team spirit (other than sports) and solidarity. It is notable how many of these men used extrovertly political language to express themeselves, despite their limited formal educational backgrounds. Unsurprisingly, they made direct reference to the difficulties they faced and would eventually face in the future in terms of becoming employable and competitive in the workplace. However, the meaning they used for issues such as ethical values, social solidarity, frugality and team grouping referred more to the need for appreciating human relations, rather than orientation to employment.

In conclusion, empowerment for such younger men arose from efforts to critically reflect on their experience and transform it into something useful with guidance from others, particuarly from their families and friends. The majority of men stated that nothing was taken for granted and that the crisis helped them to test their own limits, challenge their egos and fight the difficulties they encountered. Finally, we found that low-skilled young men were critical of the media and the social and political context in Europe. For all men interviewed, the media (television in particular) are simultaneously sources of information, a good reason to challenge their convictions and also to help change the current socio-political reality in Europe. One man's words encapsulated their disbelief in the current situation in Europe and the way that the crisis had escalated.

> I don't feel particularly well when I leave my comfort zone, but I find it essential because this is how I grow out of this [unemployment]; my family, my friends, my girlfriend are the most valuable 'others'. What I really find disturbing, however, is how the media try to present us: as lazy anarchists, disoriented, terrorists even. The focus of the media is on an image somebody took during a picket or a protest … and all young men are stigmatised. We all need to take our distance from this. Not [from] the image, the image is real … the way it is interpreted is false. We all need to distance ourselves from what holds us back . It is true [that] I don't have a particular goal in my life, what to do in the next ten years or where I will be working; I am low skilled; at this moment I feel as a refugee in my own country; not many jobs are around for someone my age with my skills; I depend financially on my parents and sister; I cannot start my own job or family; does this makes me less valuable for society? No! … This is what really matters. (Michalis, 22)

This quotation illustrates the complex interaction of different factors and perceptions at a personal level, which combine to determine the impact of the current financial crisis. It illustrates how disadvantaged young men actively reflect and respond to their roles in society, as well as how and what they learn from their disadvantage. Learning is not essentially related to an organised educational environment, nor does it relate to employment. It is essentially realised as a process of assimilation to what is not yet entirely comprehended: a process of meaning-making that asks for time for reflection and developing new codes and new 'schemas'. Learning is essentially approached as the new representation of reality that is not distorted by the media.

This research provides a powerful glimpse of how some young men in Greece are learning from the current economic crisis. It does not necessarily imply that these men are sufficiently empowered to lead their own ways in life. Empowerment asks for the support of others: this support does not seem to be anywhere apparent in the near future. As a researcher, I often wonder where the young unemployed men in Greece are. Where are they hiding and why are they not in the streets protesting anymore? My conclusion is that most are disempowered – by the system, by the media and by the stereotypes the media typically creates against them.

Conclusion

The current financial and economic crisis has resulted in the worst global recession since World War II. Greece has been one of the European nations most affected by the crisis and is not on the way to immediate recovery. Men of all ages, particularly unemployed men, are very much affected by the crisis. While much of the literature on successful and productive ageing focuses on the personal characteristics of individuals as determinants of the types and amount of learning activities in which to engage, there is no particular formula for empowering men (younger and older) to take responsibility for their own learning. Rather, there is a multiplicity of interacting factors that vary depending on the way these men view themselves and their situation. What directions do they need, and how can the current social system provide the conditions for empowering these men through learning?

Malkoutzis (2011, p. 5) stresses that, apart from addressing a lack of employment opportunities, learning schemes can encourage entrepreneurship that can bring about a change in approach. To address this situation, new ways need to be found to give men of all ages better access to learning and a respectable standard of living, to produce a workforce that reflects the needs of the market as well as their own needs. Our research also suggests the need to create spaces for empowering men to gain a voice. Many young men in particular lack a political voice, as mainstream political parties have lost touch with their generation, creating the basis for antagonistic relationships. To remedy all of this at a time when the economy is continuing to shrink is a tall order. Unfortunately, the Greek government has not yet taken up this challenge. It seems certain that if no substantial steps are taken, Greece faces the prospect of losing both a generation of older men and younger men.

There are steps that Greek society can take to improve the situation. These include better guidance for younger and older jobseekers, training programmes that reflect the country's market needs (especially in sectors like farming, shipping, tourism and energy) and incentives and support for new entrepreneurs. What these men need most is an effective tool to provide support in accessing and participating in meaningful learning, relevant to their current experiences, options and lives. It suggests the need for an active learning inclusion strategy that does not refer exclusively to employment and financial resources. Non-material values such as human dignity, respect of differences, participation in civic duties, involvement in social and cultural activities and access to lifelong learning should also be addressed. All of the above are essential elements for ensuring that both younger and older men are empowered and actively participate in Greek society.

References

Age Platform Europe (2012) *Older People also Suffer Because of the Crisis*. Report released in November 2012. Retrieved 18 February 2013 from www.age-platform.eu/images/stories/EN/olderpeoplealsosufferbcofthecrisis-en.pdf

Bettio, F., Corsi, M., D'Ippoliti, C., Lyberaki, A., Samek Lodovici, M. *et al.* (2012) *The Impact of the Economic Crisis on the Situation of Women and Men and on Gender Equality Policies*, Synthesis Report. Brussels: Expert Group on Gender and Employment/European Commission.

Candy, P. (1991) *Self-direction for Lifelong Learning*. San Francisco: Jossey-Bass.

Carré, P. (2002) 'Aprés tant d'années … Jalons pour une théorie psychologique de l'autodirection', in P. Carré, and A. Moisan (Eds.), *La Formation Autodirigée: Aspects Psychologiques et Pédagogiques*. Paris: L'Harmattan, pp. 19–31.

Courtney, S. and Rahe, S. (1992) 'Dimensions of self-directed learning in personal change: The case of weight loss', in H. Long, *et al.* (Eds.), *Self-directed Learning: Application and Research*. Oklahoma: Oklahoma Research Center for Continuing Professional and Higher Education, University of Oklahoma, pp. 355–80.

Deligianni-Kouimtzi, V., Sakka, V., Psalti, A., Frosi, L., Arkoumani, S. *et al.* (2000) *Gender Identities and Life Choices: Final Report*. Thessaloniki: Aristotle University of Thessaloniki (published in Greek).

European Commission (2007) *Demography Report 2007: Europe's Demographic Future: Facts and Figures*, SEC 638. Brussels: European Commission. Retrieved

11 January 2013 from http://ec.europa.eu/employment_social/spsi/docs/social_situation/sec_2007_638_en.pdf.

EUROSTAT (2012) *News-release Euro-indicators*, No. 171/2013. 3 December 2012. Retrieved 3 February 2013 from http://epp.eurostat.ec.europa.eu/cache/ITY_PUBLIC/3-03122012-AP/EN/3-03122012-AP-EN.PDF

EUROSTAT (2013a) *News-release Euro-indicators*, No. 31/2013, 1 March 2013. Retrieved 8 March 2013 from http://epp.eurostat.ec.europa.eu/cache/ITY_PUBLIC/3-01032013-BP/EN/3-01032013-BP-EN.PDF

EUROSTAT (2013b) *News-release Euro-indicators*, No. 40/2013, 14 March 2013. Retrieved 20 March 2013 from epp.eurostat.ec.europa.eu/cache/ITY_PUBLIC/2-14032013-AP/EN/2-14032013-AP-EN.PDF

Foucher, R. and Gousellin, A. (1995) 'Commitment to learner autonomy at Quebec-telephone: A case study of internships and formal recognition of self-acquired knowledge', in H. Long, *et al.* (Eds.), *New Dimensions in Self-directed Learning*. Norman: University of Oklahoma, College of Education: Public Managers Center, pp. 345–66.

Greenwald, B. (2011) *What is Crisis?* Retrieved 12 March 2013 from www.uic.edu/orgs/convening/crisis.htm

Jones, J. (1994) 'Self-confidence and self-directed learning: An overview from social-cognitive psychology', in H. Long *et al.* (Eds.), *New Ideas about Self-directed Learning*. Norman: Oklahoma Research Center for Continuing Professional and Higher Education, University of Oklahoma, pp. 23–38.

Koronaiou A. (2010) 'Women's leisure in Greece: Fighting for "a time of one's own"', in M. Texler Segal (Ed.), *Interactions and Intersections of Gendered Bodies at Work, at Home, and at Play* (Advances in Gender Research, Volume 14), Emerald Group Publishing Limited, pp. 257–73.

Malkoutzis, N. (2011) *Young Greeks and the Crisis: The Danger of Losing a Generation*, International policy analysis report. Berlin: Friedrich-Ebert-Stiftung. Retrieved 16 March 2013 from http://library.fes.de/pdf-files/id/ipa/08465.pdf

McCune, S., Guglielmino, L. and Garcia, G. (1990) 'Adult self-direction in learning: A meta-analytic study of research using the Self Directed Learning Readiness Scale', in H. Long, *et al.* (Eds.), *Adult Self-directed Learning: Emerging Theory and Practice*. Norman: Oklahoma Research Center for Continuing Professional and Higher Education, University of Oklahoma, pp. 145–56.

Oliveira, A., Vieira, C., Lima, M., Nogueira, S., Alcoforado, L. *et al.* (2011) 'Developing instruments to improve learning and development of disadvantage [sic.] seniors in Europe: The PALADIN Project', Paper to The Future of Education Conference, Florence, 16–17 June. Retrieved 11 October 2012 from http://projectpaladin.eu/wp-content/uploads/2011/06/ConferenceFlorence.pdf

Page, N. and Czuba, C. (1999) 'Empowerment: What Is It?', *Journal of Extension*,

37 (5). Retrieved 10 May 2013 from www.joe.org/joe/1999october/comm1.php)

PALADIN (2009) *Promoting Active Ageing and Learning of Disadvantage Seniors.* Retrieved 27 June 2013 from http://projectpaladin.eu

World Bank (2013) Poverty Net, Retrieved 27 June 2013 from http://web.worldbank.org/WBSITE/EXTERNAL/TOPICS/EXTPOVERTY/EXTEMPOWERMENT/0,,contentMDK:20272299~pagePK:210058~piPK:210062~theSitePK:486411~isCURL:Y,00.html

Ziogou-Karastergiou, S. (2006) *Investigating Gender: Historical Dimensions and Contemporary Questioning in General, Vocational and Continuing Education.* Thessaloniki:Vanias (published in Greek).

CHAPTER THIRTEEN

Men's learning in China

Aijing Jin, Zhao Tingyan, Liang Hua and Barry Golding

Introduction

China has attracted a huge amount of interest from around the world
over the last two decades because of its rapid and vigorous economic
development. This growth has brought with it significant social and
structural changes, which have influenced Chinese people's lives in
many different ways. While this chapter will focus on how this has had
an impact on learning by older people, in particular by older men, it is
important to stress at the outset that research based on gender, and of
older men's learning in particular, is not common. This is an exploratory chapter seeking to define the field for future research for possible
international comparisons.

Leading Chinese sociologists describe this period as not simply involving change but 'social transformation' (Han, 2002; Huang, 2002; Liu, 2002;
Guo, 2003; Song, 2003; Wu, 2003). This transformation has involved four
main shifts. First, Chinese society has shifted from traditional to modern
forms of authority. A second shift is evident in the transition from an
agricultural to an industrial and information-based economy. The third
shift is from a relatively 'closed-down' society to one that has 'opened
up'. The fourth shift is from a centrally planned system for managing the
economy to one which is market orientated (Han, 2002; Huang, 2002;
Song, 2003; Wu, 2003).

The symbolic representation of this social transformation is most
noted in the growth and expansion of the economy. China's gross
domestic product (GDP) has been increasing at about eight to nine per

cent per year since the early 1990s, a situation which is unparalleled anywhere else in the world (Huang, 2002). With the population shifting from rural to urban locations, China has been forced to rethink many aspects of its social life and cultural identity that were previously taken for granted and to rethink issues and tensions that are played out in the pursuit of social harmony. A further central issue for China is that the country is becoming an ageing society (Zhang, 2012).

This chapter is focused on older people's education and learning, their learning needs and the channels which they have for accessing learning to improve their overall wellbeing and the quality of their lives. Where possible, the data relating specifically to men and their implications are highlighted.

Social background of older people's learning in China

Chinese older-age education is associated with the social reform and the opening up policy since the 1980s. Deep social transformations have directly affected the content and form of this education. In order to study Chinese older men's learning, we need first to look at several social factors that have influenced their learning. First, the identification of China as an ageing society is steadily becoming a reality. According to China's sixth national census, as of November 2010, the population was 1.34 billion, with 178 million aged 60 or over. This accounts for 13.3 per cent of the population as a whole. It is estimated that the number will reach 216 million by 2015, accounting for 16.7 per cent of the national population (Zhang, 2012). In most urban areas, for most professions (except for professors, doctors, lawyers and the like), 60 years is the age to retire for most men and 55 years is the retirement age for most women. This means that most adults will still live another 20 to 30 years beyond working age according to today's life expectancy in China (Yue, 2012). This puts huge pressures on Chinese society to improve services for old age and to ensure the wellbeing of older people.

Secondly, the process of urbanisation in China is changing the traditional family model. Traditionally, Chinese culture promoted the family structure of up to four generations living together under the same roof with the common view of 'bringing up children for their old age'. A big family was also synonymous with being vigorous, energetic, prosperous, powerful and successful in society, according to traditional Chinese values. Today, rapid social change and the market economy are challenging traditional cultural values. As a result, more and more big families are being replaced by smaller, nuclear families and at least two generations of people are becoming separated from the family residence. Historically, China has been a big agricultural nation, with 80 per cent of the population living in the countryside. Since the 1980s, much of the rural population has moved into urban areas and urbanisation is predicted to reach 50 per cent and beyond by the end of 2013 (Yue, 2012).

Thirdly, from the late 1970s, a 'one couple, one child' policy was put forward as a strategy for controlling population growth. Now, China's first generation of 'one children families' have grown up and have their own families and careers. Their children, the second 'one child' generation, are now young adults. This trend will continue to define mainstream Chinese families in the immediate future, especially in urban areas where substantial changes in values and lifestyles have occurred. This has also contributed to an unravelling of the traditional Chinese family structures in the past two decades. Now a large number of 'empty-nests' (families with no children left at home) are appearing in China (Yue, 2012). According to the sixth national census statistics, as of November 2010, there were 32 per cent empty-nest families among older families in China, bringing huge and diverse demands for public elderly services (Pan, 2012).

In response to this situation, the Chinese government is now promoting a lifelong learning model for older people, put into practice through older people's universities, community activities and social services (Wang, 2012a). Currently, very few programmes focus specifically on older men. Older people's universities are normally organised under the direction of the government, which provides financial support.

Overview of aged people and men's learning in China

As mentioned earlier, Chinese society was traditionally family-oriented. After retirement, while some older men sought re-employment to earn an income to support their families, most preferred to stay at home to look after grandchildren and enjoy the family union and were less willing to participate in social and educational activities aimed at older people. In recent decades, with the increased percentage of aged people in urban areas, elders' education is getting more attention and is developing

(Wang, 2012b). There are a number of different ways of understanding older-aged education. For the majority of older people, learning is understood as comprising a combination of leisure activities, promoting health, keeping fit and preventing loneliness. For the government, academics and other experts in later-life learning, it has been viewed in three ways. One is about the purpose of learning. Here, it is believed that later-life learning should focus on the educational activities that could help improve the quality of their ideological and moral dimension, and in doing so increase knowledge, enrich lives, cultivate character and improve health. Another understanding is linked to the notion of learning across the lifespan. Here it is argued that later-life learning is the final stage of life's journey. The third perspective is related to the intention of the aged learner. Here it is felt that aged people's learning should include activities that add to knowledge, skills and physical and mental health (Zhang, 2012).

Research does not currently distinguish between the needs of men and women. Later life learning is taking place both in formal and informal settings. For older people with professional and business backgrounds before retirement, there is a strong interest in formal learning that fosters the development of new knowledge, enhances social interaction and skills and fulfils their social needs. The vast majority of ordinary people is more interested in informal learning that aims to enrich post-retirement life and meets their spiritual and physical health needs. They do not emphasise knowledge, skills and values, but rather seek a sense of pleasure and happiness. In addition, most older adults are put off by costs of formal learning, which in China is not free. In reality, the government gives more attention to organised, formal education, providing resources and other kinds of support (Wang and Tan, 2009).

The mechanisms and channels of older men's learning in China

The Committee on Ageing and the Civil Affairs Department in China are the main government departments that set policy for later-life learning in China. Education services, especially higher education, are not directly involved in education policy for older people. There are also not enough services offered to older people by the state-run public service system, such as public libraries. While most of the services are provided at community level, with the support of community organisations, planning for older people's education is still in the early stage of development. At the moment, there are four different channels to support older people's learning in China, as summarised below.

1. The Older People's University: A formal institution of education for older men

Older people's universities (老年大学) in China receive government financial support. In most large and medium-sized cities there are a number of such institutions. The organisation of the school buildings, staff, programmes and school terms is similar to other education sectors. Anshan is a medium-sized city in northeast China, where the Older People's University was first established in 1993 under the leadership of the Urban Office of Ageing. Mr Huang Hua, Principal of Anshan Older People's University, said that:

> By the end of 2012, the city's elderly population reached 578,600. However, our school buildings can only arrange and accommodate 800 trainees learning at the moment. The programmes cover courses such as: tai chi, calligraphy, painting, photography, folk dancing, social dancing, traditional Chinese music instruments, paper cutting, and so on. All courses have been designed to promote the health and wellbeing of older people, the demand for arts and humanities subjects, and leisure interests and skill learning. The activities are for men and women and there is no specific gender focus. The main problem is the limitation on numbers and only a small proportion has the opportunity to enrol in the Older People's University, thus making it a kind of 'elite' education. Because of the limited capacity, resources and the popularity of activities which attract the same students year after year, it is only possible to allow a ten per cent entry each year, with a long waiting list resulting. (Personal communication with the Principal of Anshan Older People's University, early 2013)

As for the gender composition of the elderly participants in older people's universities, women are much more likely to be involved than men in most of the universities throughout the country. A survey about the learning needs of elderly college students conducted by Yue and Bao (2003) indicated that the ratio of male and female students was 3:7, similar to ratios in many cities across the country. This situation is expected to continue to grow. The reasons for this are a) that women retire earlier than men, according to China's current policy with the requirement of 60 years for men and 55 years for women; b) on average, females live longer than males and this means that the elderly female population is larger than the male one; c) women usually pay more attention to nutrition and health and as a result they have a better health status than men of the same age and have more energy to participate in learning activities (Yue and Bao, 2003).

2. Community learning: The main channel of learning for most older people

Community learning in China is a local government supported activity. In terms of older people's education and learning in the community, the informal programmes/courses are provided with the guidance of the departments for the civil affairs, health, culture and ageing, based on China's political, economic, cultural, social and ecological situations. Generally, there are three different ways to organise community activities for older people.

a. Flexibly conducting community education for older people based on current community resources and service capacity. For example, by using community libraries and reading rooms to provide health and wellbeing information and knowledge through reading books and journal articles. The community may invite guest speakers to provide seminars or lectures about the information and knowledge of health, legal and policy aspects of education to update their knowledge.

b. The establishment of 'fancier (support) associations', such as, the support association for Beijing Opera (京剧票友会), the chess enthusiast association (棋迷协会), aged choir (老年合唱团), aged fashion team (老年时装表演队), Sunset Red Orchestra (夕阳红乐队), aged rural folk dance (老年秧歌队) and the tai chi association (太极拳). Most participants are male in chess, Beijing Opera and tai chi groups (Zhou, 2010). Older men can exchange ideas and learn from each other to stimulate self-education, self-management and self-motivation while developing a speciality hobby

c. Competition and exhibition activities including painting, calligraphy, paper cutting and photography, to enrich learners' knowledge and lives. All of these activities promote healthy leisure behaviours with the purpose of helping older people with their beliefs, emotions, attitudes, knowledge, skills, education and improving their quality of life.

3. Social service agencies: The new starting point for elderly male education

In China, community services specifically for older people are still in the early stage of development. For example, we will look at the current situation in Shanghai, China's biggest city and most economically developed area. The data from an investigation into the demand for public services in the community and social organisations conducted within 1,709 social service organisations in seven districts of the Shanghai area (Wang *et al.*, 2013) indicated that, despite 24 per cent of these organisations having an older people's service function, the number one ranked issue for older people was the gap between supply and demand. On average, each service organisation attempts to meet the needs of over 3,000 people. The research indicated that 91 per cent of communities hope to develop organisations providing educational services for the elderly. At the same time, services to address older men's education and learning professionally are still in the stage of government policy planning and have not really taken off yet in practice (Wang *et al.*, 2013).

Most existing professional service organisations are located in Shenzhen and other economically developed areas, such as the establishment of Shenzhen JiuJiu older people's classroom in December 2010. Under the leadership of the local Bureau of Civil Affairs and Ageing Committee, the aims of the classroom are said to promote community harmony and improve the overall wellbeing of older people. It is a non-degree programme, involving non-profit, later-life learning that provides a variety of activities for the elderly in the community, such as cultural learning, sports and entertainment, health care, laws and regulations. Older people can choose to participate in different activities based on their own interests and hobbies in order to improve their skills. Consistent with the underlying concept of 'edutainment' (寓教于乐), the activities are organised in a practical manner to meet the diverse needs of older people in the community.

4. Other forms and means of education for aged people

In addition to the above modes of education, the most popular way of learning for older people in China is through self-education, connected closely to the cultural traditions of self-reflection and self-improvement. Learning can occur watching TV, listening to radio broadcasts and reading newspapers and magazines specifically for older people: for example, 'ageing newspapers' and 'health news', subscribed to largely by the older age group. The internet is also a popular way to access a variety of information for older people aged 60 to 70 years who have good educational backgrounds and economic capacity. In this field, men dominate (Wang, 2012a). There is also a Labour Office (or Union) in most state-owned enterprises, government departments and agencies, schools, and other institutions that provides health counselling, cultural entertainment, social activities and other services for older people, which has become a unique form and channel of education and learning for many. However, it has not yet formed a gender-based elderly male education and learning system.

Conclusion

Due to the improving economic conditions and social security system for older people, the rapid process of urbanisation, lifestyle changes, family structure changes with the one child policy, as well as government-led expansion of the construction of a harmonious society, the conception of education for older people in China has been established, bringing many changes. However, changes are still at an early stage of development and little research has been focused on the needs of older men. Most of the educational programmes and learning activities for older people are aimed at both genders. With resource constraints for formal and organised learning, the main methods of older people's learning are non-formal and lack clear learning goals. Factors such as educational level, economic power and pre-retirement professional experience directly affect older people's learning and achievement levels. The improvement of older people's material life will lead to the pursuit of the spiritual life, which is consistent with human development. The increase of 'empty nest' older families is becoming a universal phenomenon of Chinese social life and a considerable proportion of older people will choose to enrich their lives through formal and informal learning and activities, which means the demand for later-life learning will continue to grow. In general, because older people's educational needs are diverse the service cannot meet these needs. In this respect, public services responsible for ageing have to be improved, professional services need to be established and promoted. Services based on gender difference may also need to be established where appropriate.

References

Guo, D. (2003) 'Chinese social transformation in the 20th century', *Studies in Ethics*, 1, 2003, pp. 7–9.

Han, Q. (2002) 'Social transformation in contemporary Chinese society', *Modern Philosophy*, 3, pp. 27–35.

Huang, L. (2002) 'Contemporary Chinese social transformation and reconstruction of values', *Sociology Studies*, 2, pp. 36–42.

Liu, Z. (2002) 'Review on characteristics of social transformation in current China', *Wuhan University Journal (Humanity Sciences)*, 55 (6), pp. 28–31.

Pan. L. (2012) 'The exploration about the function and mechanism of older people's education in China', *Adult Education*, 2, pp. 78–81.

Song, L. (2003) 'The trend, sacrifice and measurement of the social transformation in China', *Sociology Studies*, No. 3, pp. 30–6.

Wang, Q. (2012a) 'Community education for the aged people and elderly socialization', *Adult Education*, 9, pp. 48–51.

Wang, X., Chao, G., Liu, B. and Yang, S. (2013) *Speeding up the process of ageing: Old before getting rich, the test to the older people's services.* Retrieved 1 May 2013 from http://news.xinhuanet.com/fortune/2012-03/11/c_111636947.htm

Wang, Y. (2012b) 'The equalization on old-age education', *Education for Senior Citizens*, 10, pp. 17–18.

Wang, Y. and Tan, L. (2009) 'Non-formal education and social participation of older people', *Journal of Population Studies*, 4, pp. 41–2.

Wu, Z. (2003) 'The basic features of Chinese social transformation in the 20th century', *Sociology Studies*, 3, pp. 98–104.

Yue, Y. (2012) 'Analysis of the current demand and potential demand for old-age education', *Chinese Journal of Gerontology*, 20, pp. 8–11.

Yue, Y. and Bao, H. (2003) 'The investigation report about elderly college students' learning needs', *Journal of Tianjin Academy of Educational Science*, 6, pp. 55–8.

Zhang, Z. (2012) 'Summary of research on older people's education in China', *Journal of Tianjin TV University*, 3.

Zhou, D. (2010) 'The characteristics of the old-age education needs based on the development of old-age education', *Adult Education*, 10, pp. 14–19.

CHAPTER FOURTEEN

Men's learning in Australia

Barry Golding and Annette Foley

Introduction

Men's learning, wellbeing and health remained relatively un-problematised in Australia until a decade ago. Women have previously (for good reasons) been identified as an equity target group in many areas of education and health, though this picture is changing. Work in Australia in many sectors of education and health services remains comprehensively gendered. Adult and community education in Australia is attempting to re-invent itself in the wake of two national reports in the 1990s alluding to it as a primarily women's (*Cinderella*) sector (Aulich, 1991; Crowley, 1997). New research has identified the difficult situation experienced beyond education and work for men. Australia's national health policy highlights concerning statistics in relation to some men's broader health and wellbeing in Australia. Particular groups of men are at risk through effective exclusion from (or opting out of) existing education and health programmes and services, particularly some Aboriginal and Torres Strait Islander (Indigenous) men, older men, men living in rural areas as well as men who have had limited success at school.

Research into the Australian men's shed movement and in diverse community settings, as elaborated in Chapter Eight, has thrown new light on the relationships between men's learning and wellbeing. There is broad national and community consensus that while Australian women remain relatively disadvantaged in many areas of employment, policies and practices, they are in ascendancy in terms of formal educational aspirations and outcomes. There is significant value in turning some of the attention to several areas of men's health and education that are perceived as ripe for change. This chapter includes the identification, description and evaluation of several examples of good practice involving men and boys, inclusive of Indigenous men's learning from different parts of Australia.

Recent trends across Australia

Martin (2007) undertook a review of Australian skill acquisition across the lifecourse. The standout demographic finding relating to men was the withdrawal of prime-aged men (between 25 and 54 years) from the labour force (p. 7). Other findings for men were that men aged 25 to 29 are increasingly likely to either live with parents or alone (p. 18). Indeed, only one-quarter of men in this age group lived with their partner. Amongst men in their 40s and also over 50, there is a trend away from couples living together and a trend towards men living alone (p. 18). Martin also found that men's work roles in Australia have declined and diversified over recent decades (2007, p. 19). However:

> *Men's declining labour force participation is not predominantly a chosen shift towards a lifecourse that does not require they work full-time though much of their adult life. Instead, it reflects declining opportunities for men, especially those with low formal skills.*
> (Martin, 2007, p. 19)

Consistent with this trend of decline in male workforce participation is a concerning trend (for governments) of the steady departure in the past three decades of qualified male tradespersons from trades occupations after their mid 20s (Martin, 2007, p. 34). Since men tend not to re-enter these trades in large numbers, there is a skills shortage in many trades which traditionally employed men. While there have been significant increases in the proportion of men and women undertaking full- and part-time study across all age groups since the early 1980s, women's participation has risen several times faster than men's (albeit from a lower base), and now surpasses that of men.

Aside from the changing numbers, the key finding of Martin (2007) relevant to our account of men learning through life in Australia is that men of all ages in this current decade (2010–19) are experiencing life transitions very differently from how their parents and grandparents experienced things. The traditional lifecourse model (Martin, 2007, p. 22) of men flowing through life from school into post-secondary education, to full-time work, partnering and marriage, skills upgrade, empty nesting and retirement at 65 has been significantly altered for many men and other family members. Aside from the longer term trend of men living longer post-retirement, the main change is that men's participation in the workforce and education have been declining and flat-lining respectively, while women have been working, earning and learning more.

These changes in roles from 'men mainly earning' to 'women learning and earning', which are partly embodied in the title of McGivney's (1999) UK book, are explicable and in many ways desirable in terms of gender equity. However, many working age men in retirement with the lowest levels of formal education and the least likelihood of re-entering paid work or learning later in life in Australia have found themselves confused, stranded and with a greatly diminished quality of later life. The phenomenal growth of men's sheds across Australia can arguably be linked to some of the demographic changes identified by Martin (2007).

Gender segmentation

Men's learning and wellbeing are important issues in Australia for men of all ages, particularly for: men not in paid work, those with lower socioeconomic status and low levels of formal education, and Indigenous Australians. The evidence comes from the workplace, from post-compulsory education, and men's health and wellbeing statistics, as well as literacy and life skills surveys.

Unlike most schooling, post-school education and training and the paid workforce remain highly segmented according to gender. Indeed, Australia has one of the most gender-segmented workforces in the developed world. Women comprise around three-quarters of employees in healthcare and social assistance and education, and men more than 75 per cent in construction, mining, essential services, transport and manufacturing (AWPA, pp. 13–14).

A report, titled *Australia's Skills and Workplace Development Needs* (AWPA, 2012), emphasises a significant decline over the past three decades in male workplace participation, almost all of it 'accounted for by men who left school early and have no further qualifications' (p. 12). Between 1970 and 1983, the employment to population ratio of men aged 60 to 64 declined from 76.7 per cent to 39.8 per cent (*ibid.*). Though the early part of this decline was associated with men in older age, in recent decades it has broadened to include younger men (age 35 to 54) and has also been linked to men with a disability or health-related problems. Of all Australians on Disability Support Pensions (DSP) in Australia in 2010, men comprise 54.5 per cent, and 35.8 per cent are men aged 45 years and older (AWPA, 2012).

Men in Australia are less likely than women to be involved in most forms of post-school education at any age, despite data showing that:

> *A lack of qualification is not such a barrier for women as it is for men, given the loss of traditionally 'masculine' low skilled jobs associated with production sectors, and the rise of jobs in female-dominated services such as retail, hospitality and the community care sector.* (AWPA, 2012, p. 12)

The importance of a range of literacies is recognised for adults of all ages, not only from the point of view of the labour market, but increasingly for an individual's ability to function in modern society. Men in most nations tend to have somewhat lower prose literacy skills ('the ability to understand and use information from various kinds of narrative texts': ABS, 2008) than women. Close to one-half (47.5 per cent) of Australian men are more likely to be at the lowest (Level 1 and 2) prose skill levels, severely limiting their understanding of texts from newspapers, magazines and brochures. While men's document literacy (essential for job applications, payroll forms, maps and tables) is only marginally higher (45 per cent of men have below minimum functional Level 3), men and women have similarly low numeracy skills, problem solving skills and very low health literacy skills (required to understand and use information on health issues such as drugs, alcohol, safe first aid and emergencies): 47.5 per cent, 59.7 per cent and 60.3 per cent below Level 3 respectively (ABS, 2008).

Lattimore (2007) conducted the most comprehensive review of men outside the labour force in Australia. Coming out of the Australian Productivity Commission, its underlying concern was the economic and social impacts of premature withdrawal from the paid workforce of many prime aged males (referred to as 'economically inactive') 'due to injury, ill health, disability and premature retirement' (Lattimore, 2007, p. xix). While age-related withdrawal was found to play 'a big differentiating role in inactivity rates' (p. xxii), four intersecting factors were identified as being associated with these high rates: men being un-partnered, having low levels of educational attainment, being Indigenous or being a migrant to Australia (pp. xxii–xxiv).

Lattimore also identified a number of key reasons for men's economic inactivity, which vary with lifecycle events (Lattimore, 2007, p. xxvii). For example, in younger age cohorts many men are not in paid work because of education and training. In midlife, it is more likely to be ill health and caring or home duties, and in later years retirement or voluntary inactivity. Lattimore concluded that the most socially and economically challenging aspect of economic inactivity by males is the significance of illness and disability as the motivation for detachment. Of particular interest in this chapter is the strong relationship between educational level, as measured by attainment of qualifications, and men's engagement in the labour force. One in 20 post-graduate men are not in the workforce, compared to one in two with Year 10 or below educational attainment (p. xxiii). Lattimore drew the obvious connection between boys staying on at school, and entering and remaining in the labour market at older ages (p. xxxii).

Lattimore's study looked at educational and occupational characteristics of men outside the labour force (Lattimore, 2007, pp. 47–50), concluding that the links between education and labour force status were so complex they warranted extra analysis (Lattimore, 2007, pp. 187–227; pp. 229–51). In the analysis of education and participation, Lattimore made several observations of interest based on a range of statistics: for example, that less educated men have become more vulnerable than other men when not in paid work, while women have not. In his analysis of education and participation, Lattimore concluded that conventional inferences saying that more education is always better for labour market performance are not well founded, particularly for 'non-academically oriented male students [who] tend to receive smaller (absolute) benefit from additional schooling than their academically oriented peers' (p. 226). In effect, more mandatory schooling 'might be seen as asking a sub-group of non-academically oriented students to do more of what has so far served them badly' (p. 226), akin to Gorard's (2010) concerns about the discourse of 'barriers' to participation, which were discussed in Chapter Two.

Lattimore's (2007) conclusions are validated by research on outcomes from lower level qualifications for prime-aged people (25 to 44) as well as from those over 45 years (mature aged) in Australia (Stanwick, 2006). Stanwick showed that 'there were no substantial vocational and further study outcomes for prime and mature aged people who had undertaken Certificate I and II qualifications', despite employment-related reasons being the main motivation for undertaking the courses, particularly for men (p. 6). Only one in ten people employed before taking up a course were employed afterwards, though men employed afterwards were twice as likely to be working full time (rather than part time) than women.

A brief history of research on men's learning in Australia

Men as a learner group were virtually un-problematised in Australia until the mid 1990s. Indeed, the 1991 Australian Senate reports, *Come in Cinderella: The Emergence of Adult and Community Education* (Aulich, 1991) and *Beyond Cinderella: Towards a Learning Society* (Crowley, 1997), were named because of the then pride within the ACE sector of attracting and meeting the specific adult education needs of women.

Approximately two decades ago, older men began to be the main object of the relatively small body of research into male learning, replacing the previous focus on boy's learning. A gerontologist (incidentally instrumental in some of the earliest Australian community men's sheds in South Australia) researching successful ageing in Australia found that men were less socially competent, less language skilled and less willing to do things than were women (Earl and Earl, 1996). The Leigh Report (1997) that investigated positive ageing in Victoria was one of the first in Australia to explicitly identify men generally (along with people from non-English speaking backgrounds and rural dwellers) as under-represented adult learners. Concern 'regarding the trauma experienced by men and the alarmingly high incidence of men's depression and suicide particularly in rural areas' in Western Australia (LCL, 2002, 2004) was provoked in part by the 1999 *Report of the Committee Reviewing Family and Parent Support Services for Men* (FCS, 1999).

A citation from Hurworth (1995, p. 37) is one of the earliest acknowledgements and explanations in Australian literature of the reasons for men's low participation in adult education. Specifically, men's low participation was seen to be associated with their perceived relative fulfilment after paid work, their preference for outdoor activities, their lack of enjoyment in joining groups, their fear of not knowing things when in learning contexts, their lack of response to structured learning environments and their perceptions of neighbourhood and community centres as 'women's domains'. Each of these themes has re-appeared in the two decades of research since, albeit in different combinations.

International dissemination of McGivney's (1999) men's learning research in the UK coincided with research since the mid 1990s in Australia into masculinities and underachievement by boys. Connell's work on masculinities in Australia (Connell, 1995) and the *Boys: Getting it Right* (2002) report brought to prominence some of the issues for Australian men, largely to do with wellbeing, as well as for boys, focused mainly on schooling. By 2003, *Campus Review* was featuring articles by Maslen (2003) with claims that 'Women are the dominant sex in education'. Marks' (2000) research linking UK health policies and lifelong learning as it applied to working-class males also combined to stir up Australian researchers and policymakers in some related fields in Australia post–2000.

Some of these ideas presumably permeated to some of the thinking in the *Keeping the Balance: Older Men and Healthy Ageing* report by the Men's Health Information and Resource Centre (MHIRC) for the NSW (New South Wales) Committee on Ageing (MHIRC, 2001). Aside from being authored and informed by Anthony Brown, an important influence behind the early men's shed movement in NSW (with a small number of community men's sheds already active in 2001 in South Australia, NSW and Victoria), the MHIRC report was influential since, as Byrne put it, it identified:

> social isolation as having a major negative impact on older men's health and wellbeing, so – apart from the course – the very act of encouraging older men to talk about their lives would have beneficial effects. (2002, p. 12)

The gendered patterns of adult learning, with women in a significant majority in education and training programmes in small and remote towns, was first identified in Golding and Rogers' (2001) study and was further elaborated in Golding (2002). This led Golding to undertake a suite of research over the next decade into men's learning in diverse community organisations in small and remote towns in Victoria (Golding *et al.*, 2005), through fire and emergency service organisations in Australia (Hayes *et al.*, 2004), community men's sheds (Golding *et al.*,

2007), a national study of older men's learning (Golding *et al.*, 2009b) and a study of men's learning in Western Australia (Golding *et al.*, 2009a). In totality, this suite of research found that men most at risk of not engaging in further formal learning were those who, for whatever reason, are not in paid work, despite also being those whose wellbeing would benefit most from the many outcomes associated with further learning.

This research challenges widespread government policy discourse that more education and training is all that is necessary to ensure that men of working age are in the paid workforce, aside from those men who don't want to work. As an example, of all Victorians not in the labour force (and not on long-term unpaid leave) in December 2010, 41 per cent would like to return to or start work (ABS, 2010). The most common reason preventing such people, who had already undertaken paid work, from returning to work was not to do with skills, as one would expect. Rather, almost one-half (49 per cent) reported personal ill health, disability, injury or having children as the main reason. One in eight (12 per cent) believed work was not available and one in ten (11 per cent) had a caring role that prevented then from taking up education.

Key mentions of men's learning in Australia that preceded or paralleled Golding's early studies of men's learning in community settings in Victoria included suggestions in the ANTA *National Marketing Strategy for VET* (Thomas, 2001) of strategies for helping promote learning for people, including men, with negative attitudes towards structured learning. Byrne undertook a two-stage study commissioned by the WEA Board 'into adult learning in clubs and other informal settings with a view to increasing the participation of males in the Discussion Group Programme [DGP]' (Byrne, 2001, p. 3, citing WEA Board meeting resolution, 4 August 2000). It specifically researched how men learnt, how men related to adult education and how the DGP met men's needs based on existing research, enrolment statistics, a very small survey and discussions.

Byrne (2001) deliberately distinguished his Stage One study for the Workers' Education Association (WEA) in Sydney from McGivney's (1999) study, though based his research heavily on some of its findings. Aside from being conducted in Australia, Byrne paid more attention to 'the learning aspirations of older men (the over 55s who constitute the bulk of male DGP members)' (Byrne, 2001, p. 4). While some of the research approaches and findings are now dated, Byrne's findings about older men's learning in Australia, based on the limited research and data then available, remain robust over a decade later. Byrne (2001, p. 12) concluded that 'Successful adult education initiatives involving older men tend to share the same characteristics': they work from the 'ground up', involve the teaching of practical skills, provide the opportunity for men to share existing knowledge or to serve the community, are specifically concerned with addressing men's issues and have come about after intensive and targeted promotion. Each of these findings anticipated many of the later learning-related findings of the community men's sheds research (Golding *et al.*, 2007).

Byrne's (2002) Stage 2 report canvassed possible strategies for improving male participation rates, including in other, less traditional, ACE environments and beyond in diverse community settings. Many of Byrne's suggested strategies, like Golding *et al.*'s adult and community education research, at least in retrospect and without naming them, pointed towards community men's sheds as one likely future solution.

Insights from studies of neighbourhood houses

Both the Western Australian *Bringing in the Blokes* (LCL, 2002, 2004) study and the *Growing the Generations* study (Harris, 2004) in Victoria came out of concerns that ACE (adult and continuing education) organisations, including learning centres and neighbourhood houses, tended not to be used by men. An earlier study of such places (Kimberley, 1998) discussed the dilemma that had grown and proliferated since the early 1970s. Largely established by women, predominantly to serve women's needs, they claimed to be inclusive of the whole community but were really not so. Golding *et al.* (2008) drew many parallels (and some differences) between the genesis and growth since the 1970s of neighbourhood houses mainly for women, and the genesis and growth of men's sheds from the late 1990s. While neighbourhood houses were in many ways a critical bridge for women between family and paid work, men's sheds were more a bridge beyond work, including for men who had experienced what the Human Rights and Equal Opportunities Commission (HREOC, 2005) described as 'broken working lives' because of unemployment or illness, not because they chose to do something other than paid work. Arguably this working pattern is damaging to men's physical, mental and emotional health; it bestows on them the overwhelming financial responsibility for family, insufficient breaks from workplace stress and insufficient time to devote to family and intimate relationships.

Principles emerging from the research

Before summarising some of the principles that this Australian research confirms, it is useful to return to some of the general findings from McGivney, who suggested that to widen participation in learning, including for men,

> *We need to recognise just how deep the economic, social and cultural divides in society actually are. Under-representation in organised learning is just one dimension of the multiple and inter-related forms of social exclusion many people face.* (2006, p. 102)

Gorard and Rees (2002) summarised what research shows overall: it is more likely that an equal society will lead to wider participation rather than wider participation in learning leading to a more equal society.

While the ways in which Australian education is perceived by boys and men is qualitatively different, these are in the most part a mirror of an historic and persistent gender segmentation in work, family and society, exacerbated by an adult, higher and vocational education system in which already highly educated and fully employed people of all ages have persistently higher rates of participation. Introducing market mechanisms into a system in which more education and more work are already self-reinforcing stands to make things far worse for adults with limited prior experiences of education, and become intergenerational for children, families and communities. Being able to talk about the systemic issues affecting and isolating some men and allowing men not in paid work to have voice and agency is essential in transforming the wellbeing of all men, boys, families and communities.

One of several difficulties is that the service sectors in which men not in paid work are more likely to interact with and potentially benefit from – welfare, aged care, community services and adult education, for example – are typically comprehensively gendered towards women in terms of staff, services and clients. On top of all these difficulties, place also plays a big part in Australian men's opportunities to access learning in any form that is accessible in terms of embedded literacies and which suits their interests, needs and pedagogies.

It is the notion that education and training is primarily or only about work and vocations that perpetuates the problem. In 1997, the *Beyond Cinderella* report complained about the conceptual inadequacy in funding mechanisms that differentiate:

> *between educational programs on the grounds of their perceived or declared vocational orientation. This vocational/non-vocational divide fails to accommodate the rich harvest of various kinds of educational experiences that make up a learning society. It also muddies thinking, distorts values, and perpetuates a whole lot of unhelpful divisions – between private gain and social benefit; between the market and domestic spheres; between men's work and women's work; between short term interests and ling term gains.* (Crowley, 1997, p. 3)

Such funding mechanisms perpetuate and exacerbate discrimination by age and income as well as by gender in both directions. Men and women who are retired or withdrawn from paid work because of family, age, disability, illness or caring roles are particularly discriminated against because, whatever they do and achieve in terms of learning, they are not necessarily valued, supported or recognised.

It is also important to acknowledge that some of the issues that men face are not to do with learning, but the un-friendliness of some work-places towards their identities as men, towards their health and wellbeing, as well as towards their age (including from employers *and* younger employees: NSA, 2010). 'It is mostly men, often fathers, who work long hours in the paid workforce' (HREOC, 2005, p. 21). Many men not in paid work are, or were previously, damaged by work and its excesses and imbalances, physically and psychologically. Others have families and lives severely affected by men's excesses at work and by their associated risk-taking and self-harming behaviour in and beyond work. Much of the 'new' un-skilled and semi-skilled, part time and casual work in Australia (most of it relatively poorly paid in hospitality, retail, personal and community services) is seen as women's work, and not inclusive of men's (and employers') perceptions and expectations of male identities, strengths and skills.

The main value of all learning for men is to their lives, including but going well beyond men's paid work, to include their identities, well-being, children, partners and communities. The pedagogies developed within and practised by the men's shed movement have as much to teach educators and other service providers as they do the men themselves. These pedagogies work to engage and connect men in learning opportunities and health and wellbeing benefits through creative and authentic approaches. Few adults enjoy being patronised as clients, customers, students or patients. Adults benefit most from learning that builds on what they know and can do and which promotes agency and mentoring, not learning which sifts and sorts them on the basis of what they do not know or cannot do from a deficit model. While some men are already passionate and self-directed learners, most men in Australia benefit from learning *through life*, particularly through activities that are safe, healthy and salutogenic (health promoting).

For men with least confidence and experience with learning, and often the most difficult experiences of life and work, the key, ironically, is not to foreground and name education, teaching, training or literacy in the activity. Promoting hands-on skills through productive, informal, practical activity in familiar safe, social and community settings re-inforces the many values of activity, friendships, fitness, health, relationships and particularly identities. As Wallace argued in an Australian study of reluctant learners, recognising learner identities is the key to educational engagement. 'By validating learners' identities, the education system develops its understanding of students, their knowledge and social context' (Wallace, 2008, p. 13). Wallace concluded that a community-centred approach to learning maintains learner integrity while negotiating other forms of knowledge, literacy and identity on learner terms, and develops pedagogies in partnership with community members rather than serving up only one form of learning.

Men with the most difficulties, both in life and with their identities, often prefer, and are more likely to progress in, contexts where men are the main participants and fellow mentors. Such approaches can be truly re-creational: aside from preparing men for possible paid work, being well is a prerequisite for re-creating and coping with other life issues, including unemployment, separation, ageing, disability and retirement. But again, the key is to encourage men to learn through developing, sharing and enjoying lives and identities beyond those associated with paid work and home.

Most powerfully, as Marks (2000) stresses, lifelong learning can address the World Health Organization's social determinants of health (Wilkinson and Marmott, 2003) and also save men's lives.

This is not wild hyperbole: if these men can find something that expands their intellectual horizons, draws them out of the narrow confines of their own lives, and shows them that there is more to life, they will have gained a reason to live … If health practitioners are similarly committed and can offer support to the lifelong learning community, then we may be able to stop the rot of misplaced masculinity and save at least one generation of men from themselves. (Marks, 2000, p. 13)

Vignettes of good practice in men's learning

The intention of this set of vignettes of good practice in men's learning in Australia is to provide pointers to others on what can work, rather than critiquing and theorising what does not.

Learning through men's sheds

Chapter Eight provides a comprehensive analysis of some learning-related aspects of community men's sheds. Their particular value lies in the ability of the shed model to be adapted to local and community imperatives. There are hundreds of good examples but we will restrict ourselves to four: sheds in a capital city, a regional city, a rural town and remote Indigenous men's sheds.

- The Fremantle Men's Shed (Fremanshed, 2012) just south of Perth was one of the earliest sheds in Western Australia. It has been a leader in education innovation through men's sheds. Two skilled ex-teachers with a vision of something better and different for men not in paid work and an excellent background knowledge of vocational and school education have used the shed, a converted pigeon club, to create a remarkable community of practice to involve a wide range of community members, including men and boys of all ages, embracing men with a disability, young Aboriginal boys and older retired men.
- The Dubbo Community Men's Shed in New South Wales has similarly been based around a two-person collaboration between an ex-policeman and a local Aboriginal elder. The shed's logo of a black and white handshake encapsulates the approach taken to improve race relations within a large regional city (40,000 people, including 12 per cent Indigenous Australians) where people's

experiences and life outcomes have previously been very much divided by race. The shed has published a book based on shedders' experiences (Dubbo, 2012).

- The Donald Men's Shed in Victoria operates as an extension of the Donald Neighbourhood House and Learning Centre. On a separate site within the local showgrounds and sports oval, the shed has undertaken numerous community projects of significant benefit to the small (population of 1,500) rural community during a protracted series of drought years. Most of the men who participate are older retired farmers and tradespeople. The Buloke Shire, the local government area that includes Donald, has a total population of only 8,000 people, including a high proportion of older rural residents. The Shire supports four other very vibrant and active men's sheds that have transformed the lives of a significant proportion of older men. The shed co-ordinator has written a practice-based account in Vallance and Golding (2008).

- Indigenous men's sheds and men's groups in mainly rural and remote Australia have achieved some traction, which client-based programmes for Aboriginal men have found very difficult to do. In recognition of this, the Australian government has had separate funding rounds to support this grassroots activity. Men's sheds and men's groups 'provide a safe, friendly and inclusive environment where Aboriginal and Torres Strait Islander males can connect with their elders and work on traditional and cultural activities' (Snowden, 2012). While the underlying aim for governments is men's health, the learning and broader wellbeing associated with active engagement in this traditional and cultural activity is significant in very small communities with minimal access to 'top-down' services.

Learning through football clubs

Though not often considered as learning organisations, the many learning opportunities facilitated through sports clubs are significant, as identified in Chapter Six. The main football codes in Australia, in order of men's participation, are Australian rules, rugby (league and union) and the 'round' football (called 'soccer' in Australia). All football codes except soccer play through the winter months and have traditionally been men's sports, though this is changing, and all are very important in terms of men's informal learning, community and social capital. At a place-based, community level, the winter football codes, typically in close association with women's netball, become the main focus for team-based weekend activity in Australia for players and spectators. In most rural towns, sport, particularly football for men and netball for women, directly or indirectly engages most of the community. As community size decreases, the importance of sport and the proportion of men involved increases exponentially to a point where around two-thirds of men are connected in some way in many towns of less than 1,000 inhabitants. Football in many remote Indigenous communities has become the main focus for the men's expression and exchange of community and Indigenous cultural identity.

The learning goes well beyond what football players learn through regular and intensive training: about working as a team, staying healthy, avoiding and recovering from injury, team strategies and individual sporting skills. Each football club relies primarily on volunteers for training, coaching, mentoring and organising the multi-ability and multi-age team competitions and weekly games and fundraising, as well as representing the club through league competitions. All of this football activity is conducted in an environment where sport, once associated with smoking and alcohol advertising, has increasingly become a focus for encouraging Indigenous and multi-racial involvement and respect, as well as for community health and wellbeing programmes. While the association between football clubs and gambling activity continues, all clubs are undertaking strategies to make themselves and their players positive role models for men and boys, which in 2012 started to include gay men at the elite levels of football in Australia. All of the associated informal learning activity is arguably more powerful and inclusive educationally than what can be achieved for men through formal and compulsory education. A number of football clubs, leagues, educational organisations and communities have recognised the potential for collaboration between football and learning, aside from Clontarf (2013), mentioned in Chapter Six.

Learning through volunteer fire brigades

There are approximately 200,000 volunteer members in the mostly rural and regional 5,500 fire services and brigades across Australia, with additional volunteers involved in emergency services and coast rescue organisations, some of whom are partly paid (mainly for training and callouts) as 'retained' fire fighters. While most fire service volunteers (around 90 per cent) are men, all Australian fire services are actively encouraging more women to join. Meanwhile, entrenched negative attitudes persist within the service to working alongside women. During the past decade, in response to the tragic death of fire volunteers and subsequent inquiries, the formality and necessity of accredited training has greatly increased.

The learning that now takes place for fire volunteers through formal and informal training, retraining and response to real incidents is typically hands-on and accredited. As with sporting clubs, as community size decreases, the importance of sport and the proportion of men and the learning involved increases exponentially. Fire and other emergency services volunteers are required to maintain competencies and readiness at any time using a wide range of skills. Again, a number of fire organisations, educational organisations and communities have recognised the potential for collaboration between fire and emergency services volunteering and learning. This voluntary sector arguably engages more men in Australia in more regular, post-compulsory accredited training than any other activity beyond paid work, and results in completion of one of the most common forms of accredited training beyond paid work that most men beyond capital cities will undertake.

Learning through surf clubs

While Australia is a huge continent, its population is disproportionately located towards the coast in the southwest and east. Indeed, 85 per cent of all Australians live within the narrow coastal strip less than 50km from the relatively high-energy coastline, where being safe on beaches in surf is an important public and community concern. With more than 153,000 members, of whom around 44,000 actively patrol over 400 Australian beaches (SLSA, 2013), surf lifesaving clubs, like fire brigades, rely almost totally on appropriately trained volunteers.

Surf Life Saving Australia (SLSA) has close to 60,000 junior members, or 'Nippers' as they are more commonly known, aged between five and 13 years, who learn beach safety and awareness skills in a fun and healthy environment (SLSA, 2013). AUSTSWIM, the national water safety organisation, has around 25,000 accredited teachers (AUSTSWIM, 2013). Surf lifesavers must be competent swimmers, as well as experienced in rescue, resuscitation and first aid. This experience is gained in a minimum of 20 hours training and followed by a written and practical examination (SLSA, 2013). The hands on, intergenerational learning, in a mostly outdoor, beach and pool environment, is highly effective for boys and men and, with its associated community education and school programmes, is designed to cut across gender, age, cultural background and physical ability (SLSA, 2013). As with fire fighting, it teaches and encourages safety and provides many men and boys with a critically important combination of valuable skills and community identities with much wider applicability beyond their specific and primary safety foci.

Learning though organisations for gay men

Being a gay man and learning about how to negotiate living an openly gay lifestyle in Australia is not easy, particularly within communities and contexts where homophobia and discrimination persists. While increasingly supported by laws against such discrimination and homophobia, it is difficult for many men to publicly 'come out' as gay because there is neither a proper community understanding of being gay (lesbian or trans-gender) nor safe places where gay men can gather and support each other.

Our research into older men's learning in Australia (Golding *et al.*, 2009b) identified clubs at the level of community that tend not to be highly visible but which provide essential mutual support for Australian gay and trans-sexual men. Community organisations included in our study included a swimming club specifically for the mutual support of HIV positive gay men in western Sydney and an organisation supporting gay men in south suburban Adelaide. Men's narratives in these studies confirmed how many aspects of learning are achieved informally through meeting in safe places. It also revealed how unsafe many such men feel when gathering in some public places: indeed the latter organisation typically meets in private. In both cases, the clubs were only able to operate with a 'filter' to screen men whose intentions were not seen as consistent with the group themes of mutual understanding and support.

Conclusion

Much of Golding's research in Australia from the early 2000s was critical of the way most adult and community education organisations in Australia tended not to acknowledge or be inclusive of men in their organisations, staffing and programmes. This has changed in part because of a number of factors and initiatives summarised below, taken from

McIntyre's (2007) evaluation of the 2005–06 circles of professional research practice in Victoria led by the chapter authors, which included men's learning research circles. McIntyre's evaluation noted the value and need for ACE to 'reach out more directly to men' through personal contact, and specifically:

- the importance of food and cooking classes in an informal atmosphere;
- the need to present and promote ACE using male images and voices;
- increasing the effectiveness of ACE through partnerships;
- the need for alternative, informal venues appropriate to men;
- the challenge for ACE to accommodate men's sheds in an ACE setting;
- constructing learning activities so there is a pathway that starts at an accessible point and the challenge of finding funding to support this;
- men's learning requires a cultural shift by a whole organisation. (McIntyre, 2007, p. 24)

Later research has identified the value of encouraging and including men on ACE centre committees and employing men with expertise in men's community engagement (Golding *et al.*, 2009b). It is of some interest (tinged also with some concern) that since these research circles and McIntyre's (2007) evaluation, the number and reach of men's sheds in Australia in 2013 significantly exceeds the number and reach of conventional ACE providers, due both to the huge growth in men's sheds and progressive government defunding of many parts of ACE's networks, programs and services across Australia.

References

ABS: Australian Bureau of Statistics (2008) *Adult Literacy and Life Skills Survey: Summary Results*, Cat. No. 4228. Canberra: ABS.

ABS: Australian Bureau of Statistics (2010) *Workplace Participation and Workplace Flexibility, Victoria*, Cat. No. 6210.2. Canberra: ABS.

Aulich, T. (1991) *Come in Cinderella: The Emergence of Adult and Community Education*, Report of the Senate Standing Committee on Employment, Education and Training. Canberra: Senate Printing Unit.

AUSTSWIM (2013) Retrieved 4 June 2013 from www.austswim.com.au

AWPA: Australian Workplace and Productivity Agency (2012) *Australia's Skills and Workplace Development Needs*. Canberra: AWPA.

Boys: Getting it Right (2002) *Boys: Getting it Right: Report on the Inquiry into the Education of Boys*, Standing Committee on Education and Training, House of Representatives. Canberra: Senate Printing Unit.

Byrne, M. (2001, 2002) *Men's Participation in the WEA Discussion Group Program*. Stage One and Stage Two Reports to the WEA Board. Sydney: WEA.

Clontarf (2013) Clontarf Foundation, Retrieved 6 February 2013 from www. clontarf.org.au

Connell, R. (1995) *Masculinities*. Cambridge: Polity Press.

Crowley, R. (1997) *Beyond Cinderella: Towards a Learning Society*, A Report of the Senate Employment, Education and Training References Committee. Canberra: Senate Printing Unit.

Dubbo: Dubbo Community Men's Shed (2012) A shed load of stories. Retrieved 28 February 2013 from http://dubbocommunitymensshed.com. au/page3.html

Earl, R. and Earl, L. (1996) *Introduction to Australian Society: A Sociological Overview*. Sydney: Harcourt Brace.

FCS: Family and Community Services (1999) *Report of the Committee Reviewing Family and Parent Support Services for Men*. Perth: FCS.

Fremanshed (2012) Retrieved 28 February 2013 from www.fremanshed.org/ content/about-us

Golding, B. (2002) 'Who's doing the hunting and gathering? An exploration of gender segmentation in adult learning in small and remote Australian communities', Paper to Conference on Lifelong Learning, Adult and Community Education, Australian Catholic University, Ballarat, 20 September.

Golding, B., Brown, M., Foley, A. and Harvey, J. (2009a) *Men's Learning and Wellbeing through Community Organizations in Western Australia*, Report to the Western Australia Department of Education and Training. Ballarat: University of Ballarat. Retrieved 1 May 2013 from http://archimedes.ballarat.edu. au:8080/vital/access/HandleResolver/1959.17/16443

Golding, B., Foley, A., Brown, M. and Harvey, J. (2009b) *Senior Men's Learning and Wellbeing through Community Participation in Australia*, Report to National Seniors Productive Ageing Centre. Ballarat: University of Ballarat. Retrieved 1 May 2103 from http://archimedes.ballarat.edu.au:8080/vital/access/ HandleResolver/1959.17/16450 and www.productiveageing.com.au/site/ publications.php

Golding, B., Brown, M., Foley, A., Harvey, J. and Gleeson, L. (2007) *Men's Sheds in Australia: Learning through Community Contexts*. Adelaide: NCVER, Retrieved 1 May 2013 from www.ncver.edu.au/publications/1780.html

Golding, B., Harvey, J. and Echter, A. (2005) *Men's Learning through ACE and Community Involvement in Small Rural Towns*, Final Report to ACFE Board Victoria. Ballarat: University of Ballarat.

Golding, B., Kimberley, H., Foley, A. and Brown, M. (2008) 'Houses and sheds: An exploration of the genesis and growth of neighbourhood houses and men's sheds in community settings', *Australian Journal of Adult Learning*, 48 (2), pp. 237–62.

Golding, B. and Rogers, M. (2001) *Adult and Community Learning in Small and Remote Towns in Victoria*, Report to ACFE Board. Bendigo: Bendigo Regional Institute of TAFE and La Trobe University.

Gorard, S. (2010) 'Participation in learning: Barriers to learning', in C. Cooper, J. Field, U. Goswami, R. Jenkins and B. Sahakian (Eds.), *Mental Capital and Wellbeing*. Chichester: Wiley-Blackwell, pp. 351–60.

Gorard, S. and Rees, G. (2002) *Creating a Learning Society? Learning, Careers and Policies for Lifelong Learning*. Bristol: Polity Press.

Harris, P. (2004) *Growing the Generations: Increasing the Participation of Men in Community Houses*. Report to Knox Network of Community Houses. Melbourne: Glen Park Community Centre.

Hayes, C., Golding, B. and Harvey, J. (2004) *Learning through Fire and Emergency Services Organizations in Small and Remote Australian Towns*. Adelaide: NCVER.

HREOC: Human Rights and Equal Opportunity Commission (2005) *Striking the Balance: Women, Men, Work and Family, Discussion Paper 2005*. Sydney: HREOC.

Hurworth, R. (1995) *Living Longer, Learning Later: Assessing the Education Needs of the Older Adult in Victoria*. Active Seniors Project Report. Melbourne: ACFE Board and Sport and Recreation, Victoria.

Kimberley, H. (1998) 'Conscientiousness and Culture: A Study of Neighbourhood Houses and Learning Centres in Victoria', PhD Thesis. Bundoora: La Trobe University.

Lattimore, R. (2007) *Men not at Work: An Analysis of Men outside the Labour Force*. Canberra: Australian Government Productivity Commission.

LCL: Learning Centre Link (2002, 2004) *Bringing in the Blokes: A Guide to Attracting and Involving Men in Community Neighbourhood and Learning Centres*. Perth: LCL.

Leigh Report (1997) *Inquiry into Planning for Positive Ageing: Report*. Chair G. Leigh, Family and Community Development Committee. Melbourne: Parliament of Victoria.

Marks, A. (2000) 'Men's health in the era of "crisis" masculinities', *Adults Learning*, October, pp. 11–13.

Martin, B. (2007) *Skill Acquisition, Activity and Use Across the Life Course: Current Trends: Future Prospects*. Adelaide: NCVER.

Maslen, G. (2003) 'Sex education: Women are on top', *Campus Review*, Feb/March, p. 19.

McGivney, V. (1999) *Excluded Men: Men who are Missing from Education and Training*. Leicester: NIACE.

McGivney, V. (2006) 'Attracting new groups into learning: Lessons from research in England', in J. Chapman, P. Cartwright and E. McGilp (Eds.), *Lifelong Learning, Participation and Equity*. Dordrecht: Springer, pp. 92–101.

McIntyre, J. (2007) *Engagement, Knowledge, Capability: Connecting Research to Policy and Practice*, Evaluation of the circles of professional research practice for Adult, Community and Further Education Board of Victoria, Final report, October. Melbourne: ACFE Board, Retrieved 28 February 2013 from www.jamc.com.au/documents/Circles_evaluation.pdf

MHIRC: Men's Health Information and Resource Centre (2001) *Keeping the Balance: Older Men and Healthy Ageing*, Report for the NSW Committee on Ageing. Sydney: MHIRC, University of Western Sydney.

NSA: National Seniors Australia (2010) *Valuing and Keeping Older Workers: A Case Study of what Workers Think about Ageing, Retirement and Age-friendly Workplace Strategies*. Canberra: NSA.

SLSA: Surf Life Saving Australia (2013) Retrieved 28 February 2013 from http://en.wikipedia.org/wiki/Surf_Life_Saving_Australia#Membership.

Snowden, W. (2012) 'Aboriginal and Torres Strait Islander men's sheds share in new funding'. Retrieved 28 February 2013 from www.indigenous.gov.au/aboriginal-and-torres-straigh-islander-mens-sheds-share-in-new-funding/

Stanwick, J. (2006) *Outcomes from Higher-Level Vocational Education and Training*. Adelaide: NCVER.

Thomas, J. (2001) *National Marketing Strategy for VET: Meeting Client Needs*. Brisbane: Australian National Training Authority.

Vallance, P. and Golding, B. (2008) '"They're funny bloody cattle": Encouraging rural men to learn', *Australian Journal of Adult Learning*, 48 (2), pp. 369–84.

Wallace, R. (2008) *Reluctant Learners: Their Identities and Educational Experiences*, Occasional Paper. Adelaide: NCVER.

Wilkinson, R. and Marmott, M. (Eds.) (2003) *Social Determinants of Health: The Solid Facts*, Second edition. Copenhagen: WHO.

CHAPTER FIFTEEN

Men's learning in Aotearoa/New Zealand

Brian Findsen

Introduction

This chapter is concerned with describing and critiquing men's learning in a geographically remote country of the British Commonwealth, Aotearoa or New Zealand. After discussing key socio-cultural features of relevance to learning in New Zealand, especially those that help shape ideas of masculinity, the chapter will traverse relevant national and localised social/educational policy that has influenced the pattern of boys' and men's participation in schooling and post-compulsory education (termed 'tertiary education'). Some men's purported (dis)engagement in varied forms of learning (formal; non-formal; informal) will be analysed, emphasising its stratified nature, especially according to age, social class and ethnicity. This investigation of the contexts in which men earn/learn will include the workplace, as well as other sites where learning takes place in selected social institutions (e.g. family or community organisations). Finally, instances of 'good practice' will be provided in regard to men's learning and explication of how existing practices, policies and research may influence future directions of male orientation and achievement in learning/education in New Zealand.

In this chapter it is important to distinguish between what is regarded as 'learning' and what is regarded as 'education'. As in the case of Withnall (2010) in the UK, the definition of these terms is crucial. 'Learning' is taken to denote changes in skills, attitudes and knowledge for individuals and groups, whereas 'education' is focused on the formalised (often assessed and credentialed), structured and systematic attainment of learning. In terms of the argument put forward in this chapter, males' strongest attachment in New Zealand has generally been towards informal and non-formal learning and less towards formal education. While discussion of 'formal', 'non-formal' and 'informal' learning follows, it is better to consider these descriptors as indicative of approaches to learning on a continuum rather than as firm entities with fixed characteristics.

It is important to acknowledge the complexities of discussing 'gender' and 'masculinities', concepts that have been treated in essentialist terms, as if non-problematic. Gender is both a biological and social construct; recent writers have stressed that gender is a social practice, not a unitary phenomenon and that 'gender relations and masculinities reflect, produce and reproduce discourses of power' (Bowl and Tobias, 2012, p. 25). Considerations of male aspirations and achievements in learning/education need to be interpreted in the complex economic, cultural and political contexts in which they occur.

Socio-cultural factors, masculinity and learning

The essential bi-cultural character of this nation is captured in the often used paired name for this country in Māori/Pakeha, Aotearoa/New Zealand, thus acknowledging its colonial nature. The Treaty of Waitangi, enacted in 1840, has been a founding document upon which relations between dominant and subordinate European and Indigenous cultures have endeavoured to set a pattern of co-operation for the future. Essentially, this was an agreement forged by men whose ideologies stemmed principally from Britain and these beliefs were transplanted to the new colony. Yet, in recent decades, significant immigration from Asia has introduced a more multi-cultural environment that challenges the prevailing bi-cultural narrative.

The colonial heritage, one of a dominant Pakeha (of European descent) over a minority Māori population, is pertinent in constructing prevailing ideologies of masculinity in New Zealand and notions of what is appropriate for boys/men to engage in, and equally what is appropriate for girls/women. This country, from a Pakeha perspective, has long been 'a bloke's world' (Phillips, 1996) built on European (mainly British) pioneers' qualities of self-reliance, physical prowess, resilience and fortitude. These were the major values which settlers brought with them and which have withstood the test of time, albeit under severe challenge as society has become more diversified. In the world of work, 'a fair day's work for a fair day's pay' was enshrined as part of New Zealand's egalitarian ethos; leisure, sport, culture and identity became intertwined, exemplified by the country's obsession with rugby football as a symbol of male prowess (though there is now a solid female rugby culture too) (Fougere, 1989). As noted by Tobias, the development of ideas around masculinity in the new colony is intimately connected to the work order of an emerging industrialised nation: 'with increasing mechanization, bureaucratization, specialization and professionaliza- tion, men's occupations in the labour market played a growing role in defining masculinities' (Tobias, 2012, p. 63). In addition, New Zealand's contribution to overseas wars, principally World Wars I and II, reinforced the availability of fit, versatile men (and some women), who were pre- pared to demonstrate loyalty to a sovereign nation.

One non-endearing feature associated with significant numbers of men, especially amid the young, is that of violence against women. In a now much more multi-cultural society, some men from every ethnic group and economic stratum are too often closely associated with vio- lence (James and Saville-Smith, 1990). Waves of feminism have tended to liberate women from traditional patterns of work and leisure but men have been slower to adopt more 'traditionally female' caring roles. In addition to this, there has been an increase in incidences of young men driving under the influence of alcohol. Globally, women's suffrage really began in New Zealand (in 1893 women gained the right to vote), thus establishing a base from which women have exercised more control over their lives and the nation. However, masculine identity has been fraught with uncertainty and ambiguity, as men in a post-modern era seek alter- natives to prevailing male stereotypes (Biddulph, 1995).

In a post-modern era, critical and feminist theorists have argued for a more problematic analysis of what masculinity means (Archer, 2006; Dalley-Trim, 2007). According to Archer (2006), hegemonic masculinity privileges a vocational and skills-based agenda for working-class men, where it is certainly not 'cool' to be engaging in higher education, for instance. Dalley-Trim has noted that the aggressive behaviour of young boys in classrooms, which effectively closes down girls' social interac- tion, is related to a 'doing' orientation to learning. The irony of such an approach is that often 'manly behaviour' of aggression and sometimes violence acts against eventual progress on the economic front, as dem- onstrated in Willis' British study with boys, *Learning to Labour: Working Class Kids Get Working Class Jobs* (Willis, 1977). Yet, it is fair to observe that the notion of equality of opportunity still has real resonance in this society, where working-class boys can become socially mobile via a purported internationally sound education system. Patterns of social and cultural reproduction are not as constraining as in older nations, and it is not unusual for working-class children to break out of comparative poverty, even in a sluggish low-wage economy.

Social and educational policy

The high emphasis given to early childhood education (ECE) in Aotearoa/New Zealand provides an effective beginning point for youngsters. Different types of ECE co-exist: kindergarten (government-sponsored education and care), playcentre (a co-operative of parents); kohanga reo (Māori language nests), Montessori preschools, and private crèche facilities, some connected to workplaces. An espoused objective of the New Zealand government, as expressed in its policy document for ECE, *Working with Te Whariki* (ERO, 2013), is to strengthen the learning experiences of pre-schoolers via principles of empowerment, holistic development, family, community and relationships. These goals do not differentiate girls from boys; gender is an invisible category. Hence, at this early stage of the lifecourse, boys' and girls' opportunities are largely the same, at least in an 'educational' context.

Another conscious effort of respective governments has been to alleviate the impact of a market forces approach to the economy with social equity initiatives in schooling: that is, providing additional resources to groups in society where severe disadvantage has been identified. In the compulsory school context, each individual school has been rated on a one to ten scale of relative poverty (decile ten schools tend to be in the most wealthy areas; decile ones in the poorest). Proportionally more funding has been made available to lower decile schools, many of which have disproportionately high numbers of Māori and Pasifika (Pacific Nations) children, to help re-address social inequalities in the wider society. This means that Pasifika boys, for instance, are in theory not marginalised by their participation in lower decile schools. In practice, however, the wealth of the contributing community, of which the school is a part, is a more defining feature of potential social mobility and life chances than the school itself.

In this country, the majority of secondary schools are funded by government. There are also significant numbers of integrated schools (those of a religious denomination but also receiving government financial support). Private schools, most of a single sex nature, are quite numerous, especially in the major metropolitan areas, such as Auckland. It would be naïve to think that differences in socio-economic background do not influence boys' life chances; a boy studying in Auckland Grammar (ostensibly a public school but one where hot competition operates for places because of its historic fine performances in New Zealand and international examinations), is more likely to gain economic benefit than a boy studying in South Auckland, a poorer socio-economic area, in a public, mixed gender, low decile school. There is generally much more variety of subjects available for children in well-heeled schools, where the 'best teachers' tend to work.

Boys in such environments are more than likely to have a wide range of subjects available to them, though there may be pressure to undertake traditional 'boys' subjects', such as mathematics, physics and chemistry, rather than arts-based 'soft' subjects usually associated with girls' education. In comparison, boys in low decile schools will have a narrower range of subjects, arguably less qualified teachers and less conducive physical facilities. Home environments will also differ – as Bourdieu (1974) has observed, the *cultural capital* of boys from higher economic echelons of society will be derived from cultural artefacts and social practices consistent with the dominant values of the ruling class. Boys from homes in a Māori or Pasifika environment will usually emerge from their early years with a different cultural heritage, where knowledge of a different character is valued from that of the majority of schools (Smith, 2012).

It is important at this point to briefly identify the key characteristics of tertiary education in New Zealand. In 2012 it included:

- eight universities, all publicly-funded;
- 18 polytechnics or Institutes of Technology focusing on technical/ vocational programmes;
- 321 Private Training Establishments in areas such as English-language providers, hospitality, hairdressing and business schools;
- three *whare wananga* (Māori-controlled and government-financed) institutions oriented towards Māori knowledge;
- 30 industry training organisations (e.g. automotive);
- 379 schools supporting adult and community education (ACE), foundation literacy and numeracy, training opportunities, youth training and workplace literacy;

- 30 rural education activities programme providers and community education providers;
- 14 other tertiary providers such as the National Association of ESOL home tutors schemes; Literacy Aotearoa Inc. (TEC, 2012, p. 4)

What have been the key policy directions and impact on men in these institutions? Given the plethora of institutions in which men participate as learners, it is not possible to provide a comprehensive response, but education policy changes and some indicators of men's preferences and participation levels are discernible. A cautionary note is needed because gender disparities on their own tell only part of the story; it is perhaps more useful to couple gender with age and/or ethnicity and social class to gain a more nuanced understanding of which men are participating and in what.

According to the Tertiary Education Commission (TEC), the key funding and monitoring performance body, adult learners are involved in the following contexts: industry or workplace learning; modern apprenticeships; literacy, numeracy and language skills development; foundation or advanced vocational skills; transition from secondary school to the workforce; and various youth programmes (TEC, 2013). The Tertiary Education Strategy (TES) highlights three areas for governmental priority: Māori; Pacific Nations peoples (Pasifika); and youth under 25 years of age. In the Māori and Pasifika populations, disproportionately large numbers of men under 25 are unemployed and left school with minimal qualifications.

That being noted, the government's targets in the above varied tertiary education contexts are concentrated in alleviating gaps in achievement, and most social equity programmes (e.g. special scholarships in universities) are designed to maximise successful outcomes for these young people. There has been a considerable tightening of entry requirements, exemplified in universities by the phrase 'managed entry' under a capped funding system, to maximise positive completion outcomes for enrolling students. In addition to 'hardening' of access (especially for older men and women who previously had open entry to universities for most disciplines), the government has four performance indicators: progression, retention, course completions and qualification completions (TEC, 2012, p. 4). Men's learning pathways in tertiary education need to be accommodated within these parameters.

Formal education: Men's engagement

In scanning the websites of both the Ministry of Education and the Tertiary Education Commission, it is noticeable how gender has become embedded in different spheres of formal education. As pre-eminence is now given to Māori, Pasifika and under 25s, gender is almost a dormant category. Explicit discussion, as in governmental publications, on the educational aspirations and achievements of men is largely absent. Statistics, including those on gender, are available for most types of tertiary education participation, but the discourse is more concentrated around ethnicity and age (although older adults constitute an invisible sub-population), related to individual up-skilling for enhancing the economic performance of the country.

Participation rates in tertiary education in recent years have shown a consistently higher rate for women. The male participation rate in tertiary education is 10.7 per cent of the population over 15 years, compared with 13.4 per cent of females, the gap increasing from 2006 to 2010 (*Education Counts*, 2012). Men tend to have lower level qualifications, especially amongst Māori and Pasifika. The New Zealand Qualifications Framework (NZQA), which attempts to integrate non-vocational and vocational education, provides a standard structure for naming and describing qualifications across ten levels and types of provision. Entry-level tertiary qualifications start at Level 1 (equivalent to the mid-point of secondary school), going up to doctorates, Level 10, in universities. There is gender differentiation in achievement at varying levels and according to the provider context.

A relatively rare, explicit comment about gender and age among tertiary students is as follows.

> *The proportion of the population holding bachelors or higher*
> *qualifications is higher for women than for men. Men continue to be*
> *more likely than women to hold tertiary certificates and diplomas.*
> *This difference reflects changes in the tertiary education participation*
> *trends over the last 15 years, with more women completing bachelors*
> *qualifications and the expansion of industry training which led*
> *to higher proportions of men gaining certificates and diplomas.*
> (*Education Counts*, 2013, p. 1)

A significant trend, partially a result of explicit government policy, has been for adult students to veer away from non-degree qualifications towards qualifications at Level 4 and above on the NZQA framework (Level 5 is linked to the first year of study at a university). According to the TEC (2011), enrolments in formal tertiary study by domestic students had fallen from 2010 to 2011 as older students opted for non-degree qualifications as a quicker route for entry into the labour market. Men with at least Level 4 and above qualifications have been better able to secure employment and gain a higher income than those beneath this threshold in comparison with women. This trend was associated with a significant demand for 'trade' qualifications, with men prevailing in numbers. The government's response has been to encourage greater numbers of both genders to enter higher status qualifications, the outcomes for which are not known as yet.

Workplace learning

Workplace learning, while industry-led largely through industry training organisations (ITOs), as in meat, dairy, leather, engineering, food and manufacturing, is funded by government and industry. Polytechnics in Aotearoa/New Zealand have tended to emphasise industry training as a prominent objective, and consequently can have a significant influence on what counts as curriculum in workplaces, particularly at the lower levels of the qualifications framework. The higher demand for accreditation by men at the lower levels (entry certificates and diplomas) is related to an expansion in industry training. 'In 2010, almost 70 percent of industry trainees were enrolled in Levels 1 to 3 on the NZQA framework' (Ministry of Education, 2010, p. 48). Workplace learning, especially for men, is a key site for training, including the Modern Apprenticeship (available to young people age 16 to 21) and the Youth Guarantee scheme introduced in 2010 for 16 and 17 years old. However, more men than women are prone to use these qualifications as an end point rather than extend on to further education and training.

In addition, there is comprehensive gender segmentation by field of study in Aotearoa/New Zealand. Proportionately fewer men enter hairdressing, tourism, the public sector and the equine industry, but proportionately more are in other fields (e.g. building and construction, agriculture, motor engineering and forestry: Ministry of Education, 2010, p. 61). Hence, gender participation in work-based learning opportunities is differentiated by level and industry. While openness to most industries continues for both sexes, there is still a lingering propensity for men to be attracted to more stereotypical 'men's domains'.

Non-formal learning/education

Non-formal learning/education does not result in a qualification and is commonly undertaken within adult and community education (ACE), an area where historically men have been under-represented in Aotearoa/ New Zealand. The three government priorities for ACE are to:

- engage learners whose initial learning was not successful;
- improve the literacy, language and numeracy of individuals and *whānau* (extended family); and
- strengthen social cohesion.

University-based ACE has a different set of priorities, more aligned to the specific purposes of university education, such as contributing to the knowledge society, disseminating research and facilitating pathways into and through university education. However, all funding to universities for ACE ceased at the end of 2012; in 2010, community education funding in high schools was cut by 80 per cent. Hence, while women were arguably more directly affected by these cuts (69 per cent of enrolments in community education were by women: Ministry of Education, 2010, p. 84), men were not exempt from having lesser access to more liberal education opportunities. In regard to tertiary contexts for ACE, men constituted 44 per cent of students in 2010; if their interests were related to targeted priority funding from government (in English language, literacy and numeracy, New Zealand sign language and Te Reo Māori), their continuing education needs were more readily met at no or low cost. Overall, ACE funding, including literacy initiatives, has been subservient to the central government agenda of harnessing human capital to increase productivity and the nation's wealth.

From the perspective of a political economy, while men in New Zealand, as in the UK, have traditionally been the 'earners' and women the 'learners' (McGivney, 2001, 2004), in which case women provided much unpaid labour to the nation, this kind of analysis is too simplistic in a post-modern world. In most Western countries, people's dominant life patterns have changed markedly away from an 'education to work to leisure' lifecourse orientation, to one where these major life transitions are carried out concurrently (see Riley and Riley, 1994, on the concept of structural lag), smashing old stereotypes of what is appropriate behaviour for men and for women at particular ages/stages. Accordingly, lifelong learning is a necessity for both expressive/communicative and instrumental needs and it is increasingly lifewide (Mezirow, 2006).

While engagement in formal education is still important for both individuals and the nation, more learning is occurring outside of this framework, bolstered by widening (though not yet universal) access to the internet and ICT more generally. However, while New Zealand espouses equal opportunity for all, it is largely a myth (Beeby, 1986). Instead, men's access and participation in education is differentiated according to social class, ethnicity and age, as confirmed by the Government's statistics. Men from a white professional class tend to profit from a lifelong commitment to continuing education. Māori and Pasifika men, proportionately more numerous among the less educated and in unskilled labour, struggle to get comparability with Pakeha counterparts.

Men's engagement in social institutions

In a sociological sense, social institutions are places where people conduct their lives and in which certain 'functions' are performed for individuals and societies (Blackledge and Hunt, 1985). In this case, men undertake patterns of learning in varied locations, such as the family, religious institutions, workplaces, community organisations and leisure facilities. In such environments there is no hard and fast distinction between 'non-formal' and 'informal' learning; the former involving systematic, organised learning and the latter associated with everyday living and incidental learning. As a truism, we know that learning for men is far more plentiful in these contexts, especially for older men, than in formal education (Golding, 2012).

Within a lifelong learning framework, men's engagement in social institutions links to major themes of lifelong learning: the economic imperative to contribute to a knowledge society; the personal fulfilment usually related to recreational learning pursuits; developing a critical citizenry in a civil society; and contributing to an inclusive learning society (Wain, 2004; Findsen and Formosa, 2011). Some social institutions (e.g. the workplace) readily map on to one or other lifelong learning theme (e.g. economic sustainability), but in reality these varied contexts for men's learning enable several purposes to be fulfilled simultaneously.

Empirical research on men's engagement in social institutions in New Zealand is scant; however, the next section points to some trends that can provide fruitful directions for future research.

Selected sites of learning

The family

Men's learning in families, in the roles of partner/spouse, (grand)father and (grand)son has been fundamental to the maintenance of family life. Early family history in New Zealand witnessed the creation of the 'family man' in pioneer days, where the social order was modelled on pre-industrial Britain and men benefited from the 'cult of domesticity'. Women dominated the private space of the family and men were the primary breadwinners, yet freer to pursue 'mateship' (James and Saville-Smith, 1990). In New Zealand, an emergent imperative for men to enact responsible diverse roles across generations became strong at a time when increasing fragmentation of the nuclear family was and is apparent. Much of what men learn is derived from observation of others (Bandura, 1986) and through experiential learning (Kolb, 1984), its character influenced by socio-economic realities. The life chances available to boys in a white professional family are significantly more than those of many in marginalised ethnic groups, where family size is generally larger. The cultural capital of boys/men from 'the ruling class' usually leads them into higher status knowledge circles. Social capital (Field, 2003), the extent of their social connectedness, enables them to cement greater educational opportunities. Hence, social reproduction of privilege operates across family types and opens up the learning potential for boys/men, even in the private domain of the family. For instance, professional men typically mentor boys to reproduce their social positioning in society.

In the Indigenous Māori context, traditional practices appropriate to the masculine gender are demonstrated on a daily basis within *whanau* (extended family) in events such as welcoming guests on to a *marae* (communal meeting area), in the strongly gendered and sacred art of carving and through the memorisation of *whakapapa* (genealogy). *Kaumatua* (older men) are commonly revered for their wisdom and given respect and authority as elders in a tribe. Again, intergenerational learning along gender lines is part of daily life and reproduces the importance of male lineage as a differentiating device for what should be learned by boys/men.

However, in a post-modern era, where more Māori are urbanised and tribal links are weaker, young Māori men frequently challenge traditional practices and values, and collective support may emerge through other social formations such as gangs. Young Māori men's over-representation in social statistics of crime, prison participation, unemployment and poverty points to major challenges for Māori leaders and wider New Zealand society. Learning approaches that emphasise positive Māori identity, usually within a *kaupapa Māori* framework, and are related to collective emancipatory action, are best placed to achieve good outcomes (Smith, 2012).

Community organisations

As has been shown by Golding (2011a, 2011b) in respect of Australian society, New Zealand also has a plethora of community organisations that provide learning opportunities for people of all ages, ethnicities, social class, geographical location and for both genders. Much of this learning is through active participation. In the context of Golding's research into men's learning and wellbeing, he has categorised community organisations into three areas of relevance to New Zealand, though there are differences in historical, cultural and economic circumstances of the two nations:

1. adult and community education and sporting organisations;
2. fire, emergency services and men's specific organisations;
3. age-related and disability, Aboriginal, Indigenous, religious and cultural organisations.

In the case of 1., men's participation has been weak in ACE but strong in sporting organisations (e.g. rugby football); in the instance of 2., men dominate the emergency services and men's specific organisations (e.g. Working Men's Clubs); in the case of 3., there are instances of formerly male-dominated organisations, such as Rotary and Probus, which have opened to women but retain a strong patriarchy. While religious institutions usually have a male hierarchical structure, participation according to gender varies from location to location, but as the ageing population increases, there are proportionately fewer males engaged in learning through church affiliation (see Findsen, 2012a, for an analysis of religious institutions as sites of learning for older adults).

Of all organisations related to men, in actual numbers of males engaged, it would be difficult to go beyond sporting and leisure organisations as sites of experiential and informal learning for most men. Since colonial times, sport has featured prominently in the New Zealand psyche, related to an outdoor-oriented society. Additionally, Indigenous Māori and Pasifika peoples have embraced this sporting ethos and new immigrants outside these ethnicities have adapted to a lesser extent to this agenda. Men have featured prominently across most sporting codes, while women have also gained prominence in female-oriented sports (e.g. netball). Hence, overall, community organisations are enmeshed in Kiwi culture and men, either through volunteering or paid positions, dominate many of them. Consequently, non-formal learning (e.g. via volunteering or training) and informal learning is massive in and through such organisations.

Vignettes of 'good practice'

The following brief descriptions of sites of men's learning in Aotearoa/ New Zealand illustrate effective adult learning principles in action, such as ownership of the learning; learning of high relevance to learners in a specific social context; cultural appropriateness; inter-generational linkages; and the emergence of strong male identities as learners.

The Rauawaawa Trust

An educational partnership between the University of Waikato in Hamilton city (via the Centre for Continuing Education) and the Rauawaawa Kaumatua Charitable Trust has operated for over a decade, enabling *kaumatua* (Māori male leaders) to learn a wide range of cultural activities. In essence, this is a programme of Māori seniors teaching other seniors important features of their culture. While some of these learning events are of mixed gender (e.g. *te reo Māori* (Māori language); *waiata* (action songs)), others are single sex. In this respect, *whaikorero* (speech-making) and *whakairo* (carving) are specialised, male tasks and considered *tapu* (sacred), in which only men may participate.

The uniqueness of the relationship between the University and the Trust has been centred on helping to meet the learning needs of older Māori people in the Waikato region where the curriculum and teachers emerge from the immediate context. A salient point of distinctiveness is in the focus on older Māori, rather than in most educational programmes where youth is the highest priority. It provides a safe place for non-formal and informal learning in Māori-oriented contexts, where collaboration rather than competition holds sway. Further analysis of this distinctive programme by Māori for Māori, where men's learning is fundamental to its success, is available in Findsen (2012b).

Men's sheds in New Zealand

Unlike the previous site of learning, where the sub-population was of mixed gender and the cultural roots are ancient, the men's sheds movement has been mainly a male-only domain and is a very recent development (post-2007 in New Zealand). As the name implies, it is a place for men to come together for diverse purposes, but mainly to complete projects, usually of a practical nature, and discuss issues in a male-centred location. Since Golding set the platform for expansion of the Australian men's sheds movement (2011a, 2011b), New Zealand has followed suit, particularly as the dominant male European culture of both nations has a close affinity. Sheds now exist in both urban and rural geographical regions and tend to reflect the character of the immediate environment and local human/men's needs. The spread of sheds across the Canterbury Plains followed and was in part associated with community reaction to the Christchurch quakes. As explained by MenzShed Aotearoa, while a national organisation provides guidelines for action, each shed is autonomous. Sheds 'drive the organization rather than the organization the sheds' (Cox, 2009, in MenzSheds, 2013).

The success of these relatively new cultural spaces mainly for and by men is based on the acknowledgment that collaborative learning and action are at their base. Diverse groups can be accommodated in one site (e.g. through strategic timetabling), even if the physical facility is modest. These are community-based men's organisations where 'shedders', as they self-describe, can learn new skills in unpretentious surroundings and undertake both personal and communal activities, such as building playgrounds for pre-schoolers, repairing bikes or helping to beautify the main street. These informal locations for learning and keeping active and well debunk the notion that (mainly older) men do not want to learn or care for themselves and their communities. They allow men to develop greater social capital (Field, 2003) to enhance health and wellbeing; they create spaces for more marginalised groups of men (e.g. un- or under-employed) to enjoy one another's company and share collective knowledge (Golding, 2011a).

While the two above-cited locations for men celebrate learning in situationally-specific arenas, boys/men also learn in hosts of other work-related and community settings. Even amid the ACE sector, where men have traditionally been under-represented, there are exciting opportunities in areas such as family literacy and rural education activities programmes, where non-formal and informal learning take precedence. When 'learning' is examined, as opposed to 'education' (Withnall, 2010), a wider range of engagement by males in New Zealand society becomes apparent.

Conclusions

Undoubtedly there are complexities in mapping men's learning in Aotearoa/New Zealand. Male identity is a social construction and practice, as much as it is a biological phenomenon. Little is inherently 'masculine' or 'feminine' but has been determined by historical, social and cultural forces, including prevailing ideologies of what it means to be a boy/man. Socio-cultural forces related to this country's origins and contemporary practices continue to influence learning behaviours of men. While some men's behaviour has been shaped by colonial attitudes as to what men can and should do, the majority are now seeing that stereotypical gender roles do not need to be followed. Nevertheless, differential opportunities for traditionally disenfranchised male groups in Aotearoa/New Zealand, particularly among Māori, Pasifika, un- and under-employed and older men also influence actual engagement.

Educational policy at multiple levels (ECE; compulsory schooling; tertiary education; ACE) has enshrined equality of opportunity as a powerful myth, but in more recent times social equity, especially for Māori, Pasifika and young people, has been a dominating discourse. Linked to setting the conditions for a more competitive economy, formal learning, especially for marginalised men, has focused on establishing a minimal benchmark of education via literacy and numeracy, training for work and youth-related initiatives. In the workplace, men have availed themselves of learning opportunities, but have tended to settle for a less credentialed pathway than for women. In the higher sphere of post-graduate studies in universities, women now outperform men in participation (Ministry of Education, 2010, p. 43).

The formal education system is not a reliable indicator of men's desire and capacity to learn. Instead, we need to look at non-formal learning sites (e.g. community organisations) or informal learning in the likes of community men's sheds, to more fully appreciate the diversity and commitment of men to continue learning, well into later life (Findsen, 2005). While women may occupy more learning sites associated with ACE, men nevertheless have their own preferences, some of which coincide with women, but others are more gender specific.

In regard to 'good practice', effective adult learning principles prevail in contexts where men feel safe to be themselves, sometimes in mixed gender environments, sometimes in a single sex context. It is wise not to be prescriptive in what men can and should learn. In Aotearoa/New Zealand, the moves against sexism are strong and, accordingly, the avenues for men and women to learn continue to diversify rather than to narrow. The challenge is for men to take advantage of these new horizons.

References

Archer, L. (2006) 'Masculinities, femininities and resistance to participation in post-compulsory education', in C. Leathwood, and B. Francis (Eds.), *Gender and Lifelong Learning: Critical Feminist Engagements*. London: Routledge, pp. 70–82.

Bandura, A. (1986) *Social Foundations of Thought and Action: A Social Cognitive Theory*. Englewood Cliffs: Prentice-Hall.

Beeby, C. (1986) 'Introduction', in Renwick, W. (Ed.), *Moving Targets: Six Essays on Educational Policy*. Wellington: New Zealand Council for Educational Research, pp. xi–xlv.

Biddulph, S. (1995) *Manhood: An Action Plan for Changing Men's Lives*. Melbourne: McPherson's Printing Group.

Blackledge, D. and Hunt, B. (1985) *Sociological Interpretations of Education*. London: Croom Helm.

Bourdieu, P. (1974) 'The school as a conservative force', in J. Eggleston (Ed.), *Contemporary Research in the Sociology of Education*. London: Methuen, pp. 32–46.

Bowl, M. and Tobias, R. (2012) 'Ideology, discourse and gender', in M. Bowl, R. Tobias, J. Leahy, G. Ferguson and J. Gage (Eds.), *Gender, Masculinities and Lifelong Learning*. London: Routledge, pp. 14–28.

Cox, M. (2009) Article by 'Martin' posted on 23 April 2009, Retrieved 31 January 2013 from www.Menssheds.org.nz/about-2/

Dalley-Trim, L. (2007) 'The boys' present … Hegemonic masculinity: A performance of multiple acts', *Gender and Education*, 19 (2), pp. 199–217.

Education Counts (2012) *Education Counts: Participation Rates in Tertiary Education*. Wellington: Ministry of Education.

Education Counts (2013) *Education Counts: Profile and Trends 2011: New Zealand's Tertiary Education Sector*. Wellington: Ministry of Education.

ERO: Education Review Office (2013) *Working with Te Whariki*. Wellington: ERO.

Field, J. (2003) *Social Capital*. London: Routledge.

Findsen, B. (2005) *Learning Later*. Malabar: Krieger.

Findsen, B. (2012a) 'Religious institutions as sites of learning for older adults', in P. Isaac, (Ed.), *Expanding the Boundaries of Adult Religious Education: Strategies, Techniques, and Partnerships for the New Millennium* (New Directions for Adult and Continuing Education), No. 133, Spring, pp. 71–82.

Findsen, B. (2012b) 'University and community engagement through continuing education: The case of the university of Waikato and the Rauawaawa Trust', in P. Jones, J. Storan, A. Hudson and J. Braham (Eds.), *Lifelong Learning and Community Engagement*. University of East London: Forum for Access and Continuing Education, pp. 43–55.

Findsen, B. and Formosa, M. (2011) *Lifelong Learning in Later Life: A Handbook on Older Adult Learning*. Rotterdam: Sense Publishers.

Fougere, G. (1989) 'Sport, culture and identity: The case of rugby football', in D. Novitz and B. Willmott (Eds.), *Culture and Identity in New Zealand*, Wellington: Blueprint Consultants, pp. 110–22.

Golding, B. (2011a) 'Social, local and situated: Recent findings about the effectiveness of older men's informal learning in community contexts', *Adult Education Quarterly*, 61 (2), pp. 103–20.

Golding, B. (2011b) 'Older men's learning through age-related community organizations in Australia', *International Journal of Education and Ageing*, 1 (3), pp. 237–52.

Golding, B. (2012) 'Men's learning through community organizations: Evidence from an Australian study', in M. Bowl, R. Tobias, J. Leahy, G. Ferguson and J. Gage (Eds.), *Gender, Masculinities and Lifelong Learning*. London: Routledge, pp. 122–33.

James, B. and Saville-Smith, K. (1990) *Gender, Culture and Power*. Auckland: Oxford University Press.

Kolb, D. (1984) *Experiential Learning: Experience as the Source of Learning and Development*. Englewood Cliffs: Prentice Hall.

McGivney, V. (2001) *Fixing or Changing the Pattern: Reflections on Widening Adult Participation in Learning*. Leicester: NIACE.

McGivney, V. (2004) *Men Earn, Women Learn: Bridging the Gender Divide in Education and Training*. Leicester: NIACE.

MenzShed (2013) MenzShed New Zealand. Retrieved 25 November 2013 from http://menzshed.org.nz.

Mezirow, J. (2006) 'An overview on transformative learning', in P. Sutherland and J. Crowther (Eds.), *Lifelong Learning: Concepts and Contexts*. London: Routledge, pp. 24–38.

Ministry of Education (2010) *Profile and Trends: New Zealand's Tertiary Education Sector.* Wellington: Ministry of Education.

Phillips, J. (1996) *A Man's Country? The Image of the Pakeha Male: A History,* Revised edition. Auckland: Penguin Books NZ.

Riley, M. and Riley, M. (1994) 'Structural lag: Past and future', in M. Riley, R. Kahn and A. Foner (Eds.) *Age and Structural Lag.* New York: Wiley, pp. 15–36.

Smith, L. (2012) *Decolonizing Methodologies: Research and Indigenous Peoples.* London: Zed Books.

TEC: Tertiary Education Commission (2011) *Profile and trends 2011: New Zealand's Tertiary Education Sector.* Wellington: TEC.

TEC: Tertiary Education Commission (2012) *Annual Report for the Year ended 30 June 2012.* Wellington: TEC.

TEC: Tertiary Education Commission (2013) *Types of tertiary education.* Retrieved 23 January 2013 from www.tec.govt.nz/Tertiary-Sector/Types-of-Tertiary-Education/

Tobias, R. (2012) 'Images of men and learning: The impact of imperialism on settler masculinities and lifelong learning', in M. Bowl, R. Tobias, J. Leahy, G. Ferguson and J. Gage (Eds.), *Gender, Masculinities and Lifelong Learning.* London: Routledge, pp. 58–71.

Wain, K. (2004) *The Learning Society in a Postmodern World.* New York: Peter Lang.

Willis, P. (1977) *Learning to Labour: How Working Class Kids get Working Class Jobs.* Farnborough: Saxon House.

Withnall, A. (2010) *Improving Learning in Later Life.* London: Routledge.

CHAPTER SIXTEEN

Men's turn to learn?
Discussion and conclusion

Barry Golding, Rob Mark and Annette Foley

Introduction

Our intention in this final chapter is to argue a case for repositioning men's learning at any age as a significant benefit not only for the men involved, but also for their families and the community, aside from the narrowly defined vocational benefits which lifelong learning policies often focus on. We seek to identify some generalisable conclusions based on the data and literature examined in the first part of this book and the national research policies and practices identified in the second part. The chapter consists of a discussion, comprising a number of important acknowledgments about the extensive theoretical and practical ground our book has covered. This is followed by a number of broad and over-arching conclusions.

Discussion

Acknowledging that this goes beyond men's learning
The first part of this book demonstrates how a lack of engagement with learning effectively locks men of all ages out of many activities and can put relationships, partners, families and children's health and wellbeing at risk. It also raises an important question about the kind of learn-ing women experience through life at similar ages and stages. Without

wishing to broaden the debate beyond men, we acknowledge four important points here.

Firstly, it is critically important to acknowledge the role of women in carving out the theoretical space in which our book has ventured, through recent decades of gender analysis, which has:

> helped women challenge unequal power relations and the stereotypes of what women should be. It needs to continue to be so … But its insights now need to be applied much more consciously and rigorously to men. (Sweetman, 2000, p. 4)

Secondly, we acknowledge that internationally most women experience significant inequities as learners in and beyond work, in part because many have been unfairly oppressed by men in patriarchal families, societies, institutions and workplaces. The 'good news' from research confirming a 'women's turn' in learning in many countries is that women with both the habitus and finances to engage in formal and vocational learning will do similarly well if not better than men, including in work afterwards, provided that women achieve equal access to school and post-school education and are equitably employed and paid. We acknowledge that these provisos are not in place for women in most world nations.

Thirdly, while the emphasis in our book has been on men's learning through life, we also acknowledge that there is a case for similarly re-positioning women's learning through life, particularly where it focuses on disadvantaged groups. As Oustrouch and Ollagnier stress:

> Women have their own particular ways of making sense of life and choose their modes of knowledge construction accordingly and do not necessarily lay great stock in ways of learning that are valued in terms of their universality. (2008, p. 22)

Fourthly, we acknowledge that men and women tend to experience some aspects of life, including learning, differently. What we are identifying is that many men who have spent a lifetime in paid work are often poorly buffered or prepared for changes beyond work, and without support from a partner, children, family or friendship networks which help them to learn to understand, adapt to and cope with this cavalcade of changes, they can and do often silently experience and endure miserable and depressing later lives. Being socially conditioned and educated in very different times and circumstances, it is unfair to anticipate that the masculinities that older men experience and subscribe to will be the same as those prevailing in the wider community. Furthermore, it is important to acknowledge that it is in the interests of adults in loving relationships with men that the men are well, happy and socially connected both in and beyond their working lives.

The evidence which comes through in all national chapters in Part Two suggests that while in general most men in work are faring relatively well compared with men not in work, work can have a dark and damaging side. The most damaging aspect of paid work, aside from the risk of becoming stressed, damaged, depressed and debilitated, is men's tendency to deny these aspects and 'soldier on'. Men who take on a 'breadwinner' role can often invest too much time in their working lives as compared with investing in relationships with their partners, children, families and communities, and become physically and mentally damaged in the process.

Without socially progressive education policies, pedagogies or funding, a hierarchical education and training system focused only on work-related learning will tend to reinforce and reproduce existing inequalities. Men who are less well educated and trained were typically disadvantaged or disengaged in the school system as boys, and will tend as adults to inherit and pass on negative attitudes towards learning and occupy less well-paying jobs. Evidence from all nations featured in our book confirms that as adults, such men tend to live in the most socially deprived and rural areas and be less likely to marry. If married, they are more likely to marry or partner with someone who is similarly poorly educated, thereby reproducing the inequities they experienced through their own children. They will also earn much less for their families, be less healthy and die earlier.

Links to boy's learning

While the focus of our book was not on boys, the link between men's and boys' participation in education is important to recognise. This link surfaces in several of the chapters. As Endepohls-Ulpe concluded:

> *It has frequently been documented girls did better than boys whenever they had the opportunity to participate equally in educational*

measures (Connolly, 2004). This was already documented in the British school system in the 1980s. (2012, p. 55)

Research in schools has shown that, where any form of education has become universal, there is a tendency for boys and young men to participate less and perform significantly less well than girls. Again, we are not arguing that there is something different between boys and girls. Specifically, our concern is for those boys penalised by a combination of narrowly defined masculinities, limited experiences of and negative attitudes towards, high stakes, school-based and other types of formal, higher and vocational learning. Again, the research shows that many of these penalties are absorbed into the psyche for life, not only for men, but also for their partners, families, schools and communities.

Our primary concern is to be aware enough as school and adult educators to know what it is that can and does engage some boys and men with learning, and to recognise, avoid and redress any form of consequent disengagement from any aspect of life. We also argue for a wider acknowledgment and understanding of:

> *the social construction of gender and a tolerance and acceptance of different practices of femininity and masculinity … Current practices of hegemonic masculinity are dangerous to some teachers, to many, many girls and to a lot of boys.* (Lingard and Douglas, 1999, p. 123)

This includes its extension to all forms of learning through life, to both women and men.

Emerging global leadership

It is pertinent at this point to briefly ask why men's learning and men's sheds, like earlier critical examinations of masculinities and boys' education in Australia from the 1990s, have been relatively warmly and widely embraced in Australian research, policy and practice. Why have these issues not got similar traction in other Anglophone nations, such as the US and Canada, for example, and why have they not progressed far in the UK since McGivney's work? Australia, a country known for exuding male dominance in the 1960s and 1970s, and better known for its athletes than its academics, was by the 1990s leading the way in relation to a critical examination of masculinities (Connell, 1995). Perhaps it was timely in a newly emerging nation, less constrained by non-Indigenous cultural traditions, for researchers to make a splash on the international arena.

On further reflection and examination, it is unsurprising that our book about men's informal learning, community men's sheds and the second national men's health policy in the world all developed most of their 'research legs' in Australia a decade after McGivney's *Excluded Men* and *Men Earn, Women Learn* (1999, 2004). As Weaver-Hightower notes in *The Politics of Policy in Boys' Education*, Australia 'stands apart in the quantity of discussion, its visibility and the lengths to which it has gone in international debates about boys' learning' (2008, p. 3). As Apple (2008, p. xii) says in the book's foreword, referring specifically to *Boys: Getting it Right* (House of Representatives, 2002), Australia was also 'the first nation of its type to actually have a federal policy on the education of boys'.

Oustrouch-Kaminska *et al.* (2012, p. 12) suggest that it is generally Anglophone researchers who have been more interested in theorising gender and adult education. Weaver-Hightower (2008, p. 187–8) provides five possible clues for why the American perspective tends not to be heard here when he points out that 'the U.S. populace tends to see gender issues as exclusively *women's* issues' (p. 187), therefore limiting 'receptivity to notions that boys might face problems *because they are male*' (p. 187); that 'focussing on boys can be seen as a distraction from, or threat to, more "traditional", accepted notions of gender equity' (p. 187), that 'males' *gendered* concerns largely lack institutional infrastructures' (p. 187) in the US; that 'social justice is aligned *against* most men's interests' (p. 187), and that 'movements towards boys' education tread a tense, ambivalent cultural ground ... due to their positions within larger, sometimes contradictory masculinity ideologies' (p. 188). Weaver-Hightower's (2008) fifth clue is particularly pertinent to Foley's painstakingly careful attempt in Chapter 5 to clear some tensions and potentially ambiguous theoretical ground, aside from but related to our arguments for creating new men's learning places and spaces beyond paid work, as acknowledged below.

The importance of learning beyond paid work

Our book acknowledges that there are many places and spaces in which men's learning through life can be and is already facilitated and enhanced. To summarise, our main concern is not focused on men already actively involved in education and training or work, but is more about men, who in McGivney's (1999) words, are 'missing' from either or both forms of provision. Most educational research confirms that the home and family are where most children get leveraged for success at school and work and that, in combination with home and family, work and the community are sites where most adults learn most of what they know or can do. It is when any one or more of the trilogy of key learning places fall over (work, home/family and community), and/or when men's health and wellbeing are affected, that the real problems start.

Our key concern, as amplified by the chapters contributed by other authors, has been to acknowledge ways of making learning accessible to men not in work. Most modern nation states recognise (and arguably become besotted with) the value of education as a subsidy to the individual as an employee, in order to benefit and service the economy. They also value the training and retraining of adults as long as they want to engage in paid work. However, most governments tend to turn a blind eye to people not in paid work, particularly the growing proportion of men who have decided (or been told) that they are beyond working and learning age.

Our key policy message is that we have got reasonably good at getting most young people into work, and retraining them for multiple jobs over a lifetime when economies are booming and while people are of working age. In Europe, where there are declining economies, this is perhaps one of the most pressing problems, as illustrated in the chapters from Greece, Ireland and Portugal. All have extremely high proportions of youth unemployed. We are very bad, and arguably getting worse, at helping men in particular to learn beyond paid work. We are also bad at helping younger men when economies inevitably turn around or plunge into crisis, as eloquently described in the Greek chapter. We are a long way from 'getting it right' in relation to disengaged boys and their view that traditional schooling is irrelevant and doesn't relate to their needs.

Our related acknowledgement is that, while we are not arguing here for an expansion of formal educational provision, we are acknowledging that adult basic education is a low and diminishing priority for most governments (Aikman and Unterhalter (2007, p. 44). There are many men, even in relatively 'developed' nations, with very low basic skills. Their multiple learning and literacy needs, and particularly the self-esteem and confidence necessary to take the 'first steps' towards learning, must first be addressed to give such men access to the second steps: access to vocational education and training, employment and further education opportunities. As Aikman and Unterhalter stress, international '[e]xperience in the non-formal sector indicates that interventions that are community-based, and that respond to context and mobility patterns, can work' (2007, p. 57).

What men experience beyond paid work is not the same everywhere, and is particularly related to factors beyond their direct control, particularly the state of the national economy. While world and national economies grow, national concerns are typically about education for jobs to meet skill shortages, and any debilitating effects on unemployment, pollution, resource depletion, worker stress, depression, health and safety as well as lack of balance between work, family and community are tolerated as economic necessities or externalities. In the good economic times, men are easy and essential fodder to meet the needs of the economy. In an extreme but real example, the Australian mining boom is now almost totally dependent on mainly male 'fly-in, fly-out' (FIFO) workers, who do extra long rosters, shifts and hours. These FIFOs commute thousands of kilometres by air away from home and family to work in areas where Indigenous and local community unemployment is endemic. The money is good but the externalities are huge.

With huge and painful irony, at the same time but on the other side of the world, the multiple and ongoing effects of the global financial crisis are biting deeply into the political, cultural, community and family capital and fabric of many nations, as illustrated in our chapters about men's learning in Ireland, Portugal and Greece. The most recent global financial crisis (there have been other similar crises, and there will be more) has showed how exposed and vulnerable nation states and men can become when the simple mantra of 'good work achieved through a good education' can and does completely break down. Unsurprisingly, when men's identities as workers and supporters of families break down and education and training no longer leads to jobs, many other parts of men's lives and identities can and do unravel. Men most able to cope are those most buffered for change through their prior education, their ability to understand the reasons for the crisis, to keep learning and changing, as well as through the support from their families and the community.

It is not in any country's interest to have a generation of bitter, angry and poorly educated, unemployed or under-employed men unable to comprehend what has changed, and turning irrationally, physically and aggressively on their fellow human beings (migrants, women, refugees, gay men, for example) as is occurring across most nations in Europe. Nor do nations experiencing population ageing want to tie up their diminishing public resources looking after older men in an ageist and patronising manner if men are able to help each other to age well and contribute to their communities. Our inclusion of Chapter Eight, about men's sheds, is to demonstrate that there are many other ways for men beyond paid work to self-organise, regain strength and wellbeing, experience positive male identities, learn and benefit, and at the same time give back to other men and boys, their families, children, partners and the community.

Diverse national experiences and narratives

There is a diversity of experiences in men's learning, and also in the nature and interpretation of the research associated with that learning captured by the national chapters in Part Two. Each of the seven countries examined is experiencing population ageing, and most of the European countries are struggling with a very high proportion of men of working age (including a very concerning and much higher proportion of young men) alienated through being unemployed or withdrawn from the paid workforce.

The diverse national chapters also emphasise that any adult with limited experiences of formal schooling can become disengaged or alienated as a consequence of limited literacies, and adversely affected by one or more of the multiple determinants of health, as teased out in Chapter Three. As a consequence, not being able to learn to adapt to change through life limits not only younger men's ability to work, but also to partner and enter into loving relationships, raise children and maintain health and wellbeing. It is men of working age who are not in paid work, defined by Schuller and Watson (2009) as being in the third age (50 to 74) or fourth age (75 plus) that are particularly vulnerable.

What is common across all seven nations in Part Two is that in the later ages and stages of life leading to 'retirement', as paid work activity typically slows for most men, changes in most other areas of life quicken. Though many of these changes are less visible in standard social statistics, older men experience rapid and quickening change as they age, particularly in relation to their health and wellbeing status, income, social networks and attachment to paid work. In the fourth age, when

251

physical dependency becomes increasingly likely and mobility becomes more limited, many older men also experience radical changes in terms of narrowing choices and opportunities: over where they live, their relationships with peers, partners, families, children and the community. Of the countries examined in this book, it is particularly China, with its traditional acknowledgement of the link between wisdom and age, which might provide alternative ways of meeting these challenges for older men.

That said, the seven nations included for closest analysis in the national chapters are at best a partial snapshot, and are far from representative of men's learning worldwide. Men in most European nations are now no better off, and many are worse off, than they were a decade or two ago, largely as a result of stalled or shrinking economies in the wake of the global financial crisis. We could have included some Eastern European nations such as Estonia, where health and longevity statistics have a serious impact on men, where despite the 'top problems' (of crime, poverty and unemployment) being strongly gender laden, their gendering is generally ignored in research, policy and practice (Hearn *et al.*, 2004, p. 115). Alternatively, if we had examined men's learning in primarily Islamic nations, where women are much less likely to be in education or paid work, our picture and conclusions might have been quite different. Finally, if we focused on the learning situation for Māori people in New Zealand, or Aboriginal and Torres Strait Islanders, who make up the Indigenous male population in Australia, we would likely find they are doing much worse than Pakeha or Gubba (non-Indigenous) men in their respective countries, but also falling well behind the Indigenous female population in accessing learning.

We observe some difficult ironies here. Indigenous peoples and cultures found in many countries, including most Pacific, Asian, African, Middle Eastern, Central and South American nations, often have traditional, highly gendered forms of work, family and labour, many of which adversely affect women in education and work, some of which systematically oppress women. Any educational or other intervention designed to redress gender inequality and oppression has the potential to also alter, undermine or destroy other positive and sometimes culturally pivotal aspects of Indigenous political and social relations. To ground this in a hypothetical but common scenario, an internationally funded programme, underpinned by feminist principles, to encourage Pacific, Māori or Aboriginal Australian women to participate on equal terms to men in education and work needs to anticipate resistance, if not backlash, from Indigenous men and communities, unless they are also actively involved in and recognised as part of the solution rather than *the* problem. The same might apply to a men's shed-type programme implemented in a new national context without regard to the traditional values and needs of women and families.

Any externally imposed 'solution' that embeds and encourages non-Indigenous values, for whatever good reasons, can serve also to de-stabilise culture, language and communities. Wherever educational outcomes have improved in the world, there has been an accelerated drift by those advantaged by the change closer to where 'good jobs' are, typically towards the largest cities (or by immigration to other nations in case of some Pacific and European nations), leaving many rural communities and less developed nations skewed towards older age. The Chinese and Portuguese chapters, for example, illustrate how older adults (including men) can become stranded without an intergenerational family or support in later life, with very limited local learning options and much diminished health and life expectancy.

The 'men's turn' literature

While the choice of fellow chapter authors and the diverse themes we have explored in our book are far from random, we did not prescribe what they should write or the methodology they should adopt. We find a version of Weaver-Hightower's (2003, p. 474) four-part aetiology (a categorisation of knowledge concerned with causes) about boys' learning, adapted by us to account for men's learning, to be particularly useful here. Reflecting on the chapters in both parts of our book, we conclude that most of us have either avoided or drawn back from an essentialist, *popular rhetorical* approach that *all* men are disadvantaged in the education process and that all men's learning is feminised. As an example of this popular, rhetorical approach towards men, we could cite Biddulph's (1995) book, *Manhood*, or Rosin's (2012) book, *The End of Men*.

Some of us have dabbled (largely on the edges) in the complex, *theoretically-oriented* literature, concerned 'with cataloguing types of masculinity and their origins and effects' (Weaver-Hightower, 2003, p. 474), examining how adult education and society produces and modifies masculinities, largely using qualitative research tools. Most of us, through our links with adult and men's education practice, have also delved into the *practice-oriented* literature, to borrow and paraphrase again from

Weaver-Hightower, concerned with developing and evaluating adult learning-related interventions, such as men's sheds, related to contemporary learning and social problems.

Finally, some have referred to the *feminist and pro-feminist* literature, which includes critiques of what might be described, using the 'boys' turn' double entendre discussed by Weaver-Hightower, as 'men's turn'; of 'moral panic' over men referred to by Bowl and Tobias (2012), of notions of some men's under-participation and achievement in some of our own research, as well as of popular rhetorical backlashes. In the case of Macdonald's chapter on men's health and wellbeing, a case is made for recognising men's diverse masculinities and the way that these play out for men of all ages. It might be appropriate in subsequent men's learning aetiologies to create a new, fifth category, embracing serious and critical *masculinist and pro-masculinist* literature, separate from the masculinist tendencies in the popular-rhetorical literature, which might seriously critique some feminist positions on men and, in particular, on ideas of both men's hegemony and hegemonic masculinities.

On reflection, we concur with two overarching perspectives by Ollagnier and Merrill in the preface of Oustrouch-Kaminska *et al.*'s (2012) book about gender in adult learning. First, that our research 'highlights the need to relate gender to other forms of inequality' (Ollagnier and Merrill, 2012, p. 7), including class, disability and race, and second, that the gender question in adult education is critically important. On this first perspective, we also agree with Bowl and Tobias (2012). We go much further in our book and argue a case in relation to men's inequality also occuring by age, location and paid work status.

We diverge from Bowl and Tobias (2012) on two main points. Our first relates to our interest in learning and recognition of the value of learning through life aside from through formal forms of education. As Ollagnier and Merrill put it, we agree that 'The gender question in adult education often brings us back to the importance of learning experiences through life' (2012, p. 8). We concur that national governments 'ignore the wealth of [men's] life experiences as an informal learning process' (p. 8). Our second point of divergence from Bowl and Tobias (2012) is our contention, supported by research across Europe (in Oustrouch-Kaminska *et al.*, 2012, p. 10) that, for whatever reasons, men are significantly less likely to formally learn. Indeed, 'The rate of women's access to education and training throughout life is now higher than men in all courses and company training' (p. 10). As an example, across

Europe in 2008, on average across 27 countries, 147 women graduated from higher education for every 100 men (p. 10).

Aside from these approaches related to learning, we have deliberately tried to weave men and wellbeing into our otherwise largely educational narratives, arguments and discourses. There is sufficient evidence in all nations included in our book that when men (and nations) become totally preoccupied with paid work (and work-based learning), men's, family and community wellbeing suffers, as does men's health, wellbeing and longevity.

As we have shown in each of the national chapters, for men beyond paid work for any reason, including in most world nations where population ageing is an issue and/or where gender intersects with rurality, race and socio-economic status (class), even voluntary, age-related withdrawal from the workplace can and does often result in debilitating disengagement from community and decline in men's wellbeing and health. As Foley makes clear in Chapter 5, there is a case for acknowledging and 'clearing the ground' and considering some men's disadvantage without applying the argument to all men.

Returning to Weaver-Hightower's four-part aetiology developed for the 'boys' turn' literature, each of these four categories and approaches exhibit strengths and weaknesses as they apply to the 'men's turn' literature we have both consulted and produced. On reflection, from an examination of Hightower-Weaver's (2003) strengths and weaknesses lists in relation to the 'boys' turn' literature, we have been more informed and responsive to practitioner and public concerns. We have tended to merely 'dip into' a theoretically-oriented academic literature on adult education, and deliberately tried to make our text widely accessible. If we are to be self-critical, we also we acknowledge the 'allure of the new' in these challenging and important discourses about men. We collectively agree with Weaver-Hightower that 'for scholars desiring to establish themselves ... finding a niche within a "new" topic or the opportunity to extend a hot debate is a powerful draw' (2003, p. 749). Men's learning, while highly relevant to half of the world's population, remains a small but desirable niche.

Conclusions

We conclude that, despite a growing concern about men's participation in education, the opportunities for men to participate in informal and non-formal learning (in particular for unemployed men and men drawn from disadvantaged backgrounds) is quite limited and in decline. This is in part due to the general narrowing of national education and training policies to focus exclusively on promoting education and training for entry and re-entry to paid work. A focus on job-related training means that many men, particularly older men who are leaving or retiring from the labour force and who are not interested in existing adult learning provision (which is largely female dominated), find themselves with nowhere to go.

One of our most pertinent findings is that certain forms of education can (and do) have the unintended effect of turning boys and men away from learning, thus adversely affecting men and their families wellbeing. A positive finding from our research is that there are ways this process can be addressed, particularly through valuing and facilitating learning through life rather than through market-based education and training, particularly if based on pedagogies that address and reverse the original turn off.

Our first overarching conclusion is that the issues are not about *all* men, but, in Weaver-Hightower's words (originally used in relation to boys), 'primarily about those [men] who suffer oppressions based on subjectivities other than gender alone' (2003, p. 480). As Weaver-Hightower puts it in relation to boys, we need to avoid assuming that all men 'are *disadvantaged* because some are, but also that all [men] are *advantaged* because some are' (p. 480). We conclude that the biggest disadvantage experienced by some men, as demonstrated in all chapters, is the debilitating effect of not being in paid work, for whatever reasons.

Our second overarching conclusion is that those men of all ages who stand to benefit most from lifelong and lifewide learning are those least likely to access it, particularly if it is packaged and presented in a way which is patronising from deficit models of provision. The research we have analysed shows that, almost counter-intuitively, the most effective learning for most men with limited prior experiences of learning is informal, local and community-based, which builds on what men know, can do and are interested in. Learning for such men is less effective if it assumes all men have a problem, that particular masculinities *are* the problem, or if it requires them to be served up curriculum and assessment for qualifications, vocational training or literacy, as students, customers, clients or patients, which presupposes a deficit. These approaches are totally inappropriate and patronising for most men and boys of any age, and most patronising for men already turned off from learning by negative prior learning experiences.

Our third overarching conclusion is that the debates and discussions generated by our research into men's learning and wellbeing have only scratched the surface in a small range of world nations, and that the debates still have a long way to run, particularly in relation to the links between lifelong learning and wellbeing. The research evidence of these powerful links has only recently been identified and has been slow to be picked up, even by many adult educators. It is the emerging research (Cooper *et al.*, 2010) on the relationships between the early developing brain, mental capital and conditions for learning that are increasingly pertinent here. While schools and teachers can and do make a difference, the biggest influence on a child's learning is closely tied up with both opportunities in early childhood and the education achieved by at least one parent. Aside from being suggestive of the need for better early childhood and family education for boys and girls, our research confirms the need for a wider recognition of the transferable value of lifelong and lifewide adult education in both directions in families between children, parents and grandparents.

Given that boys become tomorrow's older men, it may be that some of what we describe for today's older men had its origins with boys raised with different masculinities in fundamentally different cultural, educational, economic, social and technological circumstances and times. As the British Council put it,

> *There is also a crisis in masculinity. A generation of men who were educated in the expectation that they would earn their living through the use of their physical skills and strengths have been deprived of these opportunities.* (2002, p. 1)

Hopefully boys in the future will get access to a greater range of masculinities and more diverse options for learning though life than many of today's boys and men. Again the British Council neatly summarises the risk of inaction in a re-structured labour market where the only jobs on offer to poorly educated men are low-paid, low-skilled and casual. Many men see such jobs as 'women's work', which they have been brought up to regard as demeaning for a 'real man'.

257

Unless there is radical change in the way in which young men are socialized, it is likely that the tension crested by this gap between expectation and reality will explode into violence, directed against self and others. (British Council, 2002, p. 1)

References

Aikman, S. and Unterhalter, E. (2007) *Practising Gender Equality in Education.* London: Oxfam.

Apple, M. (2008) 'Foreword', in M. Weaver-Hightower (2008) *The Politics of Policy in Boys' Education.* New York: Palgrave Macmillan, pp. xi–xiv.

Biddulph, S. (1995) *Manhood: An Action Plan for Changing Men's Lives.* Melbourne: McPherson's Printing Group.

Bowl, M. and Tobias, R. (2012) 'Ideology, discourse and gender', in M. Bowl, R. Tobias, J. Leahy, G. Ferguson and J. Gage (Eds.), *Gender, Masculinities and Lifelong Learning.* London: Routledge, pp. 14–28.

British Council (2002) *Gender and Economic Restructuring in the UK.* Retrieved 12 May 2002 from www.britishcouncil.org/governance/gendev/ecres/ecres4.htm

Connell, R. (1995) *Masculinities.* Cambridge: Polity Press.

Connoly, P. (2004) *Boys and Schooling in the Early Years.* London: RoutledgeFalmer.

Cooper, C., Field, J., Goswami, U., Jenkins, R. and Sahakian, B. (2010) *Mental Capital and Wellbeing.* Chichester: Wiley-Blackwell.

Endepohls-Ulpe, M. (2012) 'Are males disadvantaged in the education system?', in J. Oustrouch-Kaminska, C. Fontanini and S. Gaynard (Eds.), *Considering Gender in Adult Learning in Academia: An Invisible Act.* Wroclaw: Wydawnictwo Naukowe, pp. 53–64.

Hearn, J., Muller, U., Oleksy, E., Pringle, K., Chernova, J. *et al.* (2004) *The Social Problem of Men: Final Report (2000–2003),* EU FPV Thematic Network: The Social Problem and Societal Problematisation of Men and Masculinities. Luxembourg: Office for Official Publications of the European Communities.

House of Representatives – Standing Committee on Education and Training (2002) *Boys: Getting it Right. Report on the Inquiry into the Education of Boys.* Canberra: Parliament of the Commonwealth of Australia.

Lingard, B. and Douglas, P. (Eds.) (1999) *Men Engaging Feminisms: Profeminism, Backlashes and Schooling.* Buckingham: Open University Press.

McGivney, V. (1999) *Excluded Men: Men who are Missing from Education and Training.* Leicester: NIACE.

McGivney, V. (2004) *Men Earn, Women Learn: Bridging the Gender Divide in Education and Training.* Leicester: NIACE.

Ollagnier, E. and Merrill, B. (2012) 'Preface', in J. Oustrouch-Kaminska, C. Fontanini and S. Gaynard (Eds.), *Considering Gender in Adult Learning in*

Academia: An Invisible Act. Wroclaw: Wydawnictwo Naukowe, pp. 7–8.

Oustrouch-Kaminska, J., Fontanini, C. and Gaynard, S. (Eds.) (2012) *Considering Gender in Adult Learning in Academia: An Invisible Act.* Wroclaw: Wydawnictwo Naukowe.

Oustrouch, J. and Ollagnier, E. (Eds.) (2008) *Researching Gender in Adult Learning.* Frankfurt am Main: Peter Lang.

Rosin, H. (2012) *The End of Men: And the Rise of Women.* Penguin Group US.

Schuller, T. and Watson, D. (2009) *Learning Through Life: Inquiry into the Future of Lifelong Learning.* Leicester: NIACE.

Sweetman, C. (2000) 'Beyond rhetoric: Male involvement in gender and development policy and practice', Report of Seminar Five: Beyond Rhetoric, Seminar hosted by Oxfam GB, with the Centre for Cross-Cultural Research on Women at the University of Oxford, Oxford, June 2000.

Weaver-Hightower, M. (2003) 'The "boy turn" in research on gender and education', *Review of Educational Research*, 73, pp. 471–98.

Weaver-Hightower, M. (2008) *The Politics of Policy in Boys' Education.* New York: Palgrave Macmillan.

Index

Aboriginal people 36–7, 217–18, 237, 252

academic identity 99

accreditation 78, 92, 220

achievement 60, 160

addiction: drugs 110, 142

adolescence 108, 167

adult and community education (ACE) 28–9, 66–8, 87–8, 221–2, 240–1

adult education 65, 69, 145, 150, 155, 169; programmes 72–3

adult learning 5–6, 20, 61, 67, 156, 254–6

Adult Learning Australia (ALA) 14

adult literacy 29, 51, 56–8

adult training 168, 189

aetiology 253–5

Africa 25, 141, 252

age 70–1, 215, 221, 226, 231–2, 235–7; discrimination 215; men and boys 97–112

Age Concern Cheshire 140

Age Counts (2000) 90

Age UK 139–40

ageing 71, 89, 123, 201, 204, 216; population 3–6, 9, 132, 237, 251, 255; productive 90, 122–4; society 50, 131–7, 186, 197–9

ageism 134, 215

agency 70–3, 79, 109, 114, 117, 120, 125, 216; community 81; development 110; individual 69–71, 74; restricted 71

aggression 228

agriculture 118, 198

Ahmed, M.: and Coombs, P. 10

Aijing Jin: *et al* 196–204

Aikman, S.: and Unterhalter, E. 250

alcoholism 54, 57, 117, 120, 159

alienation 98, 251

Almeida, M. 166, 175–6

Amâncio, L. 167

anger issues 104, 110

Anglo-Irish Agreement (1985) 157

Antonovsky, A. 80–1

anxiety 57, 181

Aotearoa *see* New Zealand

Apple, M. 248

apprenticeships 44, 100, 105, 231–3

Archer, L. 228

Armagh Men's Shed 158–9

Asia 7, 90, 227, 252

assessment 78–9, 124, 256

Association for Education and Ageing (AEA) 138

at-risk individuals 97–102, 107

Attention Deficiency Hyperactive Disorder (ADHD) 42

Aulich, T. 210

Australia 26–7, 36–7, 65–8, 83–91, 98–108, 113–24, 138–9; Department of Health and Ageing 45; learning in 205–25; National Male Health Policy 39, 44

Australian Assistance Plan (APP) 66

Australian Indigenous Health*InfoNet* 36

Australian Longitudinal Study on Women's Health (ALSWH) 35, 39

Australian National Training Authority (ANTA) 212

Australian Workplace and Productivity Agency (AWPA) 207; *Australia's Skills*

and Workplace Development Needs (2012) 207
authority 196
autonomy 14, 73, 126, 180

Bailey, I.: and Coleman, U. 25
Baldry, A. 44
Bao, H.: and Yue, Y. 200
barriers 25, 67, 83; attitudinal 83; educational 71; learning 24, 161; participation 84, 209
Barton, D. 79
Beckett, D.: and Helme, S. 66
behaviour: issues 101; learned 43–4
Belfast Agreement (Good Friday Agreement [1998]) 150
Beyond Cinderella: Towards a Learning Society (Crowley) 210, 215
bi-culturalism 227
Biddulph, S. 253
Big Lottery funding 138
Black, P.: *et al* 126
Blanchardstown Area Partnership (BAP) 156–7
border shed 157–8
boredom 55, 59, 114
Bourdieu, P. 23, 230
Bowl, M.: and Tobias, R. 30, 68, 79, 227, 254
Boys: Getting it Right (2002 & 2004) 211, 248
boys' education 100–1, 246–7
Bringing in the Blokes (LCL 2002) 213
British Council 257–8
Brown, A. 211; *et al* 37; Gethin, A. and Macdonald, J. 118
budgeting 122
bullying 43–4, 98, 103–5
bureaucratisation 228
Burke, P. 80
Byrne, M. 211–13

Caffarella, R.: and Merriam, S. 14
Canada 6, 21, 29, 99, 108, 113, 247
capabilities 69–74, 81, 125
capital 17, 23; community 250; cultural 230, 236, 250; family 250; human 125, 234; mental 16, 134, 257; political 250; social 15, 86, 125, 134, 218–19, 236, 239
Carragher, L.: Evoy, J. and Mark, R. 148–63
Catholic Nationalism 149
Chamberland, C.: and Ellenbogen, S. 98–9
Changing Ageing Partnership (CAP) 49, 53–60
Chase, S. 101
Cherrington, R. 138
children: boys' education 100–1, 246–7; disadvantage 143
China 199, 252–3; Bureau of Civil Affairs and Ageing Committee 199, 202; learning in 196–204
class 13, 70, 86, 98, 150, 166, 254; lower middle 187; middle 65; social 52, 100, 125, 148, 226, 231, 235–7; working 6, 44, 55, 138–9, 211, 228–9
Cleary, P. 83, 92
co-ordinators 101–4, 107, 122
coaching 86, 219
Coleman, U.: and Bailey, I. 25
collaborative learning 239
Colley, H.: Hodgkinson, P. and Malcolm, J. 21
Come in Cinderella: The Emergence of Adult and Community Education (Aulich) 210
communication 49–55
communicative learning 80
communitarianism 16, 88
community 81, 114, 117–19, 156; activities 61, 198; agency 81; capital 250; development 151; education 9–10, 58, 149–51, 201, 221, 231, 234; engagement 120, 222; identity 86; involvement 53, 126, 153–5; movements 88, 113–14, 121; organisations 59–60, 110, 118, 121, 172, 199–202, 235–9; participation 52, 65, 69, 97; pedagogy 131; services 202, 214
community learning 91–2, 144, 160, 201–2, 212, 216, 256; centres 92, 155

Community Learning Pilots 137
community men's sheds 101, 113–14, 119–20, 155, 211–13, 217, 240–1
compulsory education 219, 229
confidence 57, 79, 249–50; building 104–6; self- 52, 73, 187
Connell, R. 4, 64, 109, 165–6, 211
constructivism 15–16
contextual learning 21
Coombs, P.: and Ahmed, M. 10
Cooper, C.: *et al* 16, 79
Cordier, R.: and Wilson, N. 116–17
corporal punishment 52
Corridan, M. 25
Cost of the Troubles Study (Fay *et al*) 149
counselling 55–6, 185, 188–9, 203
course-based learning 4
course-based training 84
Courtenay, W. 65–6
crisis 118, 190–1; financial 91, 151–2, 179–80, 184–6, 189–92, 249; global financial (2008) 3–6, 10, 28, 125, 132, 151, 250–2; learning from 189–92; in masculinity 166, 257
cross age mentoring 86, 124
Cross, K. 25
Crowley, R. 210, 215
Cully, M. 123
cultural capital 230, 236, 250
cultural identity 197, 219
cultural learning 202
cultural participation 180, 186
curriculum 78–9, 99–102, 107, 233, 256
Czuba, C.: and Page, N. 185

Dalley-Trim, L. 228
Deci, E.: *et al* 41–3
deficit 115–17, 216, 256
democracy 49, 126, 166; liberal 23, 64
depression 17, 54, 110, 117, 159, 186, 250
deprivation 71, 134
developed nations 3, 28, 81–2, 90
disability 134, 148, 181, 208, 212, 215–16, 254
Disability Support Pensions (DSP) 208
disadvantage 144, 148, 151, 159, 229, 246,

256; children 143; educational 148, 153; men 11, 61–5, 148, 180–1, 184–9, 246, 256; social 50, 151; women 11, 205
disc 5
discouragement 89
discretionary learning 180
discrimination 4, 9, 71, 166, 221; age 134, 215; gender 4, 121, 215, 241; income 215; race 121; religious 121
Discussion Group Programme (DGP) 212
disease 35, 38, 41, 81
disempowerment 184, 192
disengagement 97, 103, 108–9, 139, 153, 246–7; older men 143–4; youth 98–100
Doctors' Reform Society (DRS) 37–8
domestic violence 37, 44
Donald Neighbourhood House and Learning Centre (Victoria): Donald Men's Shed 218
Douglas, P.: and Lingard, B. 247
drugs 117, 120; addiction 110, 143
Dubbo Community Men's Shed (NSW) 217–18
Dwyer, P.: and Wyn, J. 98

Earle, L. 114
early childhood education (ECE) 229
economic crisis *see* financial crisis
Eden Alternative (1991) 114
education 42, 134, 203, 252; access to 11, 25–6, 149; adult 65, 69, 72–3, 144, 150, 155, 169; adult and community (ACE) 28–9, 66–8, 87–8, 221–2, 240–1; barriers 71; boys' 100–1, 246–7; compulsory 219, 229; disadvantage 148, 153; early childhood (ECE) 229; engagement 216; exclusion 205; formal 20–5, 108, 168–9, 219, 227, 232–3, 251; further 9, 212, 233, 250; higher 28, 78, 139, 199, 214, 247, 255; informal 10, 144, 165, 168–9, 201; institutional 88, 92; lack of 5, 184; liberal 234; lifelong 185, 257; mainstream 149; market-based

256; non-formal 139, 144,
169–70; non-vocational 232; older-age
197–9; opportunities 184, 236, 255–6;
participation 68–9, 89, 133, 148,
233–5, 246, 255–6; partnerships 238;
policy 132, 151, 199, 226, 229–31,
240, 246; post-compulsory 24, 67, 83,
92, 207–8, 226, 245; post-secondary
207; primary 13, 51; problems 100–1;
quality 52; secondary 44, 229–31;
structural 170; tertiary 27–9, 84, 100,
173–4, 231; vocational 65, 99, 155,
214, 217, 250
Education Review Office (ERO) 229
educational attainment 30–1, 68, 99,
152–3; low 97, 152, 209
Edwards, R.: *et al* 80
egalitarianism 166, 175, 228
Ellenbogen, S.: and Chamberland, C. 98–9
embarrassment 52, 59
emotional health 213
employment 23–4, 98–9, 134, 149–50,
191–3, 205; high 139; history 138;
insecurity 37; opportunities 192; paid
9–17, 28–30, 71–3, 114–16, 121–5,
207–16, 252–6; part-time 190; security
5, 233; skills for 109; women 11; youth
190
empowerment 49–62, 66, 120, 160,
179–80, 184–93, 229
End of Men, The (Rosin) 253
Endepohls-Ulpe, M. 246–7
engagement 22–5, 67, 99, 103, 209, 235;
education 216; learning 141–4; social
16, 235–6
English Longitudinal Study of Ageing
(ELSA) 133
enjoyment 57, 66, 101, 160
Epstein, D.: *et al* 43
equal opportunities 229, 235, 240, 245
Equal Opportunity Commission
(Australia) 121
equality 11, 70; gender 118, 148–9, 207,
248; rights 64
equity 3, 11, 24, 65, 205, 229–31; gender
207, 248; social 229–31, 240

ethnicity 13, 166, 226, 231–2, 235–8
Europe 85–90, 108, 152–3, 191–2, 227,
239, 251–2
European Commission (EC) 90–1
European Social Fund (ESF) 54
European Society for Research into the
Education of Adults (ESREA) 8
European Union (EU) 13, 150, 158,
180–1, 186
European Year of Active Ageing and
Solidarity between Generations (2012)
116
European Youth Capital (EYC) 190
evening classes 133
Evoy, J.: Mark, R. and Carragher, L.
148–63
ex-offenders 103, 133
*Excluded Men: Men Who are Missing from
Education and Training* (McGivney) 7,
133, 248
exclusion 50, 151; education 205; social
86, 116, 148, 156, 159, 181, 186
experiential learning 53–4, 159, 236–8

failure 67, 108
family 98, 119, 180; capital 250
Family and Community Services (FCS)
210
Fay, M.: *et al* 149
feminism 11, 15–16, 30, 63–4, 118, 228,
252–4
Feminism and History (Scott) 8
Field, J. 15, 69, 79
financial crisis 91, 151–2, 179–80, 186,
189–92, 249; global (2008) 3–6, 10, 28,
125, 132, 151, 250–2
financial support 175, 198–200
Findsen, B. 89, 226–43; and Formosa, M.
133
fire and emergency services organisations
86–7, 122, 211, 237
fishing clubs 172–5
Foley, A. 63–76, 248, 255; and Golding,
B. 97–112, 205–25; Golding, B. and
Mark, R. 244–59
Ford, G.: and Soulsby, J. 134

formal education 20–5, 108, 168–9, 219,
227, 232–3, 251; low levels 207; state-
funded 136
formal learning 101, 125, 133–5, 161, 199,
203–4, 245–7
formal literacy 3–4, 14
formal qualifications 3–4
formal training 4, 14, 60, 84, 160
Formosa, M. 29; and Findsen, B. 133
Foster, V.: Kimmel, M. and Skelton, C. 100
Foucault, M. 23
Fragoso, A.: Marques, J. and Lança, M.
164–78; and Ollagnier, E. 172
Freire, P. 185
Fremantle Men's Shed 217
friendship 72, 98, 102, 109, 123, 160,
174–5
full-time work 98, 207
Fuller, A.: and Unwin, L. 82
functional literacy 6, 13, 20
funding 67, 152, 157, 215, 229–31, 234,
246; Big Lottery 139; European Union
150, 171; government 117, 151, 229,
234; international 252; National
Lottery 139–40; short-term 136–9;
state 136, 151; withdrawal 80, 151
further education 9, 212, 233, 250
Further Education Means Business (DEL
2002) 151

GalGael project 141–2
Geert, T.: and Severiens, S. 4–5
gender 7–12, 68–71, 98–100, 164–8,
237, 252–6; difference 85, 90, 138,
169, 175, 204, 231; discrimination 4,
121, 215, 241; equality 118, 148–9,
207, 248; identity 26, 85, 152, 165;
inequality 27, 64, 166–8, 252; mixed
241; order 7, 165; regime 85, 165;
relations 26, 168, 174; roles 109, 164–6,
174–5; segmentation 172, 207–10, 214;
stereotypes 152, 165
gendered pedagogy 9
gendered spaces 63–4, 68, 73, 74
gerontology 114, 120, 210
Gethin, A.: Macdonald, J. and Brown, A.

118
Gissler, M.: *et al* 43
global financial crisis (2008) 3–6, 10, 28,
125, 132, 151, 250–2
Golding, B. 20–33, 77–96, 113–28,
171, 211–12, 221, 237–9; *et al* 72,
83, 102, 116, 123, 213; and Foley, A.
97–112, 205–25; Mark, R. and Foley,
A. 244–59; and Rogers, M. 211; and
Vallance, P. 218
Good Friday Agreement (1998) 150
Gorard, S. 23–4, 209; and Rees, G. 214
government: funding 117, 151, 229, 234;
policy 143, 212, 232–3; support 88,
201
Gradman, T. 73
Graham, H. 41
Gramsci, A. 165
grassroots movement 67–8, 87–8, 101–2,
113–14, 119–21, 125, 218
Greece 185, 249, 250; learning in 179–95
gross domestic product (GDP) 196–7
Growing the Generations (Harris) 213
Grummell, B. 151
Grundtvig Learning Partnership (2012)
134
guidance 185, 188–91

Hager, P. 22
hands-on activities 118, 124, 154, 161,
216
Harris, P. 213
Hattam, R.: and Smyth, J. 99
Hayes, R.: and Williamson, M. 116; and
Williamson, S. 68
health 64–5, 69–73, 121–5, 133–4, 201–5,
249–52; benefits 63, 66–8; care 43,
187, 202; emotional 213; ill 40, 81,
208–9, 212–15; and learning 39–42;
men's 7, 34–48, 206; mental 37–8,
42, 54, 65–6, 71, 133, 143, 159, 213;
physical 38, 42, 54, 65–6, 71, 133, 213;
policy 7, 34, 39, 211, 248; poor 148;
promotion 41, 91, 115, 120, 199
Hearn, J.: *et al* 13
hegemonic masculinity 64–5, 126, 165–8,

175–6, 228, 247, 254
Helme, S.: and Beckett, D. 66
Heseltine Review (2012) 139
higher education 28, 78, 139, 199, 214,
    247, 255
Hodgkinson, P.: Malcolm, J. and Colley,
    H. 21
Horgan, G. 153
Howard, J.: and Langworthy, A. 81
human capital 125, 234
human rights 15, 70–3
Human Rights and Equal Opportunities
    Commission (HREOC) 213
humanism 12–15
humiliation 52
Hurworth, R. 210

identity 21, 71, 101, 109, 124, 228, 240;
    academic 99; cultural 197, 219; gender
    26, 85, 152, 165; masculine 73, 134,
    159
ill health 40, 81, 208–9, 212–15
illiteracy 49–50, 153
incidental learning 69, 72, 171, 176, 235
inclusion 23, 126, 148; social 85, 156–7
income 11, 17, 134–6, 169, 251–2;
    discrimination 215
Index of Multiple Deprivation (IMD)
    134
Indigenous people 85, 205–9, 217–19,
    227, 236–8, 250, 253
industry training organisations (ITOs)
    230, 233
inequality 63, 71, 151, 254; gender 27, 64,
    166–8, 252
inequity 63, 71; social 65
informal education 10, 144, 165, 168–9,
    201
informal learning 49–53, 59–61, 72–4,
    133–5, 168–76, 238–40, 254–6
Informal Learning in the Community
    (McGivney) 10, 91
informal pedagogy 131
informal segregation 52
innovative learning 11
innovative pedagogy 110

Inquiry into the Future for Lifelong Learning
    (Schuller and Watson) 10–12
institutional education 88, 92
instrumentalism 80, 83
intergenerational learning 97, 101, 107–9,
    173–4, 214, 220–1, 236
intergenerational mentoring 110
intergenerational role modelling 108–10
International Adult Literacy Survey
    (IALS) 13, 49–50
International Fund for Ireland (IFI) 157
International Journal on Education and
    Ageing (2010) 89
intervention 41, 120, 181–2, 254;
    learning-related 254
Ireland 29, 49–51, 68, 114, 117–21, 139,
    249–50; learning in 148–63; Northern
    53–5, 140, 149–51, 159–60; Republic
    of 149, 155–6
Irish Men's Sheds Association 141, 153,
    156
Isle of Man: Southern Community
    Initiative 139
isolation 55, 140, 148; social 91, 211

Japan 90, 124
Jarvis, P. 89
Jenkins, A.: and Mostafa, T. 133–5
Jha, J.: and Kelleher, F. 26
jobs see employment
Johns, S.: and Kilpatrick, S. 84

Keddie, A.: and Mills, M. 108
Keeping the Balance: Older Men and Healthy
    Ageing (MHIRC 2001) 211
Kelleher, F.: and Jha, J. 26
Kentra Anihtis Prostasias Ilikiomenon
    (KAPI) 188
Kilpatrick, S.: et al 83; and Johns, S. 84
Kimmel, M.: Skelton, C. and Foster, V.
    100
knowledge sharing 58, 107–8
Kral, I.: and Schwab, R. 78

labour market 132, 168, 181, 189, 208–9,
    228, 233

Lalor, T.: *et al* 51, 153
Lança, A.: Fragoso, A. and Marques, J.
  164–78
Landcare movement (Australia) 88
Lane Cove Men's Shed 115
language problems 100
Langworthy, A.: and Howard, J. 81
later-life learning 199, 202–4
Lattimore, R. 208, 209
Lave, J.: and Wenger, E. 21
Leach, F. 4–5
learned behaviour 43–4
learner-centredness 15, 123
Learning Centre Link (LCL) 213
*Learning How to be a Man: Constructing
  Masculinities* (Amâncio) 167
Learning Later (Findsen) 89
*Learning for Life: White Paper on Adult
  Education* (DES 2000) 151–3
Learning Through Life (Schuller and
  Watson) 79
*Learning to Labour: Working Class Kids Get
  Working Class Jobs* (Willis) 228
*Learning and Wellbeing Trajectories Among
  Older Adults in England* (Jenkins and
  Mostafa) 132–3
Leigh Report (1997) 210
leisure 123–4, 180, 199, 202, 228, 235
Leonard, B.: and Myint, A. 40
Lesches Filias 189
Levitas, R. 81
Lewis, S. 87
liberal democracy 23, 64
liberal education 234
life expectancy 36, 132, 197, 253
life transitions theory 22
lifecourse 12, 15–16, 23–4, 28–30, 207,
  229; learning through 34–48
lifelong education 185, 257
lifelong learning 4–14, 20–3, 72–3, 122,
  169–70, 216–17, 256–7
Lifelong Learning in Later Life (Findsen and
  Formosa) 134
Lifelong Learning Programme (LLP) 179
limitations 5–6
Lingard, B.: and Douglas, P. 247

literacy 3–4, 50–1, 54–6, 60–1, 67, 230;
  adult 29, 51, 56–8; formal 3–4, 14;
  functional 6, 13, 20; learning 53–4, 57;
  problems 49, 52–3, 61, 97, 100, 160;
  programmes 55, 61; skills 56, 60, 208
Livingstone, D. 21
local schools 101, 110
localism 86, 138–40
Locke, J. 100
loneliness 110, 114, 199
longevity 45, 65, 252, 255; increased 132
lower middle class 187
loyalism 160

Macdonald, J. 34–48, 254; Brown, A. and
  Gethin, A. 118
McGinn, C. 84–5
McGivney, V. 5–11, 20–2, 91–2, 131–4,
  207, 211–14, 247–9
MacInnes, J. 166
McIntyre, J. 222
McMillan, J.: and Marks, G. 99
McNair, S. 28, 125
mainstream education 149
Malcolm, J.: Colley, H. and Hodgkinson,
  P. 21
Malkoutzis, N. 189, 192
Malta 29, 172
Manhood (Biddulph) 253
Māori 227–32, 235–40, 252
marginalisation 65, 68, 134, 151, 229, 236,
  239–40
Mark, R. 49–62; Carragher, L. and Evoy,
  J. 148–63; *et al* 159–60; Foley, A. and
  Golding, B. 244–59; and Soulsby, J.
  131–47
market-based education 256
Marks, A. 211, 216–17
Marks, G.: and McMillan, J. 99
Marmot, M. 45
Marques, J.: Lança, A. and Fragoso, A.
  164–78
Martin, B. 206–7
masculine identity 73, 134, 159
masculinity 7–12, 25–6, 34–7, 117–18,
  226–9, 256–7; crisis in 166, 257;

diverse 254; dominant 85; hegemonic 64–5, 126, 164–8, 175–6, 228, 246–7, 254; ideologies 227, 248; negative 126; positive 108–10; traditional 167

Maslen, G. 211

Maslow, A. 22

Mechanics' Institutes 137

Medeiros, F. 164

media 83, 121–2

memorandum of understanding (MOU) 107

Men Earn, Women Learn (McGivney) 7, 248

Men's Health Information and Resource Centre (MHIRC) 211

men's sheds 69–71, 100–1, 106–10, 113–28, 222, 247, 251–3; community 101, 113–14, 119–20, 155, 211–13, 217, 240–1; in Ireland 153–5; as learning centres 139–41; learning through 217–18; movement 73, 87, 162, 205, 215–16; in New Zealand 239–40; non-funded 155–7

Men's Sheds Network 140

mental capital 16, 134, 257

Mental Capital and Wellbeing (Cooper et al) 79

mental health 37–8, 42, 54, 65–6, 71, 133, 213; problems 159

mentoring 58–9, 97, 101–2, 107–10, 216, 219; cross age 86, 124; intergenerational 110

Merriam, S.: and Caffarella, R. 14

Merrill, B.: and Ollagnier, E. 254

middle class 65

Millennium Development Goals (MDGs) 26

Mills, M.: and Keddie, A. 108

Misan, G. 16; *et al* 116

modernity 166–8, 180

Morrison, R. 124

Mostafa, T.: and Jenkins, A. 132–5

motivation 22, 98; self- 201

Mousaferiadis, T. 27

multi-culturalism 227

Myers, K.: and Myles, M. 29

Myint, A.: and Leonard, B. 40

National Adult Learning Survey (NALS) 134–5

National Adult Literacy Agency (NALA) 25, 49–53, 153

National Centre for Vocational Education Research (NCVER) 21, 98

National Institute of Adult Continuing Education (NIACE) 7, 133–5

National Lottery funding 139–40

National Male Health Policy (Australia) 39, 44

National Marketing Strategy for VET (Thomas) 212

National Men's Health Policy (DoHC 2009) 153

National Seniors Productive Ageing Centre 90

National Youth Action 181

Nationalism 150, 158; Catholic 149

Navarro, Z. 23

negative masculinity 126

neighbourhood houses 67–8, 71, 213

neoliberalism 30, 149–51

Network on Gender and Adult Learning (NGAL) 8

networks: social 99, 115, 175, 251–2

New Zealand Qualifications Framework (NZQA) 232–3

New Zealand/Aotearoa 28, 68, 108, 114, 119–21, 139, 252; learning in 226–43; Ministry of Education 232

non-formal education 139, 144, 169–70

non-formal learning 78, 135, 175, 227, 234–5, 238–40, 255–6

non-government organisations (NGOs) 187

non-vocational education 232

Northern Ireland 53–5, 140, 149–51, 159–60

numeracy 51–6, 67, 208, 230; problems 52

Nussbaum, M. 70–3

occupational segregation 9

O'Connor, M. 51, 152

Ohsako, T. 90

Oldenburg, R. 81–2
Older Men: New Ideas (OM:NI) 123
older men: disengagement 144–5
Older Men as Active Learners in the
    Community (OMAL) 134, 171–2
older people's university 200–1
older-age education 197–9
Ollagnier, E.: and Fragoso, A. 172; and
    Merrill, B. 254; and Oustrouch, J. 245
opportunities 53, 257; economic
    36; education 184, 236, 255–6;
    employment 192; equal 229, 235, 240,
    245; lack 192; learning 56, 67–8, 82,
    154–5, 214, 218, 237; training 230
oppression 160, 166, 252
Organisation for Economic Co-operation
    and Development (OECD) 27–8
organised learning 78, 203, 214, 235
O'Rourke, R. 9
Oustrouch, J.: and Ollagnier, E. 245
Oustrouch-Kaminska, J.: *et al* 248, 254
out-of-school programmes 103–4, 108
Owens, T. 25, 148

Page, N.: and Czuba, C. 185
paid employment 9–17, 28–30, 71–3,
    114–16, 121–5, 207–16, 252–6; easier
    access to 172; learning beyond 248–51
Pākehā 227, 235, 252
part-time employment 190
participation 51, 58–9, 68–70, 83, 168,
    237; adult learning 13; barriers 84, 209;
    community 14, 52, 65, 69, 97; cultural
    180, 186; decline 206; education 68–9,
    89, 133, 148, 233–5, 246, 255–6; group
    115; improving 213; learning 169,
    179, 188, 193, 201, 214, 231; older
    men 173–4; primary 26; social 22, 72,
    79, 90, 186; tertiary education 27–9,
    173–4; training 89; women 63, 118
partnerships 97, 101–2, 108–10, 222;
    educational 238; learning 164, 171–2
Pasifika 229–32, 235, 238–40
patriarchy 64, 165–6, 180, 237, 245
Payne, G. 85
Peabody Trust 140

pedagogy 17, 77–8, 97, 113, 123, 215–16,
    246; community 131; gendered 9;
    informal 131; innovative 110; place-
    based 11; possibility of 109
peer groups 98, 109
personal development 56, 79, 104
personal services 89
personal support 58
physical health 38, 42, 54, 65–6, 71, 133,
    213
policy 23, 91; context 150–2;
    development 131; discourse 155;
    education 132, 151, 199, 226, 229–31,
    240, 246; government 144, 212, 232–3;
    health 7, 34, 39, 211, 248; social 150,
    181, 226, 229–31
policymakers 61, 72, 101, 211
political capital 250
Politics of Policy in Boys' Education, The
    (Weaver-Hightower) 248
Pollak, A. 150
Pollard, A. 23
polytechnics 230, 233
population ageing 3–6, 9, 132, 237, 251,
    255; rapid 132
Portugal 28, 122, 249–50, 253; learning in
    164–78
positive masculinity 108–10
post-compulsory education 24, 67, 83, 92,
    207–8, 226, 245
post-compulsory learning 6
post-compulsory training 220
post-secondary education 207
post-structuralism 15, 23
poverty 144, 148, 153, 156, 181, 186–7;
    relative 229
power 23, 64–6, 83; relations 180
primary education 13, 51
primary participation 26
private schools 230
Private Training Establishments (PTEs)
    230
productive ageing 90, 122–4
professionalism 36, 78, 89
professionalisation 228
Program for the International Assessment

of Adult Competencies (PIACC) 13
Promoting Active Learning and Ageing
   of Disadvantaged Seniors (PALADIN)
   179, 185–9
Protestant Unionism 149
provision 136–7, 249; deficit 115, 256;
   welfare 181
public services 204

qualifications 5–6, 23–4, 60, 133, 256;
   acquisition 30; entry-level 232; few 50;
   formal 3–4; lower level 232; nationally
   recognised 135; New Zealand
   Qualifications Framework (NZQA)
   232–3; non-degree 233; trade 233
quality education 52
quality of life 70, 133, 136, 188, 197, 202

race 70, 86, 100, 148, 217–18, 254–5
racism 121
Rauawaawa Kaumatua Charitable Trust
   238–9
reading 52–3
recreation 84–6
redundancy 11, 83
Rees, G.: and Gorard, S. 214
reference group theory 22
rehabilitation 54–6
relational learning 21
religion 118, 150, 237
religious discrimination 121
*Report of the Committee Reviewing Family
   and Parent Support Services for Men*
   (FCS 1999) 210
Republic of Ireland 149, 155–6
respect 103–6, 110; self- 52, 57
retirement 88–92, 115–17, 121–5, 198–9,
   207–9, 215–16; early 152, 208; post-
   116, 199, 207
retraining 152, 249
Rhodes, J. 109–10
rights 70–1; equal 64; human 15, 70–3;
   women 11
Rogers, M.: and Golding, B. 211
role models 44; intergenerational 108–10
Rosin, H. 253

Rowan, L.: *et al* 63
Rubensen, K. 12–13
Ruxton, S. 79–80

Sage, G. 85
Säljö, R. 14
salutogenesis 80–1, 84, 126, 216
school life expectancy (SLE) 25–6
schooling 42–4, 97, 217, 247, *see also*
   education
schools: local 101, 110; private 230
Schugurensky, D. 171
Schuller, T.: and Watson, D. 10–12, 16, 79,
   251
Schwab, R.: and Kral, I. 78
Scotland 83, 87, 114, 141
Scott, A.: and Wenger, G. 29
Scott, J. 8
secondary education 44, 229–31
sectarianism 150
segregation 150–1; informal 52;
   occupational 9
self-confidence 52, 73, 187
self-directed learning 164, 171, 176,
   185–9, 216
self-esteem 55–7, 60, 73, 79, 187, 249–50;
   lack 181; low 98
self-image 189
self-motivation 201
self-respect 52, 57
self-worth 45, 60
Sen, A. 70–2, 125
Severiens, S.: and Geert, T. 4–5
sexism 4, 121, 215, 241
Shared Future Policy (2005) 150
sheds *see* men's sheds
situational learning 14–15
Skelton, C. 85; Foster, V. and Kimmel, M.
   100
skills 134–6; acquisition 30; development
   58; transferring 58; vocational 137,
   231
Smith, M. 14, 22
Smyth, J.: *et al* 109; and Hattam, R. 99
social capital 15, 86, 125, 134, 218–19,
   236, 239

social class *see* class

social determinants of health (SDOH) 34–5, 39, 42–3

social disadvantage 50, 151

social engagement 16, 235–6

social equity 229–31

social exclusion 86, 116, 148, 156, 159, 181, 186

social inclusion 85, 156–7

social inequity 65

social isolation 91, 211

social learning 14–15, 115

social networks 99, 115, 175, 251–2

social participation 22, 72, 79, 90, 186

social policy 150, 181, 226, 229–31

Social Problem of Men, The (Hearn *et al*) 13

social services 52, 198, 202

socialisation 4, 117, 169–76

socio-cultural factors 226–9, 240

socio-economic status 153, 255; low 108, 121, 171, 207

socio-economics 98, 230, 236

socio-politics 191

Solid Facts, The (WHO 2003) 38

Soulsby, J. 124, 138; and Ford, G. 134; and Mark, R. 131–47; and Underwood, L. 143

Southern Community Initiative (Isle of Man) 140

Southern, N. 80

spelling 56

sport 84–6, 237

Stanwick, J. 210

state funding 136, 151

stereotyping 134; gender 152, 165

Strategic Framework for European Cooperation in Education and Training (CEU 2009) 153

stress 37, 54, 159, 213, 246, 250; relief 57

structural education 170

Structural Funds Programme 158

structured learning 211

substance abuse 17, 54, 159

success 108

Success through Skills: Transforming Futures (DEL 2012) 151

Success through Skills (DEL 2009) 151

suicide 35–6, 39–40, 117, 181; prevention 186

support: financial 175, 198–200; government 88, 201; personal 58

suppression 159

surf clubs 220–1

Surf Life Saving Australia (SLSA) 220

Sweetman, C. 245

Tasmania 102

technical vocational education and training (TVET) 27

tertiary education 84, 100, 231; participation 27–9, 173–4

Tertiary Education Commission (TEC) 231–3

Tertiary Education Strategy (TES) 231

Tett, L. 9

third age learning 181

Thomas, H. 212

Thomas, W. 114

Thomson, N.: *et al* 36

Tobias, R. 228; and Bowl, M. 30, 68, 79, 227, 254

Tonts, M. 86

Tools for Self Reliance (TFSR) 140

trade qualifications 233

tradespersons 121, 124, 206

traditional masculinity 167

training 134, 219; absence 124; adult 168, 189; course-based 84; employment-related 256; formal 4, 14, 60, 84, 160; opportunities 230; participation 89; post-compulsory 220; programmes 193; vocational 27, 78, 152, 169, 256

Transforming Learning and the Transmission of Knowledge 91–2

trust 103–5

Tse, T. 123

underachievement 25–7, 30, 100, 211

underfoot syndrome 124

Underwood, L.: and Soulsby, J. 142

unemployment 53–4, 98–9, 116–17, 151–2, 181–6, 190–2, 250–1; history

50; long-term 148, 152; rising 28, 79, 89, 189–90; support 156; youth 157, 179, 249

Unionism 150, 158

United Kingdom (UK) 28–9, 66–8, 79–80, 226, 234, 247; Department for Innovation, Universities and Skills (DIUS) 135; Government 135–6, 144; learning in 131–47

United Nations Development Programme (UNDP) 26

United Nations Educational, Scientific and Cultural Organisation (UNESCO) 50

United States of America (USA) 6, 13, 85–90, 98, 108, 122, 247–8

university 57, 198, 230–4; older men's 200–1

University of the Third Age (U3A) 29, 88, 123, 138–9

Unterhalter, E.: and Aikman, S. 250

Unwin, L.: and Fuller, A. 82

urbanisation 197–8, 203

Vallance, P.: and Golding, B. 218

Victorian Certificate of Applied Learning (VCAL) 100, 107–8

Victorian Certificate of Education (VCE) 100

View Dale Community Health Centre (Victoria) 107

View Dale Men's Shed (Victoria) 106–8

violence 50, 103, 149, 228; domestic 37, 44

vocabulary 56

vocational education 65, 99, 155, 214, 217, 250; non- 232; programmes 100–1, 110, 230

Vocational Education and Training (VET) 28, 100, 123

Vocational Educational Centre (Dundalk) 158

vocational learning 78, 135, 245–7

vocational skills 137, 231

vocational training 27, 78, 152, 169, 256

volunteerism 86–7, 91, 122, 143–4, 150, 219–20, 238

vulnerability 82, 134

Waitangi, Treaty of (1840) 227

Wallace, R. 216

Watson, D.: and Schuller, T. 10–12, 16, 79, 251

Weaver-Hightower, M. 248, 253–6

Welcome to the Learning Revolution (DIUS) 135

welfare 90, 121, 214; provision 181

welfare state 81

wellbeing 3–13, 81–3, 119–25, 159–61, 237–9, 249–51, 255–7; benefits 66; boosts to 133; capabilities for 69–73; community 117; diminished 17; enhancement 77, 80; improved 7; men 34–49; older adults 132; programmes 107; promotion 115, 120; strategy 7; subjective 172

Wenger, E.: and Lave, J. 21

Wenger, G.: and Scott, A. 29

Williamson, M.: and Hayes, R. 116

Williamson, S.: and Hayes, R. 68

Willis, P. 44, 228

Wilson, N.: and Cordier, R. 116–17

Withnall, A. 226

women: access to education 254; disadvantage 11, 205; employment 11; learning 66–9; participation 63, 118; rights 11

work-based learning 44–5, 233

Workers' Educational Association (WEA) 151, 212

working class 6, 44, 55, 139, 211, 228–9

Working Men's Clubs 138

Working with Te Whāriki (ERO 2013) 229

workplace learning 82, 231–4

Workplace Men's Health Program 45

World Bank 185

World Health Organisation (WHO) 17, 34, 38, 90, 216

World War I (1914–18) 228

World War II (1939–45) 192, 228

Wyn, J.: and Dwyer, P. 98

youth 98; disengagement 98–100;
    employment 190; programmes 231;
    training 230; unemployment 157, 179,
    249
Yue, Y.: and Bao, H. 200

Zarifis, G.K. 179–95